Striking chords

STRIKING CHORDS

Multicultural literary interpretations

Edited by Sneja Gunew and
Kateryna O. Longley

ALLEN & UNWIN

First published 1992
Allen & Unwin Pty Ltd
8 Napier Street, North Sydney NSW 2059 Australia

National Library of Australia
Cataloguing-in-Publication entry:

Gunew, Sneja.
  Striking chords: multicultural literary interpretations.
  Bibliography.
  Includes index
  ISBN 1 86373 089 3.
  1. Australian literature — Minority authors — History and criticism. I.
  Longley, Kateryna O. II Title
A820.9920693

Set in 10/11pt Sabon by Adtype Graphics, Australia
Printed by Kin Keong Printing, Singapore

Contents

v

Part III: Author studies

Part IV: Subversive re-readings

Part V: Re-writings

Acknowledgments

Versions of the following have appeared in *The Age Monthly Review*:
Dewi Anggraeni, 'Irritations', Brian Castro, 'Necessary Idiocy', Zeny Giles, 'Move Over Shahrazad', Rosa Safransky, 'The Goulash Archipelago'. A version of the Introduction appeared in *Antipodes: A North American Journal of Australian Literature*, vol. 2, no. 2, Winter 1988. Sneja Gunew's 'PMT Post modernist tensions' appeared in *Meanjin*, vol. 49, no. 1, Autumn 1990. Ivor Indyk's 'The Migrant and the Comedy of Excess in Recent Australian Writing' appeared in *Thalia: Studies in Literary Humour*, vol. 10, no. 2, 1989. A longer version of Antigone Kefala's statement appeared in *Displaced Persons*, eds K.H. Petersen & A. Rutherford, Dangaroo Press, Sydney, 1988. An earlier version of Efi Hatzimanolis's paper 'Big Words, Little Words (naturally): An unnatural reading' was published in *Span* no. 29, October 1989. Poems by Silvana Gardner from *With Open Eyes*, Silvana Gardner, Queensland Community Press, Brisbane, 1983.

We would sincerely like to thank the following for their help in typing the manuscript: Diana Clegg at Murdoch University and, at Deakin University, Judy Waldie, Val Lestrange and Bev Bartlett.

Contributors

Walter Adamson was born in Germany in 1911 and emigrated to Italy in 1938. He arrived in Australia in 1939 and worked as an interpreter in Italian for the Australian military forces during the war. He taught English in Bolivia 1949–53 and then returned to Australia. Since 1969 he has been a full-time writer published in Germany and Australia. The following work has appeared in Australia: *The Institution* (1976); *Australia of All Places* (1984); Adamson's *Three Legged World* (1985); *The Man with the Suitcase* (1989).

Dewi Anggraeni arrived in Australia in 1970 and is the author of two novels; *The Root of All Evil* (1987) and *Parallel Forces* (1988). She is also the Australian correspondent for *Tempo*, the leading news and current affairs magazine in Indonesia.

David Carter teaches Australian Studies and Literary Studies at Griffith University, Brisbane. He is the editor of *Outside the Book: Contemporary Essays on Literary Periodicals* and is writing a biographical study of Judah Waten's literary and political careers.

Paul Carter is the author of *The Road to Botany Bay* (1987) and of the forthcoming *Living in a New Country* (1991). He has written a number of radio and performance works including 'What is Your Name' (1986) and 'Mirror States' (1988), which explore the language of psychic displacement. He is currently a Research Fellow at The Australian Centre, University of Melborune.

Con Castan was born in Australia the son of Greek migrants. He has taught at the universities of Athens (Greece), Leicester (UK) and Queensland. He is the author of two books on Greek-Australian literature, *Conflicts of Love* (1986) and *Dimitris Tsaloumas: Poet* (1990), as well as many articles on migrant/ethnic/multicultural literature.

Brian Castro is the author of *Birds of Passage* (1983), *Pomeroy* (1990) and *Double-Wolf* (1991).

Margaret Coombs was born in Mudgee, NSW, and has lived as well in Sydney and London. She has an MA in Government from the University of Sydney and has published two novels: *Regards to the Czar* (1988) and *The Best Man for This Sort of Thing* (1990). Her short fiction has appeared in *Uneasy Truces* and *Speaking with the Sun*.

Anna Couani is a Sydney writer who is also the publisher of Sea Cruise Books. She works as an art teacher with students who are new arrivals. Her most recent book, with Peter Lyssiotis, is *The Harbour Breathes*, which is available from 28 Queen St, Glebe 2037.

Zeny Giles (Zenovia Doratis) was born in Sydney in 1937 of a Cypriot father and Castellorizian mother. She won the *Age* Short Story Award in 1981 and has published one novel, *Between Two Worlds* (1981), and a volume of short stories, *Miracle of the Waters* (1989). She has also written two plays.

Yasmine Gooneratne was born in Sri Lanka and arrived in Australia in 1972. She is Professor of Literature and the foundation director of the Post Colonial Literatures and Languages Research Centre at Macquarie University. Her fourteen books include: critical studies of Jane Austen (1970), Alexander Pope (1976), Ruth Prawer Jhabvala (1983) and James D'Alwis (1986); anthologies of poetry from Asia (1979); three volumes of poetry (1971, 1972, 1983); and *Relative Merits: A Personal History of the Bandaranaike Family of Sri Lanka* (1986). She was awarded the Order of Australia in 1990. Her first novel is *A Change of Skies* (1991).

Sneja Gunew is Associate Professor in Literary Studies at Deakin University. She has edited and coedited four anthologies of women's and multicultural writings (*Displacements: Migrant Storytellers, Displacements 2: Multicultural Storytellers, Beyond the Echo: Multicultural Women's Writing, Telling Ways: Australian Women's Experimental Writing*). She has published numerous critical essays (in Australia and overseas) on feminist literary theory and on multiculturalism in its various forms.

Efi Hatzimanolis teaches in the English Department at the University of Wollongong and is completing her PhD on Multicultural Women's Writing 1970–90.

Loló Houbein has published a collection of short stories, *Everything is Real* to be reissued as *The Sixth Sense* (1992); a novel, *Walk a Barefoot Road*, which won the ABC Bicentennial Fiction Award in 1988; and an autobiography, *Wrong Face in the Mirror: An Autobiography of Race and Identity* which won the Dirk Hartog Literary Award in 1988.

Ivor Indyk lectures on Australian Literature at Sydney University.

Manfred Jurgensen is a poet, novelist and critic. His latest publications include the poetry volumes *My Operas Can't Swim* and *The Partiality of Harbours*, the literary diary (in German) *Deutsche Reise*, the film script *Native Poison* (*Das Gift der Heimat*) and a history of German-Australian writing, *Eagle and Emu*. Jurgensen is the founding editor of *Outrider* and holds a Personal Chair at the University of Queensland. He has published over 30 books.

Jim Kable has taught English at Nelson Bay High School since 1986 and more recently has been an exchange teacher in Japan. He edited two textbooks for Oxford Australia in 1990, *Made in Australia* and *An Arc of Australian Voices*, both of which explore Australian cultural diversity.

Vasso Kalamaras was born in Athens and now lives in Perth, where she is a lecturer in Modern Greek. She has published poetry, short stories and plays in Australia and Greece and has won awards in both countries. Her books include *Other Earth* (1977); *Twenty-two Poems* (1977); *Bitterness* (1982); *The Bread Trap* (1986); *Landscape and Soul* (1980). *The Same Light* won the WA Premier's Award for prose in 1990.

Antigone Kefala was born in Romania of Greek parents. She has lived in Romania, Greece, New Zealand and, since 1960, in Australia. She has a BA and MA from Victoria University in Wellington, New Zealand, and has worked as an arts administrator. She has published three books of poetry (*The Alien, Thirsty Weather, European Notebook*) and three volumes of prose (*The First Journey, The Island, Alexia*).

Maria Lewitt was born in Poland in 1924 and arrived in Australia in 1949. She began writing in English in 1967 and has written four books: *Come Spring* (1982); *Just Call Me Bob* (1976), *No Snow in December* (1989) and *Grandmother's Yarns* (1985). She has won the Alan Marshall Award and the NSW Ethnic Affairs Commission Award. Various short stories, poems, articles and reviews have been published in anthologies and literary magazines.

Kateryna Olijnyk Longley is a Ukrainian Australian who came to Australia in 1949. Educated in Adelaide, Melbourne and Sussex, she is a

Senior Lecturer in English and Comparative Literature at Murdoch University in Perth. Her published work includes *Beckett's Later Fiction and Drama* (1987) and numerous articles on Australian and postcolonial writing.

Satendra Nandan was born in Fiji where, in 1987, he became a minister in Dr Timoci Bavadra's Coalition Government. He has published two books of poetry *Faces in a Village* and *Voices in the River*, and coedited the collection *Creative Writing from Fiji*. His first novel *The Wounded Sea* was published in 1991. Dr Nandan has edited the 1980 ACLALS proceedings *Language and Literature in Multicultural Contexts*. He lectures at the University of Canberra and is President of International PEN, ACT.

George Papaellinas is the author of *Ikons, A Collection of Stories* (Penguin 1986). Various stories and articles have been published in a variety of anthologies and journals. He is the founding organiser of Writers in the Park and of Dis/Unities, the literary component of the annual Carnivalé festival in Sydney. He has also worked as a Lecturer in Creative Writing at the University of Technology, Sydney, an editor and a reviewer. He now lives in Melbourne.

Nikos Papastergiadis is part of the editorial team of *Third Text* and doing research on the theme of exile at the University of Cambridge.

Gaetano Rando was born in Rome and arrived in Australia in 1949. He is a Senior Lecturer in the Department of Modern Languages at the University of Wollongong. His publications include *Italian Writers in Australia: Essays and Texts* (1983), *Dizionario degli anglicismi nell'italiano postunitario* (1987), *Italo-Australian Prose in the 80s* (1988), *Language and Cultural Identity* (1990).

Rosa Safransky is completing her first collection of short stories, *Can a Morris Minor Break the Speed of Sound and Other Stories*. She won the ABC Bicentennial Short Story Prize and the Canberra Times National Short Story Award in 1988 and was awarded a fellowship from the Literature Board.

Lidija Simkus-Pocius arrived in Australia in 1949. She has published three collections of poetry in Lithuanian: *The Second Longing* (1973, USA), *Anchors of Memory* (1982, USA) and *Wind and Roots* (1991, Lithuania). She has read her poetry at many conferences in Australia and overseas. She studied Lithuanian language, literature and history by correspondence and at Vilnius University: her articles on cultural topics and poetry translations have been published in numerous Lithuanian and English journals.

Peter Skrzynecki was born in 1945 of Polish/Ukrainian descent. He emigrated to Australia in 1949 and grew up in Sydney. He is the author of six books of poetry, the most recent being *Night Swim*, a collection of short stories, *The Wild Dogs* and a novel, *The Beloved Mountain*. He edited an anthology of multicultural writing, *Joseph's Coat*. He has won the Grace Leven Poetry Prize and the Henry Lawson Short Story Award. He lectures in English at the University of Western Sydney, Macarthur.

Thalia was born in Greece in 1952 and migrated to Australia in 1955. She lives in the inner suburbs of Melbourne and started writing in 1972. Her work has been published in various magazines, journals and anthologies. Her concrete poems have been exhibited at festivals and galleries in Australia, Brazil, Canada, Russia, Italy and America.

Aina Vāvere is a playwright and author of prose works in Latvian, and of a thesis on the history of Australian repertory theatre. She holds the degrees of Bachelor of Agricultural Science and Master of Arts (Drama). She is a member of the Latvian Writers' Association and the South Australian Writers' Centre. Her first collection of short stories in English, *The Blue Mountain in Mujani*, was published by Penguin in 1990.

Walter Veit arrived in Australia in 1967 and is Associate Professor in German Studies at Monash University. He has edited and authored numerous books and articles. His books include: *Captain James Cook— Image and Impact* (2 vols. 1970; 1980) and *Antipodean Enlightenments: Festschrift für Leslie Bodi* (1987).

Cornelis Vleeskens was born in Holland in 1948 and emigrated to Australia in 1958. He has a BA in English Literature from Queensland University. He was on the editorial staff of Makar Press 1977–80 and has been the editor/publisher of Fling Poetry since 1980. He is a writer, translator and editor who has published twenty books of his own work and whose poetry, stories and reviews have appeared in numerous magazines. His most recent volume is *Treefrog Dreaming* (1990).

Ania Walwicz was born in Poland and arrived in Australia in 1963. She has published two collections of short fiction: *Writing* (1982 and reprinted 1989) and *Boat* (1989). The latter won the Victorian Premier's Award for New Writing in 1990. Her next collection, *Red Roses,* will appear in 1992 and she is working on a collection titled *Voyages*. Her play *Elegant* was staged in 1990. She has performed her work in England, France and Switzerland and has been published in 46 anthologies.

Birimbir Wongar (Sreten Bozic) was born in Serbia and emigrated to Australia in 1960. He has written extensively on Aboriginal culture and the environment. His works, including novels, short stories, poetry and non-fiction, concern the impact of European civilisation and industrial development on tribal people in Australia. Among his several awards are an Unsung Writer's Award given during the 1986 PEN Congress and two senior writer's fellowships from the Literature Board.

Introduction

Sneja Gunew and Kateryna O. Longley

I. A POLEMICAL FRAME: THE EXCLUSIONS OF AUSTRALIAN LITERATURE

History, as Salman Rushdie informs us, 'has been described as an interview with the winners' (Rushdie 1988: 37). Much the same may be said
about literary history. It is no surprise to us to read of the English and
Irish connections of Australian literature, but these are not
conceptualised in terms of cultural difference or ethnic specificities.
Such terms are reserved for the outsiders, the marginalised: Aborigines
and those migrants who have come from places other than England or
Ireland. If a national literature is formulated in terms of the ranked
writings of the winners, then yes, Australia has one. If, however, we
think of a national literature as composed of all the varieties of ways in
which the inhabitants of a country construct and represent their experiences over a certain time, then Australia does not yet possess a national
literature. What it does have is a subset of English literature.

Until the last decade this subset has been composed predominantly
of the writings of white, male Anglo-Celts.[1] More recently we have seen
the inclusion of Anglo-Celtic women and a very few Aboriginal writers.
But what about those non-Aboriginal Australians who write from other
than English or Irish cultural antecedents and languages? Are they generally perceived as participating in Australia's national literature? Certainly there are many from those groups who do write, sometimes in
languages other than English, but often—particularly if they are from
second- and third-generation immigrant families—in English. Nonetheless, on the whole the work of these writers is not considered to be part
of our literature, that is, if literature is defined as a textual domain
institutionally constructed and patrolled by reviewers, publishers, university and school curricula. It is a domain described by the British critic
Frank Kermode (1988) as governed by the invention of canons and

periods: works produced by so-called great writers within certain temporal contexts. In Australia, for example, the works of Lawson, Paterson and Furphy are celebrated for their role, in cooperation with the *Bulletin*, in the country's literary development, and the period of the 1890s is seen as crucial to any understanding of Australia's literary and political growth towards independent nationhood. Less obvious, until we introduce the concept of cultural difference, is the narrowness of scope and vision provided by such canonical texts and historical high points.

A national literary history exists to provide narratives of identity and of destiny for a nation and these narratives provide an illusory cohesiveness. Edward Said has defined nationalism in the following way:

> Triumphant, achieved nationalism . . . justifies, retrospectively as well as prospectively, a history selectively strung together in a narrative form: thus all nationalisms have their founding fathers, their basic, quasi-religious texts, their rhetoric of belonging, their historical and geographical landmarks, their official enemies and heroes. This collective ethos forms what Pierre Bourdieu, the French sociologist, calls the *habitus*, the coherent amalgam of *practices linking habit with inhabitance*. In time, successful nationalisms consign truth exclusively to themselves and relegate falsehood and inferiority to outsiders (as in the rhetoric of capitalist versus communist, or the European versus the Asiatic). (Said 1984 a: 162) [our emphasis]

That schema may easily be adapted to the Australian context. Such national histories are predicated on exclusions, at the very least of other nations, but the exclusions operate internally as well. Those who don't fit into the dominant historical narrative, who are not assimilated, either exist as boundary markers, token figures, or are consigned to the margins and thus either to invisibility or to permanent opposition. In the case of the oral traditions of Aborigines and of certain groups of first-generation immigrants in Australia, the mechanisms of exclusion are especially simple since the oral texts upon which these cultures depend cannot even enter the discursive arenas of control (Arthur 1988).

In Australia's drive towards autonomy in every sphere, including the cultural, we must learn to accommodate a spectrum of differences instead of working predominantly with the old binary opposition Australia–Britain. As far as literature is concerned, it is not simply a matter of adding more new names to the existing canon but of learning to read differently, in other words, to read via cultural difference. Slowly and painfully we are learning to read in terms of class and gender distinctions, but cultural difference is not yet an inevitable category in the interpretative process. To give you an example of how this might shape our reading, the theme of exile would not simply conjure up the figure, say, of Christopher Brennan's Wanderer but would be complicated by personae drawn from the poetry of Dimitris Tsaloumas or Gün

Gencer, or from those many other writers who fled postwar Europe and, more recently, war-torn Lebanon, Vietnam, etc. Exile for those groups has been filtered through other literary traditions and, of course, other languages. In simple terms, these literary traditions must contribute both to an *informed* reading of these new writers and to a re-reading of the old so that, for example, the specific ethnic antecedents of Brennan's work, and of the work of all those hitherto traditionally labelled simply Australian writers, become visible. To read the old literature via cultural difference renders visible (instead of leaving it as invisible and hence as universal norm) the extent of the English and Irish elements which dominate Australian writing. In the scales of proportional cultural representation, this leaves about one-third of Australians *un*represented.

In the critical terminology of recent postmodernist criticism, unified historical narratives such as those which purport to 'explain' Australian literature have been linked with a liberal humanism whose key terms include: 'autonomy, transcendence, certainty, authority, unity, totalisation, system, universalisation, centre, continuity, teleology, closure, hierarchy, homogeneity, uniqueness, origin' (Hutcheon 1988:57). This cluster of organising principles has been implicated in, and indeed been seen by a wide range of contemporary cultural theorists to be responsible for sustaining a tradition of Eurocentric imperialism and colonialism (Bhabha 1990; Said 1979; 1984; Spivak 1987; Trinh 1989). Certainly one could argue this in relation to the history of Australian culture which, in public terms, has been presented as a culture of the English colonial winners. Where one positions oneself in this historical exchange, as interviewer or interviewee, is a key question.

If there are winners, inevitably there are also losers. The Aborigines who have chosen to make use of European forms of writing are rewriting our national history and literature. The recent work of many writers included in this volume has centred on the others, hitherto invisible: the exiles who settled here, particularly after the Second World War, but who did not bring with them the requisite English legacy. In order to determine how a consideration of their texts might modify our national literature, their absence must first be made conspicuous. They exist, they write, but where is their writing? We might consider here Edward Said's claim that 'Modern Western culture is in large part the work of exiles, emigres, refugees' (Said 1984 a:159). To wilfully shut ourselves off from their contribution is to handicap ourselves and our cultural autonomy on the international stage. Currently their differences provoke censorship rather than curiosity. They are not much published, nor seriously reviewed, nor put on school or university curricula. It is hoped that this collection will provide a starting point for those who wish to reverse this pattern.

Since Australia is predominantly Anglophone, there is some logic in using the English literary tradition as one kind of reference point. But why does it remain so dominant? Why, for example, do our literature departments almost invariably continue to be departments of English literature? Why are they not departments of Australian literature, juxtaposed with Canadian, New Zealand, American, Caribbean, Anglo-Indian, Irish and other literatures? In recent decades spectacular disruptions of the traditional concept of English writing have emanated from the old and new Commonwealth. Indeed, Britain itself, with its complex regional and political groupings, is by no means a homogeneous entity.

In spite of this growing recognition of cultural diversity within traditional national groupings, it still appears that living in the country for several generations is not sufficient qualification for being considered Australian if one does not have the right cultural roots. One is still expected to filter one's perceptions through the terms of a tradition of representation which may generally be described as Oxbridge-endorsed British culture and literature. Oddly enough, any visit to London in particular confirms that non-Oxbridge varieties of English writing are booming there and that the English language is being eloquently re-written. In Australia, too, one could argue that Australian English is also being re-written outside the constraints of received standard English, witness the work of Π.O., Ania Walwicz and many others. Literature written in English is a very different proposition from English literature. It is time we distinguished between these two categories and changed our orientation to literature written in English, as well as acknowledging the linguistic diversity of the rest of Australian writing. The mythologising and representation of this place needs to occur inclusively if we are to take full collective responsibility for the definition of our national literature rather than waiting for the old metropolitan and cultural centres to come up with their own partisan constructions.

Simmering at the back of this discussion is always the vexed question of literary or artistic value. There is still an assumption, even amongst people who should know better, that somehow excellence streaks ahead and that the 'good' writer transcends any contexts of history, class, gender, race. But who decides? Who is even considered eligible for the preliminary heats in this process? The mechanics of choice for 'excellence' are always invisible. Here is Frank Kermode again:

> The reasons we give for choosing periods and authors always change,
> along with changed valuations ... That the choices made in all these fields
> are controlled by the desires of the mind and even by the desire for power
> I cannot contest, though conscience may also have its part ... (Kermode
> 1988: 125)

E.D. Hirsch, one of the best-known defenders of value in literature, distinguishes between interpretation as a type of consensual 'meaning' attached to a notion of linguistic competence and what he calls 'significance', which is more partisan and changes over time according to who is doing the interpreting. Unfortunately, there are many relative rather than absolute aspects in this process, and this is not always made clear. In the old days we students of literature were constantly being told that reading great literature would make us better people. A recent critic has suggested that to argue for this kind of creation of an ethical subject (a better person) simply by exposure to an aesthetic culture is to deny the influence of the political differences which inhere in any social grouping (Lloyd 1987: 171). In other words, positioning oneself as interested only in great art', as a *neutral* arbiter of taste, has a huge political advantage precisely because it renders the politics of the situation, the power differentials, invisible.

For example, the little reviewing of writings by non-Anglo-Celtic Australians which does occur is often implicitly carried out from such a position of apparent neutrality. That the reviewers are uninformed about the literary and cultural traditions from which the writer produces her or his text is never an issue. The measure is always, whether explicitly or not, that of English literature as it is traditionally conceived. It is an illuminating exercise to examine the reception of this body of multicultural writing. The analogous case is that of women writers. Whereas today there would be an outcry if an anthology containing no women's writing appeared (though women are still by no means given equal representation), the principle that one-third of an anthology of Australian literature should be devoted to non-Anglo-Celtic Australian writers is still far from being accepted. Their absence from such compilations is still rarely remarked upon.

What, then, might the strategies be for including this group? In the first place, as with Aboriginal and women's writing, we need simply to show the extent of the talent. This is slowly happening through the appearance of anthologies like *Joseph's Coat* (Skrzynecki 1985) and *Beyond the Echo* (Gunew & Mahyuddin 1988). As well, a great deal of bibliographic and archival research needs to be carried out in order to uncover lost writers whose work did not receive wide circulation.

It is now accepted that the value of a literary work can never be fixed once and for all. It is agreed upon by a community of readers within a specific cultural setting. There is no doubt that the upsurge of interest in Aboriginal writing is related to the belated recognition and respect being given to Aboriginal cultures by the government and the media and therefore by the wider community. We believe that the time is now right for multicultural writing to enter the literary arena with more strength than ever before. Its value to the community is immeasurable. As in the case of Aboriginal writing, we have to consider not only the contribution of specific works but also the collective effect of the body of multicultural writing on public awareness and national self-understanding. Within a specific work, if value, or excellence, is measured (as it often is) according to the complexities 'contained' (or opened up) by a text then it is crucial to understand the traditions operating behind that text. For instance, even when these non-Anglo-Celtic texts are written in English, their allusions may be predominantly to Greek or Italian or European literature. In Judah Waten's case, for example, Russian and Yiddish literature were arguably dominant influences. We have not even begun the work needed to interpret in an informed way the writers who draw upon the Chinese, Vietnamese, Turkish, Lebanese and other traditions. An alertness to cultural networks can only enrich our national culture and will help to situate Australia more self-consciously within our actual geographic context, the Pacific region, which is culturally dominated by Asia rather than Europe.

To call such claims for inclusion in the national culture marginal can work in two ways. The margin may be a position of strength on the one hand; on the other it can operate to reinforce the claims of a self-styled centre. Edward Said has argued compellingly that the margin, the place of exile, is often the site for a healthy scepticism where borders are breached and a useful distrust of orthodoxy and dogma is bred: ' Exile is a life led outside habitual order. It is nomadic, decentred, contrapuntal . . .' (Said 1984a: 172).The notion of a contrapuntal existence is very appealing. Said also warns, however, that membership of one marginal group may blind one to competing claims. For example, concentration on gender oppression may render one unreceptive to racial and cultural differences. That the margins may produce a necessary critique of the centre is exemplified by Said himself (a Palestinian operating in the United States). That they also engender creativity of other kinds is illustrated by writers like Kafka[2] and Salman Rushdie. The latter has, incidentally, stated that he is 'beginning to suspect that there is no such thing as a homogeneous culture' (Rushdie 1988: 37). What we must guard against, however, is the incorporation of merely token figures from the so-called margins who exist as a type of alibi for claims that the culture is inclusive and fully representative.

II. THE INCLUSIONS OF FUTURE AUSTRALIAN LITERATURE

How would the inclusion of non-Anglo-Celtic Australian writing redefine our national literature? In the first place, it would highlight the fact that until now the terrain labelled Australian literature has been shaped by very specific cultural perspectives: those emanating from England and Ireland. In other words, this shaping would no longer appear 'natural' and thus would be opened up for further analysis. There are proposals, for instance, which would re-read Australian culture from the perspective of German Australians (who have also been here for many generations). As part of his program of such re-readings, Mudrooroo Narogin (Colin Johnson) (1988: 3) has given non-Aboriginal readers an impression of what Les Murray's poetry looks like from a particular Aboriginal viewpoint.

A very generalised view of non-Anglo-Celtic Australian writing could describe it as falling roughly into three areas which may all occur in the same writer and are by no means constructed as an evolutionary model. The first corresponds to Said's contrapuntal vision insofar as it deals with those texts which juxtapose the old and the new cultures. Such writing, often nostalgic and elegiac, is usually perceived to be the only form that so-called migrant writing may take.[3] And indeed, this is the only group which can properly be termed *migrant* writing.

The second group often corresponds with the second generation after immigration and may be described as taking up the position of translation and mediation, contrapuntal in other ways. At home in both languages and cultures, these writers translate one reality into the other and mediate between the two. Names which spring to mind are Loukakis, Skrzynecki, Dell'oso, Giles, Papaellinas, Baranay, Safransky and others.

The third group is made up of those who forge new languages and new representations. This may be true to some extent of all the writers mentioned but one thinks here in particular of Π.O., Ania Walwicz, Anna Couani and others. They foreground the transgressive possibilities of incorporating elements from other languages and other systems of representation into the more conventional forms, not least in their blurring of the traditional boundaries between speech and writing. Their 'Australia' looks very different; indeed it is illuminating to compile a group of writings, including the work of these cross-cultural experimental writers, around the proper name Australia (Goodwin & Lawson 1989:292–330).

Part I comprises essays which deal with theoretical perspectives in a broadly abstract way. What are the wider implications of looking at cultural difference? As a writer sensitive to ambiguities, Brian Castro aptly opens the volume with his tantalising examination of the wellsprings of creativity and the tensions provided by too much contact with public controversies. Multiculturalism, he asserts, demands a pluralism which decrees that there are only margins and that the centre constitutes an absence. Paul Carter examines the ways in which language, in the form of personal memoirs intersecting haptically with place as 'the arrangement of buildings and spaces', functions to redefine our whole way of being in the world and in history. Examining imported architectural accessories, he sees them as camouflaging the lack of fit between our migrant culture's inner space and the outer place it inhabits. Kateryna Longley looks at the ways in which postwar migrants to some extent constitute a new world, a fifth world of the displaced. Manfred

Jurgensen sets up aesthetic frameworks and concepts for multicultural writing, thus taking on board the question of aesthetic value. For him the 'multicultural imagination' is by no means synonymous with migrant writing. Sneja Gunew's essay places contemporary discussions concerning minority literatures within the context of debates around postmodernism and postcolonialism.

Part II emphasises specific studies of particular language groups. Such work is being done by pioneers like Marko Pavlyshyn for Ukrainian Australians, by Leslie Bodi, who recently retired as Professor of German at Monash, by Serge Liberman, who has produced his monumental compilation of Jewish-Australian writings, by George Kanarakis, whose anthology of Greek-Australian writers (1987) was a landmark in multicultural literary studies, and by others. Sadly, we have not been able to include their work in this anthology, but we are conscious that this compilation would not have been possible without their endeavours. We fervently believe that this volume is only the beginning and that many more studies will follow.

Included in Part II are essays by Con Castan and Gaetano Rando, who have worked to establish Greek- and Italo-Australian literature respectively. We have produced their selected bibliographies in appendices in order to provide models for further studies of this kind. What we hope these sample bibliographies will achieve is a new awareness of the fact that there are a hundred or more such bibliographies possible though not present here. This is the future which needs to be constructed–an exciting task. Included in this section of the literary history is, as well, the enthusiastic response of Jim Kable who has worked for many years to have cultural differences acknowledged within secondary school curricula. We have placed in conjunction with these essays the personal statements of writers such as Walter Adamson, who ruefully concedes that his preserved German functions as a kind of Latin when he visits his homeland. Maria Lewitt argues for an inclusive model of literary life within Australia, while Anna Couani details the discursive and political shifts which may operate within a writer's life. Lidija Simkus-Pocius eloquently describes the pull of the home culture, particularly when that culture exists freely only in its diasporic forms. Peter Skrzynecki delineates the bitter-sweet experience of returning to a homeland that is both familiar and foreign. With her habitual elegance and concision, Antigone Kefala charts the perils and challenges of straddling several cultures and languages. All these writers draw attention to the ways in which their personal histories as artists have intersected with the public culture of Australia.

Part III deals with individual author studies, revealing that they inevitably provide theoretical frameworks, though not always as explicitly as those essays included in Part I. David Carter sets up a challenging study of Judah Waten, who, for many years, has been regarded as the founding father of multicultural writing. Carter emphasises the need for putting categories like migrant or ethnic writer within a historical framework which appreciably changes their significance. Yasmine Gooneratne looks at the work of the Punjabi-Australian writer Mena Abdullah. Nikos Papastergiadis examines the work of Antigone Kefala and in the process refashions our general ways of reading migrant writing and Greek-Australian writing. Rather than taking these categories as givens, he asks us to look at the conceptual space which exists between these yoked terms. His essay constitutes a dialogue with Castan's earlier chapter. By juxtaposing Malouf's *An Imaginary Life* with a poem by an Austrian writer and with extracts from a German explorer's journal, Walter Veit looks at interculturalism and 'foreignness' in relation to hermeneutic interpretation and so distinguishes intercultural criticism from traditional comparative literary criticism.

Margaret Coombs rightly questions various cultural and literary categories with respect to the individual subject who invariably has alliances all over the place. Loló Houbein, whose pioneering work can arguably be said to have begun the mapping of multicultural criticism, here charts her own progress as a writer who refuses stereotypes of culture and gender. Vasso Kalamaras poignantly recreates her Greek childhood and shows how its influences penetrate her writing even now. Aina Vāvere, by way of a characteristically wry parable, suggests that the appearance of multicultural pluralism within Australian culture testifies to its having reached a certain maturity.

In Part IV the accent is on those who foreground the tensions and contradictions that surround traditional ways of reading migrant or multicultural writings. Ivor Indyk analyses the humour many of these works exude, and Efi Hatzimanolis looks at the layers of irony produced by Silvana Gardner's poetry. In drawing our attention to the Pacific, Satendra Nandan produces a different cultural perspective, which exposes our Western cultural bias. His essay chimes to some extent with the view provided by Gooneratne's essay. Dewi Anggraeni displays with grace and humour the absurdities generated by stereotypical responses to her as an Indonesian writer. George Papaellinas, with his customary adroitness, provides a highly satirical account of the ways in which multicultural debates and terminology circulate within the wider community. Rosa Safransky recreates the surrealistic milieu of growing up as a second-generation migrant Martian and Cornelis Vleeskens depicts the stages in his rediscovery of his Dutch culture within an Australian context.

In Part V the narratives are not so much expository as laterally suggestive. These exemplify some of the new directions which multicultural writing promises. Thalia's concrete poetry undoes our received perceptions concerning the intersections between literature and a specific language. Zeny Giles collects and tells stories, as does Birimbir

Wongar, who has spent a lifetime negotiating the terrain between migrant and indigenous cultures. Ania Walwicz closes the volume with her unique style of rewriting the personal.

These are beginnings. Other volumes will follow, with detailed studies of writers not represented here, but this will take time and concerted effort. We need to assemble many more books in order to persuade institutions to recognise this area of study so that researchers may have access to a centralised body of necessary material.[4]

All these activities need to occur contrapuntally with what has hitherto been designated Australian literature in order to reconstruct the history of that field and to redirect its future so that it becomes receptive to changes in ways we cannot even predict. As Stuart Hall has put it: 'Identity is formed at the unstable point where the "unspeakable" stories of subjectivity meet the narratives of history, of a culture' (Hall 1987: 44). The interview between winners and losers must metamorphose into a mutually informed dialogue in order for us to create a more representative national literature which recognises that there are simply all of us, here and now, in Australia.

Part I: Theoretical perspectives

1 Necessary idiocy and the idea of freedom

Brian Castro

I would like to tell you a simple story. This story comes to me by way of Robert Bly, the American poet. Writers, he says, need to preserve their frogskins. Frogskins, not foreskins; though writing can be something of a circumcision when forced into categories—something between public ritual and private pain. To counteract this phallocentrism let me offer you the metaphor of writing as woman, not only as the repressed, but as the source. Bly relates it this way. It is, in fact, an old Russian fairy tale:

> A father orders his three sons to shoot arrows as ways of choosing their brides. The first of the brothers shoots his arrow and lo and behold! it lands beside the daughter of a prince. The second brother shoots his arrow and ends up marrying a general's daughter. The youngest son's arrow, however, falls into a pond, out of which a frog hops, carrying the arrow in its mouth. He marries the frog. He is terribly ashamed. A few years on, and after many crises, his bride offers to appear at the king's ball as a human being, shedding her frogskin and leaving it at home. She entrances everyone at the ball with her beauty. Her husband, similarly entranced and seeking permanence, rushes home to burn the frogskin. Tragedy, of course, ensues.

This story provides us with a whole map of misreading. One interpretation is that writers burn their frogskins in many ways: by becoming public, by selling out, by writing too many reviews. Writing, ideally, should be something private, a discipline, perhaps even an experience of grief. If we burn our frogskins we lose our way back to the source.

For many years, I declined invitations to speak at arts festivals, at literary luncheons and on other public occasions. This was not because I hankered after some kind of notoriety as a reclusive writer, but because of a feeling of being marginal, and a feeling that this marginality gave me the impetus to write. It was my way, as it were, of keeping the frogskin wet. It seemed to me that there were two kinds of writers:

those who courted publicity and who then let the publicity generate their future writing, and those who lived only for writing, though writing doesn't permit you to live, and who suffered from being unknown and unread. Though it is eccentric and lonely to write for the desk drawer, it is equally a misfortune to become the sport of one's reputation or the mouthpiece of others; namely, to be living outside of oneself.

At that time, I also read something by the Peruvian novelist Mario Vargas Llosa, whose works I very much admired. Vargas Llosa tells how on 2 December 1969, another Peruvian novelist, José Maria Arguedas, shot himself in a classroom of La Molina Agricultural University in Lima. Some days later, people began receiving letters from him explaining his suicide. In the letters, Arguedas revealed that he had been living a dilemma, that he had spent his life torn between different cultures and societies. Raised among the Indian peasants in the Andes, he was obliged, when he became a writer, to fulfil certain social responsibilities of which he felt he was incapable. In a way, he suffered the classic dilemma of facing his own art while being overcome by the self-conscious idea of culture.

I agonised over the Arguedas affair for a long time. I debated with myself over such issues as whether books can ever change people's minds, whether polemics can shape history, or whether the writer can be truly independent. On the other hand, I asked myself whether entertainment is a truly worthwhile activity, whether art can maintain its loftiness quite apart from incidents of racial hatred, intimidation and repression. Each time I came up not with contradictions but with paradoxes. Language simply refused to be categorised. Language which ceased to be functional in fact opposed any power position framed by categories.

It was with something akin to this sense of liberation a few years before, that I began to write *Birds of Passage*. It was written entirely without a sense of context. The Asian question in Australia was simmering, as it had been doing for well on 130 years. There had not yet been any outburst in the press, no media coverage of so-called debates, no rabid nationalism. But within a year of the book's publication, the historian whose words appear quoted in the epigraph to my book had suddenly made a speech based on the racial selection of migrants, on the value of cultural homogeneity and on the virtues of Anglo-Saxon ethnocentrism. Things exploded. Suddenly anyone was given a licence to categorise, to anthropologise, to authorise. It was of particular interest for me to note that the Australian chapter of the National Front adopted as its literary mascot Henry Lawson—one of Australia's most famous sons, a social realist and also one who couldn't come to terms with his own racism. I received publications from this group, long articles filled with racial invective. In a way, I was more than a little flattered to think that I had somehow privately pressed one corner of the psychic fabric of the nation, whose history of radical nationalism and Anglo-Saxon conservatism has always demonstrated this extremity.

My reaction was a strange one. I sat down and began to read, all over again, Proust's *Remembrance of Things Past*. I think I needed to recover a language which I believed came from the interior. And it was this language in Proust that showed me the way out of the dilemma. It showed me that writing was on the outside, that language was a process which continually remade itself as an object, in the spaces between events. It taught me that writing was the constant process of experience sliding into thought; that it relinquished the past as nostalgia for a future possibility which would resist the gratification of immediate understanding and possession. Above all, it taught me that it came out of a crisis of contradiction. For instance, the more I admired Proust for the subjectiveness of language, the more mimetic my own writing became. The more I tried to underpin its illusions with reality, the more it strove to be antihistorical, becoming fiercely determined to establish its own ineffable truth.

Yet the need to say 'no' to the standard exigencies of culture is not a moral position. The need to dissent is to carve out a life apposite to what is after all a way of life, not a lifestyle, but a life of writing, which can exist only in interrogating the assumptions of culture. The speculative nature of dissent allows a rational ideal to be won back by its will to be free. For that is what culture is: an absorption and a surrendering; a dynamic give and take, not a static decree. And it suddenly became clear to me that culture was not only being reified but appropriated in such a way as to generate a division between society and culture. It was what Thomas Mann referred to so many years ago, when he talked about the German *Innerlichkeit*, the inwardness which dispensed with social responsibility in the name of identity. It was this problem of identity which depressed me most, for it seemed to me that in its name some Australian intellectuals failed to speak for responsibility. And this, I suppose, was the difference between intellectuals and writers: essentially non-active, writers drowned in ambiguity. They had the special encumbrance of feelings to overcome before thought could surface. Thought needed long pauses, and these pauses often became novels.

Asians, some of these people rationalised, scarcely needed defending. Like the Jews in Europe almost 50 years ago, they ran businesses. They survived. Even those who were refugees from Vietnam needed little help. They had undergone such atrocities, why worry over a little bit of racism? This was how the argument ran. And this became the treason of the intellectuals. By exploiting the essential conservatism of Australian society, they conveniently neglected society in their definition of culture. In their deriding of metaphysical universality they nevertheless raised the mythical concept of nation over civilisation. It was with some irony, therefore, that I used to read about the search for identity, identity which, as Theodor Adorno pointed out many years ago, was the pretext for the suppression of heterogeneity.

It seemed to me that identity had become more important than writing, with the inevitable consequence of writing becoming invisible. It fell into the danger, for example, of neglecting the basic premise of the novel, which, as Milan Kundera has pointed out, must make a discovery. What most novels seemed to be doing was affirming what was already an accepted view—not only of life, but of literature. The novel was moribund, we were told. Writers should instead concentrate on their *craft*. This journeyman approach to writing, of course, did nothing to threaten the status quo. In a country in which conservatism used to dictate change in minutely perceptible degrees, it came as no surprise that in literature, it was the realistic short story that held sway instead of the novel with its looming, brooding menace. The short story had all the panache of a minor skirmish. The short story owed its allegiance to craft and message. Quickly read and quickly forgotten, used up in its moment, it remained incidental. This functional notion of literature as representation remains to this day.

It was to the credit of people of vision that writing in Australia, the 'dun-coloured realism', as Patrick White called it, changed. These people saw to it that Australia was connected to the wider world, recognising that the isolationist mentality, so prevalent for so long, mirrored its own destruction. And I think more people are beginning to realise that we are more free when we struggle, more free even when we encounter friction between cultures, than if we wrapped our lives in cotton wool. Cultural collectivity arises out of its knowledge of its presence in the world, out of its internationalism. It is therefore no coincidence that such a radical realisation should send the conservative political parties in Australia to consider legislation based on race. Conservatism based on isolationism had been forced into an extremist role.

You will have gathered by now that what I have to say about writing cannot be disassociated from a social context. I don't for one moment mean to say that writing must deal with it, even in an allegorical way. What I'm saying is that on a very basic level, even to publish depends on that psychic fabric, that climate in which your writing is made possible and in which your writing can exist for others. It is possible that it is only in the past ten years or so that migrant writers began to be read. It is also possible that it is only as a result of the advent of multiculturalism and the efflorescence of publishing of the literature of 'foreigners' in Australia that I am here today, with the help of translators, editors, commentators and members of the Literature Board of the Australia Council who have taken such an interest in promoting Australian writing abroad. For what is being written now in Australia demonstrates the full range of this release from identity. What is so exciting about it is that it is beginning to subvert assumptions about literature itself, enabling the body of ideas to brush against the very ephemeral texture of language without the necessity to remain economically viable. I am thinking particularly of current Australian writers like Gerald Murnane, Mark Henshaw, Rod Jones, Marion Campbell and David Brooks, among others. For this, surely, must be the pleasure of the text, the revisitation of the field upon which philosophy and literature do battle without a primary allegiance to an unquestioning acceptance of place.

I am not in the mainstream of Australian literature. I do not want to be there. This is because I do not think a mainstream exists, in any particular culture. Far from seeing multiculturalism as a set of humanistic platitudes concerning culture-bridging (which derives from a soporific assimilationist ideology; literary assimilation follows the same paths), or as a series of folkloric dances and ethnic festivals, I see it as the idealisation of pluralism. And the ideal pluralism is when everybody exists on the margins, because the centre, which is like the centre of writing itself, is an absence.

How, then, can an absence be categorised? It has always seemed to me that 'nation' exerted too much pressure on the writing process. Paradoxically, any form of nationalism both promoted writers and destroyed them. I have always preferred to stay well away from that paradox. When I speak of dissent, I speak not of some kind of facile opposition, but of a measuring of displacement, not in terms of overturning the system but of forcing a presence upon old prejudices.

But even as I speak, accelerated time and compressed historical consciousness have defeated any evolutionism. It is too late already to define. There are other ways of reading, other ways of seeing. The story of the frog unfolds. I prefer now to read the story this way: I prefer to read the experience of grief as the critical edge, the constant and infinite experience of failure and difference, built in, but also visible, at the point at which a literary experience forces itself into thought. I prefer to see failure as the x-ray of writing, as that which exists, more than anything else, as the memory of death, as the end of the limit of presence and the beginning of possibility. For just as memorisation entails the loss and erasure of recollected experience, criticism creates a crisis by warring over the control of an absent centre long vacated by the real experience. And so the creative, which flickers momentarily, glimpses its negative, a conceptualisation which writing recognises in the context of its being re-written. The *re*-vision, then, is primarily something that simulates this re-writing. And the *re*-view, this seeing again, is also a writing again, at once public and self-reflective. It mirrors the text, and simulates a monologue briefly interrupted in the continuous flow of words. If there is a battle, then, between writer and spokesperson, it is present in this dual nature of writing and rewriting and not in an external circumstance of performing two roles; present as a mute allegory of truth within the text, the cost of which is the consumption of the source.

7

All the same, I thought of José Maria Arguedas. His legacy to me was the realisation that existence and language were two aspects of the same question and that writing was the asking of this question. Perhaps he asked it more deeply than any of us.

About a month before I left Australia I noticed that there was a conference called Dis/Unities, a conference based on differences and dissent. A conference in which the word 'multiculturalism' would not be interrogated, but would be understood as a fait accompli. Its debates over differences, over dissent, seemed to me to have come a long way in a short time. This was either a ray of hope or the ultimate anodyne. What did it do for writing? It convinced me that writers do not set out to communicate anything. They set out to create a particular world which thrives on being different, and which may not necessarily coincide with their views as a person. To expose it to discussion was to risk stepping into another world, to see too clearly why one's face once wore the mask of 'necessary idiocy' and, indeed to cease writing altogether by burning one's frogskin. The difference, then, is between the world of the written and the world of the writer as human being. One transgresses limits, the other tries to speak for its excesses in a very puzzled way.

Writing knows no boundaries. Its metaphors, its translations, are part of a migratory process, birds of passage which wing from the subliminal to the page, leaving their signs for the reader. Meanwhile the writer stands a little to the side, shooting arrows into the wind, with an expression of alarmed uncertainty as the traces disappear into the eternal roar of society's unconscious.

This chapter originally formed part of a paper given in France on the occasion of the translation of *Birds of Passage*.

2 Lines of communication: Meaning in the migrant environment

Paul Carter

The meaning and significance we attribute to our lives are closely bound up with a sense of place. Places—memorable arrangements of buildings and spaces—give us a sense of orientation. Conversely, a totally homogeneous environment is disorienting, it has no human meaning. There is an influential school of architectural criticism which argues that buildings and urban spaces are, or should be, projections of the human body. The features of public and private space—verandas, footpaths, flights of stairs—should make the human individual feel at home. There should be a proportion between our own size and form and the scale and design of our surroundings. Integration with the built environment is not achieved visually, but *haptically*: by experiencing the place you live in with your body rather than by simply looking at it through a car windscreen. Haptic spaces are those that satisfactorily externalise our deep emotional need for community; they create places to embrace and inhabit, places that speak to us.[1]

The corollary of this argument is that the inhabitants of environments which lack haptic values are likely to feel physically and emotionally disoriented, literally out of touch. Their attempts to give meaning to their lives are likely to be reactive rather than interactive, reflecting alienation from the surroundings, not a sense of oneness. Writers and artists will focus on the failure of the environment to communicate human values; they will draw attention to the draining of language of all deeper meaning, to the instability of visual appearances and, more generally, to the lack of connection between the environment they inhabit and the words and images available to them to describe it.

Melbourne's north-western suburb of Brunswick, where I live, offers none of that stability, that feeling of natural forces gathered and *located* that, for writers like Norberg-Schulz, constitutes the *genius loci* of true cities. Legislative fiat, not an organic rapport with the local topography, marked Brunswick's beginnings—and its boundaries. There is a story

9

that the local Aborigines' name for the area where Brunswick is sited was 'windy place' (*Jubilee History* 1907: 33). Like most Aboriginal etymologies applied to Australian place names, this one is probably false. In reporting it, local historians alluded not to some divine afflatus blessing the site but to the absence of any sign that this plain was marked out by nature as a nurturing, sheltering place.

What is true of Brunswick is more generally true of the majority of Australian suburbs and towns established by act of parliament and laid out, with little regard for the local topography, in the decidedly non-haptic form of a rectangular grid. As the late-baroque towns of Sicily demonstrate, the surveyor's grid did not necessarily prevent the rapid emergence of a fully human habitat. But the circumstances in which Australia's colonial settlements emerged were different. In particular, if the new towns of Noto and Catania were intended to arrest the movement of the local population, and focus it on the urban centre, the nineteenth-century towns pegged out in Australia aimed to facilitate the passage and dispersal of people (Carter 1987: 217).

The main streets of Australian country towns and suburbs exhibit a melange of Italianate forms. But the function of the neoclassical pediments and pillars, the quattrocento pilasters and roundels, the baroque aediculi and lean-to verandas is not haptic: unlike the European originals they so eclectically quote from, their object is not to project a complex body image, to entice the body in with a promise of inner spaces that will at once enlarge and enclose it. On the contrary, their function is to sell space *in the absence of an inner space*. Their visual rhetoric is designed to project an air of solidity in the absence of any secure economic foundations or tradition of occupation. Their speculative facades mirror the nature of the activity that occurs within them. Businesses move in and, a few months later, move out again. The passage these buildings promote is pecuniary rather than pedestrian and their purely visual rhetoric signifies the emptiness of appearances rather than promoting any sense of stability or local identity.

It is not surprising that the most prominent form of self-expression these environments inspire is invisibly perpetrated graffiti—messages of love and hope, injunctions to save the air, to fight rape. The site of these messages is as important as their content. They are written over the very surfaces that signify the death of that haptic environment on whose existence, the graffitists imply, our own existence depends. But there is a further irony: the graffitists' efforts are insignificant in comparison with the welter of signs that legally dominate the visual landscapes of our major streets. Windows, architraves, first floor ledges and rooftops, not to mention every available wall space, exist not as architectural units but as writing places, projecting a steady, constantly changing stream of prices, brand names and even, solipsistically, notices of their own sale and demolition.

In a situation where buildings exist to provide a surface for signs, where the traditional relationship between signifier and signified is reversed, spray-canned messages urging us to shoulder our human and environmental responsibilities have a sharp pathos. No doubt they express a nostalgia for architectural spaces (and faces) that might speak for themselves, that might face us fair and square and enter into dialogue. But the walls, it seems, have lost all touch with haptic reality. They are simply *writing places*, scaffolding for signs. In writing on them our nocturnal moralists cannot help but emulate the advertisers who, long ago, recognised the profitability of a billboard landscape and accordingly adapted their messages to the eyes of passing motorists.

But even if, miraculously, our colonial and postcolonial built environment did possess the emotional and expressive values associated with the great cities of the old world, it is not clear how this would contribute to that spirit of outer place so essential, we are told, to the development of a meaningful inner life and its translation into resonant social and aesthetic forms. For the instability of our architecture is a reflection of the instability of the bodies that lodge there. Nearly three-quarters of the people living in Brunswick were born overseas; of the remaining one-quarter, the majority were born elsewhere in Australia. And of the total population living here, perhaps half will die elsewhere. Migration, from both without and within, has been endemic in Australian social and cultural life ever since European occupation.

It is often said that a sign of our contemporary condition is our sense that the world no longer affords us a home, that by our own actions we have rendered ourselves exiles on our own planet. But, less apocalyptically, a similar perspective informs much nineteenth-century Australian social commentary. The author of *Land, Labour and Gold* (Howitt 1972, vol. 2: 173) described the squatter as a 'nomad by his very name', and, according to the 'Emigrant Mechanic', Alexander Harris (1964), the working population of mid-nineteenth-century Australia was incessantly on the move. Vernacular architecture reflected this mobility: no 'old' countryside contains more ruins than Australia, remains of temporary houses dating from a period when history was geography and places remained to be defined. The truth is that our prefabricated suburban cottages and jerry-built terrace houses, clinging to the sides of channels of traffic, have not served as living places so much as camp sites, stopping places along the way; and, although the final destination may have remained unrealised, the dream of moving on has often prevented migrant residents from ever accepting *this* as the place where they live.

The doubletalk of real-estate advertising accurately expresses the provisional nature of suburban occupation. The dwellings it promotes are simultaneously timeless and affordable. They have a charm and character all their own, but invite adaptation to your 'lifestyle'. It is easy to ridicule the language of property promotion, its devaluation of superlatives through their persistent attachment to inappropriate objects (and recip-rocally, the emptying of buildings of any integrity they might possess by describing them in terms that are transparently inappropriate), but the rhetorical techniques employed are representative of the way public language is used more generally in migrant environments.

The point that real-estate journalism makes clear is that, as with public signs, so with private dwellings the distinction between signifier and signified has collapsed. The language of real-estate promotion circu-lates without reference to perceptible objects. It constitutes its own signified. It promotes a way of life that exists nowhere outside its own discourse. The built environment serves only as a writing surface, a place to affix signs that advertise the non-existence of buildings apart from their circulation in the market.

The nausea this destruction of meaning brings on, the nostalgia it creates for a more stable human and architectural community, should not be underestimated. In a recently published autobiographical memoir as remarkable for its structure as for its content, R.A. Baggio (1989) begins not by describing his own birthplace (Little River, Victoria) but with a rapturous evocation of Cittadella, his father's birthplace in north-ern Italy. When, in his forties, Baggio visited the town, his father's stories came back to him. He greeted the church, 'a touchingly simple and ancient structure'; as for the stone inside containing the imprint of a medieval saint's buttocks, 'I recognised [it] immediately, like an old friend who had not been seen for a long time' (Baggio 1989: 2). It is symptomatic of the psychic importance of this temporary haptic reintegration that half the photographs in Baggio's wholly Australian narrative depict *palazzi*, *piazze* and doorways in Cittadella and neigh-bouring Padua. There is not a single picture of 'home'.

Baggio has never felt 'at home' in Australia; his surroundings here have not provided him with a satisfactory body image, a mothering space that both nurtures him and helps him define his own difference. But the psychic deprivation he feels as a migrant to Australia is not only haptic: it is also linguistic. The instability he experiences arises from a sense of not being *at home in language*; he does not *dwell* in language, language does not *shelter* his innermost thoughts. Language, like architecture, is a means of structuring reality. The naming of things, like the imposition of perspective, is a means of defining one's own place and identity. But if one's own name is unstable, then so, too, is one's sense of place. In a passage too long to quote here, Baggio lists all the mispronunciations to which his surname has been prone, commenting how well-suited it was for 'invention, improvisation, innovation and fantastication' (Baggio 1989: 15).

In Australia, his name ceased to be a fixed point of reference and identity: it acquired the migrant virtues of adaptability and self-effacement. It was almost as if each new situation demanded a new name. At any rate, no two people in Australia pronounced his name in the same way, and as a consequence, his surname ceased to signify a personal history and came to refer instead only to *this* situation, this negotiation with a neighbour or employer. Beyond that it had no meaning whatsoever, for even its anglicised form was without stability and would be subject to further change tomorrow. His name was a swag he shouldered, a means of travelling from one human situation to another, but it no longer provided him with a house of his own, a place from which he could speak.

In the migrant environment, then, the desire to make sense of the world suffers a double setback. The provisional nature of occupation undermines that sense of place which is so essential a foundation, we are told, of an integrated psychic and emotional existence, while the provisional nature of language undermines the migrant's attempt to map his surroundings, to place over it a firm semantic grid. Further, as I have suggested, these two difficulties are related, for language is in many senses a virtual architecture. Dialogue, for instance, depends on the give and take of language across a space; and the echo we listen for in the voice of the other is also an experience we welcome in buildings.[2]

At the same time, though, this critique of the migrant environment, and the assumption that it is hostile to the formation of a sense of community (in an imaginative as well as social sense), arouses a certain unease. Even if the culture of the quarter-acre block is deficient in architectural meaning, the fact remains that it has been a historical and social success. The average suburban streetscape may be postmodernist before its time—a parodic collage of architectural styles from every period and centre of Western building—but the layout, the organisation of space into a repeated pattern of rectangular units, has been an efficient means of promoting and controlling the twin processes of colonisation and migration. As I have argued elsewhere (1987), the appeal of the grid plan lies precisely in the fact that it does *not* resemble a place: the grid is a meta-place, it offers a spatial grammar which permits the articulation of as many places or homes as there are squares; every allotment occupies the same space; each allotment dwelling can be utterly individual.

The grid permits newcomers to occupy a new country without embracing local manners or local topography. It is a means of articulating human presence in the absence of a mutually intelligible language (a tradition of occupation, a background of shared values). Each person, each property owner, knows where he stands, even if he stands nowhere. Similarly, neighbours can enter into a kind of dialogue, even if they have neither language nor culture in common. The gift of the grid is not meaningful places but a system of divisions—fence lines, road edges, pavements—that lend the inhabitants a provisional difference, a complementary otherness that can provide the basis of a kind of exchange.

The grid may not project the human body but it does make manifest another human need—the desire to communicate, to make contact *even when there is nothing to say*. The orderly streets of the colonial grid are lines of communication and, even if the pavements are empty, the telephone wires underground are humming with messages.

A parallel exists between the function of the urban and suburban grid and the role of language in the migrant environment. The grid is not a place, but it provides the grammar and syntax from which an infinity of places may be generated. Similarly, in a colonial and postcolonial context, English (or whatever transplanted European tongue constitutes the official language) acts, not as a means of self-expression, but as a language in the absence of a language of one's own. English provides a vocabulary of signifiers that, while they have no deep resonance for the speaker (no poetic power), enable him to go through the motions of speech. And, like the quarter-acre block, the elements of language are also susceptible to extreme variations: just as no two houses are alike, so no two usages of the lexicon are likely to be identical.

Baggio may despise the pidginisation of his name but, from another point of view, its instability is liberating: the mutation of its vowel sounds, the variety of stress patterns it can be made to bear, become the oil of social intercourse. When, for example, the Italian word 'cappuccino' becomes pidginised as 'cup-o-chino', the meaning of this word, the humanising wit that makes it acceptable, consists in its double aural deformation of English and Italian. The only resemblance the new word has to, say, 'a cup of China tea' is phonic, punning: no semantic connection is implied. We welcome an etymologically absurd word as meaningful because we recognise there the residue of an authentic migrant dialogue, one in which meaning is erected not on the firm foundation of semantics but on the shifting sands of sound.[3] To warp sound (unfamiliar words and phrases) into words that, for the purposes of this dialogue, make sense, verbal 'invention' and 'fantastication' are essential.

Speaking English, the migrant may not be able to say anything significant, but he can at least signify his desire to speak; in the absence of a distinctive place from which to speak, he can articulate his desire of a speaking place, a position that may endow his voice with depth. Although the signifier (speech) may be its own signified (the desire of speech), it still signifies something, namely what cannot be said. And that, however minimally, is to delineate a place of one's own. Hence, when an Italian immigrant fruiterer writes his name on his shop sign as 'Fresh E. Day', he simultaneously uses English and usurps its claim to authority. Parodying its power to name, he is able to name his own difference. This difference may only be articulated by a silence—by drawing attention to a place where his name is *not* written—but still, and albeit negatively, a kind of expression has been achieved.

The usurpation of linguistic (and architectural) authority can be interpreted psychoanalytically. It is no accident that Baggio's sense of being unnamed in Australia leads him to make a pilgrimage to his father's birthplace. In recovering his male lineage he legitimates himself. But there is an irony here. For in seeking his roots, Baggio aims to reclaim the very past that his father cheerfully rejected. In a sense Baggio is seeking the father *for him*—not his biological father, but his psychic father. And, in this respect, he may simply be reversing the decision his father made when, 40 years earlier, he moved from Italy to Victoria.

For a counterforce impels the migrant, a secret, Oedipal desire to throw off the incubus of the fatherland, its traditions, language and even family ties. And, while a genuine liberation may be experienced in embracing a destiny of one's own (however humble it may prove to be), it is not achieved without considerable cost. The father's indifference to his past is a measure of the psychological and emotional price he has paid. His silence becomes the pledge of his continuing liberation, his refusal to countenance returning. But by the same token, the son interprets this silence as a rejection of *him* and, bypassing his father, feels impelled to go back, to articulate what has been suppressed. In this sense it is not only the migrant father who murders his father, but the son who, against his father's wishes, re-establishes kinship with the old country—a country which, to him of course, is new, unoccupied.

One value of a psychoanalytical account is, perhaps surprisingly, that it shows how the migrant experience is a cultural as well as a physical and psychic phenomenon. The nostalgia and sense of displacement that the children and grandchildren of migrants may feel are not derived from any personal memory of another place: they are culturally mediated, a reaction to the deprivation of the migrant environment as much as a genuine desire to 'go back'. This helps explain why perhaps this identity conflict is not confined to ethnic minorities but also finds expression in the oscillation in Australian speech between 'correct' English usage and 'ocker' Australian—an instability of linguistic register typical, rather than exceptional, in male Australian conversation—and which, incidentally, also characterises the prose of a displaced autobiographer like Baggio.

The problem with a psychoanalytical description of the migrant's search for meaning is that, like Baggio, it regards the improvisatory nature of the migrant environment with deep suspicion. Just as Freud considered parapraxes as signs of suppressed drives, so those who decry the distortions to which migrant language and architecture are subject in migrant cultures always have in mind an ideal form, a true word that names directly, a human house that proportions exactly, our desires. From this point of view the improvisations and fantastications that characterise the construction of migrant meaning can only be regarded as forms of repression, veiling a psychic deprivation too shameful to confess. But in reality, the provisional character of migrant names and building forms does not represent the transference of unresolved private dreams into the public arena: the provisionality begins outside as the condition of migrant communication.

A better way of describing how meanings emerge in the migrant environment is by way of the model of dialogue. The phenomenological stress on haptic experience idealises the human subject, imagining him in solitary rapport with his surroundings. But the psychoanalytical model of psychic integration is no less idealising: even when stripped of its mentalism and taken as a semantic model, it pays insufficient attention to the dialogical nature of the individual's existence in the world. And both accounts underestimate the contingency of experience, the simple fact, daily illustrated by the dynamics of dialogue, that in making sense of things we project sounds and forms *in the hope that they will find a home*, an answering voice or recognisable shape (Gadamer 1976: 5).

The success of dialogue in creating a common place of meaning depends on both parties coming halfway. It depends on their not remaining stubbornly attached to their own points of view, on their willingness to improvise new meanings and thereby to create a common ground of understanding. In this sense, dialogue in the migrant environment does not make a regression from the 'high' dialogue we associate with, say, the bourgeois novel or the Edwardian stage. On the contrary, and in contrast with these dialogue genres which take the dialogue form for granted, the sometimes stuttering efforts of people trying, in the absence of a common tongue, to make sense of each other recovers the original urgency of dialogue, its spatial and performative core as a means of marking out a common place of utterance where, in the future perhaps, sounds and meanings may settle down and become social bonds.

But it is clear that, so long as we insist that the migrant's integrity depends on retreating more fully into himself psychically and physically, no dialogue is possible and the migrant environment will remain alien and threatening. Possibly at the instigation of his editor, Baggio includes in his memoir some examples of the pidginised Italian spoken by 'most Italians' in his district. It is a language which, as Baggio explains, evolved orally, amongst people who were largely illiterate: 'This speaking English by ear approach was a principal reason, I think, for the invention and rapid spread of a lingua franca which might be called Taglian or Hightalian' (Baggio 1989: 67). The resulting speech is neither English nor Italian, although it exploits to the full casual phonic resemblances. It is an improvised tongue, a dialogical formation without legitimate father or mother that, precisely because of its lack of genealogy, 'is a conveniently expressive form of communication . . . it is still spoken . . .'

A recognition that meaning in the migrant environment is rooted in the contingency of communication and is more to do with improvising new forms than with faithfully reproducing old ones has a number of broader implications. A stress on the performative nature of dialogue and its restoration as an epistemological tool, a method for making sense of existence, has clear aesthetic possibilities. It provides a theoretical reason for writing and performing work whose meaning is inscribed phonetically and syntactically rather than lexically and grammatically. It also suggests the value of cultivating art forms that are environmental rather than monumental in character. Far from signifying a zone of expressive deprivation, the migrant landscape may provide the conditions for the emergence of deeply liberating forms of expression.

Here, though, it may be more relevant to note that the stress on improvisation not only explains how lines of communication are put in place in the migrant environment: it also offers us a critical position from which to judge the haptic argument with which we began. How true is it to say that good architecture offers a generalised body image? Is there not missing from this formulation a recognition that the body's primary mode of expression is movement, its primary attachment to space? In other words, it is the process of interaction, the dance of spatial dialogue, that constitutes the core of architecture's appeal—and not its power to mirror us monumentally.

Again, we may well ask whether writing (or any other process of intellectual synthesis) has ever drawn its strength and authority from the writer's sense of place. On the contrary writing, like speaking, begins and ends in the imagination of somewhere else, the other country of the reader, without whose collusion the writer remains wingless, unable to migrate, unable to become someone else. Of course, this said, it remains true that the potential expressiveness of the migrant environment remains largely unrealised. The incubus of a historical tradition that continues to evaluate local forms in terms of their supposed derivation from originals elsewhere, and which tends to regard innovations as mere fantastications, less authentic, less deep than the styles they so lightly and irreverently subvert, continues to prevent recognition of the creative impulse at the heart of even the most ordinary migrant life.

Improvisation, an ability to coexist with ambiguities, stand-in signs and, more than this, an outgoing ability to embrace hybridised sounds and forms: these are the faculties and dispositions that give the migrant environment its complex meaning. Of course it may be objected that the aesthetic consequences of this migrant attitude remain largely unexplored—although one thinks of Salman Rushdie's *Satanic Verses* as an exemplary migrant fiction. But the improvisatory spirit faces the future as much as the past, and these remarks are improvised in the same spirit. Their aim is to open a dialogue about living here rather than to add to the litany of monologues lamenting why here is not (and never was) there.

3   Fifth World

Kateryna O. Longley

The Western practice of numbering worlds is a convenient shorthand not just for identifying them but also for putting them on a scale of economic and political power. Like the even broader labels of East and West, the terms are vague and sweeping, and provide a cover for all kinds of stereotyping and 'othering'. As an immigrant Ukrainian who had, by the age of five, lived in Poland, Germany, Italy and Australia, I was for many years totally baffled by the terms East and West, globally applied. East of where? On the spherical surface of the Brighton Primary School library globe of the world I found no more answers than I did on a tennis ball. It was only after years of history, literature and even mathematics lessons, years of kings and queens, daffodils and glades, links, chains and perches, that I grew to understand where the bearings were all taken from. Even then, the recognition came imperceptibly. This simply became part of what I knew and worked from, but it always remained a puzzling, arbitrary thing rather than the permanent given that it was presented as. Similarly, the world-numbering system seeps into people's vision, colouring their ways of mapping worlds and placing themselves in relation to others. These labels that conveniently defined the world for those who gave themselves the power of naming and numbering, highlighted a special dilemma for postwar immigrants: *they* seemed to belong to no category at all.

Now, half a century after so much of the physical remapping was done, all the labels are coming unstuck. In using the term 'Fifth World' for postwar immigrants I aim to:

- create a stronger communal identity for a vast, world-scattered migrant population of disempowered people who have lost their cultural, linguistic and political bases. The words 'immigrant' and 'migrant', by referring to the moment of displacement, implicitly define people as *not* belonging where they are and also as being on the move;

• dislodge further the hierarchical scale and geographical basis of numbering worlds by showing all such worlds to be regrouping and changing, with shifting patterns of power born of very specific historical circumstances;

• by means of the broad Fifth-World framework, to provide a stronger structure for specific groups to be separately recognised, just as the term 'fourth world' allows this to happen for indigenous colonised peoples.

But first, let's look at the origins of the existing terms. Leslie Wolf-Phillips's article 'Why "Third World"?: Origin, Definition and Usage' (1987) traces the history of the term 'Third World' back to 1952 in France. From the beginning, the idea of a 'third force' was implied, a non-aligned world that could add weight to the fulcrum of the balance of power, a group of nations that could wedge themselves between the first (Western capitalist) and second (communist) positions. There is no doubt that as it was first conceived the very process of naming was seen as an empowering act which gave solidarity to previously scattered and voiceless groups and made them visible in the US–USSR dominated world arena. However, as with all acts of naming, the other side of the coin is the danger of homogenising diverse interests and ideologies under the one bland heading. This is an inescapable problem and one which is faced by all social and political movements, since the interests of the group can never satisfy all individual interests.

Representing those who oppose the linking of a hugely diverse group under a single sign is Shiva Naipaul, who has written on the subject in his article 'The Myth of the Third World' (1985):

> The Third World is a form of bloodless universality that robs individuals and societies of their particularity ... Blandly to subsume, say, Ethiopia, India, and Brazil under the one banner of Third Worldhood is as absurd and denigrating as the old assertion that all Chinese people look alike. People only look alike when you can't be bothered to look at them closely ... a Third World does not exist as such ... it has no collective and consistent identity except in the newspapers and amid the pomp and splendour of international conferences ... The idea of a Third World, despite its congenial simplicity, is too shadowy to be of any use.

It is impossible not to agree with Naipaul's comments at one level, but I believe it can be a greater danger to be without any name at all or to have a denigrating name such as 'refugee' or 'displaced person' or 'underdeveloped country', all terms that specify the point of vulnerability in relation to the naming authority. If these labels can be shaken off by using a stronger and broader banner there is little to lose and much that may be gained, especially now, at this extraordinary moment in history, when even the entrenched first- and second-world positions are beginning to lose their distinguishing features. It's worth remembering that the word black, while totally insensitive to individual differences, has been a powerful tool precisely because it has submerged differences that no one denies.

In numbering systems the idea of a hierarchy is almost impossible to avoid, but as with the words 'black' or 'woman', there is no reason why hierarchies, like binary systems, need to hold their traditional positions. In fact, the act of creating new groupings that do not conform to traditional world power groupings has the effect of destabilising the mythology of the original set, just as the contemporary use of 'Fourth World' to signify something other than 'worse off even than third' has already done. A major Fourth World conference is being organised in the United States, and this will further consolidate that term's usage for indigenous or native peoples colonised in their own countries and now forming links worldwide. That does not mean that Fourth World people have to subsume their specific ethnic and local allegiances to the wider group; that would be to lose the very thing that worldwide linking enables: solidarity which recognises and respects difference. This is not to say that the problems of difference are solved by such linking, but simply that they can be be confronted more positively under the pressure of common cross-cultural goals. In all cases, self-definition can only be a strategically shifting process, not a fixed mark, whether it is the whole group that we are considering or its countless subsets. In this context, it's worth recalling Gayatri Chakravorty Spivak's comment to black independent film-makers in London on the dangers of worldwide grouping and naming:

> You are diasporic Blacks in Britain, and you are connecting to the local lines of resistance in Britain, and you are therefore able to produce a certain idiom of resistance; but don't forget the Third World at large, where you won't be able to dissolve everything into Black against White, as there is also Black against Black, Brown against Brown, and so on. (Spivak 1990:65)

In spite of such dilemmas of micro/macro, specificity/homogeneity, and in spite of early derogatory connotations, the term Third World, like the term Black, has been enabling. As Trinh Minh-ha (1989:98) has argued:

> Exploited, looked down upon, and lumped together in a convenient term that denies their individualities, a group of 'poor' (nations), having once sided with neither of the dominating forces, has slowly learned to turn this denial to the best account. 'The Third World to Third World peoples' thus becomes an empowering tool, and one which politically includes all non-whites in their solidarist struggle against all forms of Western

dominance ... What is at stake is not only the hegemony of Western cultures, but also their identities as unified cultures. Third World dwells on diversity; so does First World ... The West is painfully made to realise the existence of a Third World in the First World, and vice-versa. The Master is bound to recognise that His Culture is not as homogeneous, as monolithic as He believed it to be. He discovers, with much reluctance, He is just an other among others.

Fourth World, on the other hand, is seen by Trinh as a disabling label, designating 'a Third World within the Third World'. Following her Third World argument through, however, would lead to the possibility that this term could equally be turned against its potentially colonialist connotations by means of the very same process of disrupting illusions of homogeneity and by running across other world boundaries. In the Australian context, the term enforces acknowledgment of a persisting colonial mentality which can then, at least, be confronted rather than remain, as it has been in the past, invisible. The world links are essential because they throw issues of racial oppression open to world scrutiny and so make national closed-door policies much more difficult to maintain. The same can be true of attitudes to Fifth World people. Even with the act of naming, there begins a process of recognition which forces attention on old cultural habits and assumptions and so throws them open to question, particularly in relation to issues of national identity. In this way, Third, Fourth and Fifth World gain power from each other by the very fact that they do not arrange themseves symmetrically and hierarchically in relation to each other or to other worlds; instead they demand a multiple focus and a global vision.

Who belongs to the Fifth World, then? Broadly, I am suggesting that those who were referred to as postwar immigrants or migrants or refugees, and those who belong to their families and communities, should take this name. If the argument is put forward that these people belong to a specific moment in history and, what is more, one that is passing, I would point out that all group naming is similarly tied to the moment even when it appears to denote a 'permanent' category. Think of Sovietsky Soyuz or Commonwealth or Empire (with any name attached) or even Asia. As the remarkable events of the past year in Eastern Europe powerfully testify, the solidity of any world is an illusion promoted for a particular purpose; so it is in this case.

What do Fifth World people have in common? Answering that question is a large project in itself, so I will touch on it only as it relates to this paper's other theme, that of the oral tradition in transplanted cultures. The Fifth World consists of resettled people who have lost their cultural and linguistic bases.They have in common the problem of finding a niche and participating in a new dominant culture without having the basic tools that make this possible—fluency of language and competence with 'the system' in its day-to-day workings, a system which

is almost invisible to those who have been born into it and move effort-
lessly through it all the time, but one which rises up everywhere for Fifth
World people as an almost impenetrable network of fences and obstacles
that exclude them. But they also have in common a range of cultural
experience that allows them to see all cultural and political systems as
temporary structures that are infinitely changeable and open to question. That is where Fifth World people have a great advantage over those
who are monocultural—they are suspicious of *all* systems. Behind everything I say there is the recognition that shared experience provides the
basis for a stronger and louder voice but also that there is really no such
thing as completely shared experience. Those of us who have heard
individual stories of dispossession and resettlement—or have lived
them—know how different each story is even amongst Ukrainians who
lived through the same political machinations at the same time and in the
same places. Ideally, the linking of expatriate groups worldwide provides
a framework for differences to be protected and celebrated.

Central to Fifth World cultures is the importance of the oral tradition
in their development. There are at least two reasons for this. First, there
were very few opportunities to communicate in print (I am referring to
Australia now, but the pattern was repeated in other countries) because
of obvious political and economic factors in the early days of settlement,
but more importantly because of fear. Even now, older Ukrainians are
often nervous about self-revelation because they understand very well
that an approved position now may well become an offensive or even
dangerous position at another time or in a different context or in the
presence of another audience. So it is for Romanians, Chinese, Germans
and so on. Even after 40 years, and with all the transformations which
have been occurring in Soviet policy, the fear has not entirely gone.

And so the reason for the oral tradition's flourishing as it has was not
simply based on circumstantial necessity: oral story-telling was chosen
because it was safer. While reasons of a disadvantaged educational or
class background could not be invoked in my direct experience of Fifth
World storytelling, it would be interesting to consider the role of such
factors for other groups. This is not the moment to go into other
reasons—connected with something like purgation—but they were
there, driving the compulsively repeated narratives, and they, too,
deserve further exploration. In this tradition there was no communal
pool of stories as there is, for example, in the Aboriginal oral tradition,
because the stories were first-hand and autobiographical and cut off
from other similar stories told within the closed circle of the family or
small friendship group. But this is not to say that a collective tradition
will not emerge amongst Fifth World groups. More frameworks are
needed for recording and preserving this wealth of individual stories

from the Fifth World oral tradition. The new Ukrainian Studies Association provides one such supportive structure. Its worldwide affiliations provide an even wider one.

Using my own limited knowledge of Ukrainian storytelling, based almost entirely on the experience of my own extended family and their friends in Adelaide, it seems to me that there are two main kinds of Fifth World stories:

- *Private stories* of intense suffering, humiliation, exclusion from all possible worlds, stories so painful that they may be untellable even now except within the security of the immediate family or deeply trusted friends. They have not yet been transformed into acceptable fictions. To tell them is almost to relive them.

- *Public stories*, often of the old world. These are anecdotes or nostalgic tales which have been cast into a known genre—romance or mystery or self-deprecating comedy. The genre provides a welcome shield between the memory and the telling, with the memory itself already a protective fiction. These are the kinds of stories I am still compulsively told whenever I go home to Adelaide, and it is one of these, told by my father, that I will now relate.

THE COMMISSAR'S BOOTS (told to me in Ukrainian)

In 1931, when I was an engineer at the factory in Kharkov, in the early days at the powerstation, I lived with Tyotya Olya. Her name was Olya Mokina. The prosecutor, or procuror, of the city lived there too. It was his flat, where he lived with his wife, Alexandra Vasilovna, and his son, Stanislau, who was a schoolboy then. Tyotya Olya had been his nanny but even though she was no longer needed, the prosecutor let her stay in her room at the back and even allowed her to let a corner of it to me. It was just a small sleeping corner and that's where I lived. At that time it was extremely difficult to find any kind of accommodation in Kharkov so I was very grateful when I heard about this room from the student friend who lived there before me. I became friendly with Stanislau and helped him with his studies. Although I had never met Tyotya Olya before, she gradually became like family to me. She was already quite old and had a hump on her back.

The prosecutor was Stepan Vasilovich, a Byelorussian. Because of the way we lived, very close together, and because I became a good friend to his son (although I was much older), the prosecutor became my friend. These were very hard times, 1931 to 1934. During this period of repression and great hunger in Ukraine, I saw some terrible things whenever I went with Stepan Vasilovich to the prisons as part of his daily work. So many people were dying there under inhuman conditions. These were things that few people were allowed to see. I remember prison cells so packed with people that they could only stand, even to sleep, and many died like that. The prosecutor was on the side of the repressed and he helped the people in the prisons as much as he could, using his power, but often he could do nothing.

In those days it was very hard to get basic food to survive, but to get good boots was absolutely impossible unless you were a military officer of high rank or a member of the Secret Police. Even then it was not always easy. Because of his position, Stepan Vasilovich could get them; he had coupons for them. In fact, he had one magnificent pair of *choboty*, made of wonderful flexible leather of a kind you couldn't usually get, but they hurt him. He just couldn't wear them, however hard he tried, and so he gave them to me. They were a bit big but I just wrapped extra rags round my feet (we didn't have socks at that time, even the army didn't always have socks because it was customary to bind your feet with *onuchi*) and I wore the *choboty* for special occasions. My everyday shoes were short boots, not *choboty*, and they were worn with galoshes over the top. Shoes and boots were very important because of the harsh winters and the deep snow.

On my wedding day in January 1934, I wore those *choboty*. It was still a time of hunger, when the only way to get food was through your factory or place of work. There was no such thing as a shop where you could buy food, even if you had the money. Every institution had a director of produce, who was in charge of distributing rations to the workers. To honour the occasion of our wedding I was given by my factory a bag of potatoes and two kilograms of meat (this was about ten times the usual monthly ration!) and Babushka (mother's mother, who came to Australia with us) made *cutleti* and *piroshki*. Of course Stepan Vasilovich came to the wedding. In fact he was our only guest because we had already lost contact with our relatives. They had all been taken away from their villages to labour camps like millions of other Ukrainians in those years under Stalin. So the wedding was very small and took place in the shadow of great fear about our relatives, but we still had a good party and ate *cutleti* for a whole week for our 'honeymoon'. We had to pay three roubles to get married. It would have been three again if we had decided to get divorced. It was a registry office wedding, of course, since the churches had long since been closed.

For years I only wore the *choboty* on very special occasions because I wanted to save them. It's difficult to explain how precious they were. Even as a soldier you couldn't get a uniform unless you had been in the army for ages, and being a soldier without boots was a terrible thing.

In 1941 Hitler attacked the Soviet Union and Ukraine and so Kharkov was occupied by the Germans, but then the Soviets came back to occupy Kharkov for the second time. At that time I was working at the margarine factory, the only factory left unharmed in our area other than the beer factory. It was a huge modern factory employing more than a thousand people. In retreat, the Germans took away the electrolysis machine which separated water into hydrogen and oxygen as part of the process of making margarine. The Germans wheeled it out late on their last evening. It was an enormous 3000-kilowatt machine. When they found that they couldn't take the whole thing, they took out its essential parts. In that factory it had been my job to maintain the electrolysis machine and so, as soon as the Soviets arrived, they sent me to search train wagons for the crucial missing sections. My Adelaide friend Avdiev worked in that factory too, and it was he who recommended me as the one they should send.

It was February and I had to go out in the freeze on foot, making my way along the railway line towards Poltava and Kiev, straight towards the front line. I wore my *choboty* but I kept them covered by my trousers so that no one could see them and demand to take them from me. It was a terrible journey. There were thousands of dead people lying in the snow. Using sleds, women and children searched amongst the bodies for their families. Some of those who were huddled in the snow were not yet dead but asking to be killed. Many were swollen with hunger. Through this nightmare I walked on. As I walked the Soviets were forcing every man they could find to attack the Germans, but they gave them no weapons and no clothes and so they had to use sticks and clubs, useless in front of the German guns. For most of them there was no chance of survival. By then the Germans had retreated to Skorohodova. After 110 kilometres of walking, I came to the front line itself, near Poltava (the place was called Iskrovka), and I could go no further.

The Soviets stopped me and even though I had documents they could check they said they would mobilise me into the army. 'You have no right,' I said. 'I am a Soviet civilian on essential business for the Soviets.' But it was no use arguing, they were not interested in my documents. They took me towards the place where the shooting was going on. On the way I saw a burning house in the fields and outside it, barefoot in the snow, was a boy—about seven years old he must have been. He was crying and saying, 'My mother's in there,' but the house was almost burnt to the ground. I was led to a small antitank gun which they put me onto for a while. Then they gave me a sealed military packet to deliver and sent me back to the Shevchenko *sovkhos* [a Soviet state farm] for reinforcements. On that journey through the fields I was shot at from haystacks. I hid behind the huge heaps of harvested sugar beet that were lying in the snow but every time I made a run for it I would hear the bullets pattering again and see them making patterns in the snow.

In this way I made my way towards the *sovkhos* and eventually arrived that same day. I delivered the packet and joined the 'army' there. They were all civilians—50 people with about ten machine guns—holding a Soviet base 100 metres from the hayfields where the Germans were with one tank next to a haystack. This was the front. Neither side attacked the other. And all this was happening practically in my village, the village where I was born and grew up, Rublivka. Because I knew the area so well I was sent to explore, reconnoitre. When I got to the next village there were only a few people there, all women—no Soviets, no Germans. 'Go to the next village,' they said. My cousin lived there. As I approached it in the dark and with snow falling, bullets began to fly out of the haystack. Out of the snow, dressed in white, came a German pointing a rifle and indicating where I should go. I put my hands up. Several others rose up and led me with guns to my cousin's village where their 'front' station had been set up. They took me into a small building, searched me and then gave me a bowl of thick pea soup. I will never forget the taste of that soup. It had been a very long time since I had eaten but this soup was wonderful. It had lumps of meat in it, probably that tinned meat that the army had, but however many times I have tried since then to make such a soup again I have never come near re-creating that beautiful taste, there in the German station.

I still had my documents to say that I was not a soldier but a civilian on important official business and that I knew the area really well and even had relatives in that very village. But when they looked at my boots they were very suspicious about me. They did not believe me but decided to test my story by asking me to take them to the house of my cousin. We went to the house and knocked on the door. No one answered. I shouted out, 'It's Petro,' and then Mariusia came out, crying. She was my cousin's wife. She hugged me and cried on my shoulder. Somehow, with the German soldiers watching, she managed to whisper in my ear, 'The Germans have taken Maria but Andriy is hiding in the trunk (soondook).' She began to ask us all to come inside but the soldiers said, 'OK. You're genuine, let's go.'

They took me to a higher military base, an office with high-ranking officials. Again my boots were a problem and I spent the night there under heavy guard on the floor of the office. In the morning a top German general arrived, accompanied by at least ten other high-ranking officers in several of those big open armoured cars. Over their greatcoats they wore long white furs. I had never seen anything like this before. They immediately began to question me about my boots. 'No ordinary civilian has *choboty* like that. You are an impostor, a spy. You must be a commissar. Come with us.' And so it happened that I was taken in the open car, sitting between the German generals, to inspect the German troops at the front line! We drove for at least 100 kilometres, perhaps even 200, in the cold and the snow, over the steppes, through villages and small towns, watching the shooting, all of it in the direction of the Soviets. Late in the evening we arrived at the German headquarters in Poltava, in the big white crescent-shaped building overlooking the central garden—it's still there. I slept in a guarded room and the next morning they interrogated me under heavy guard. However hard I tried,

I could not explain my boots in a way that convinced them. 'These are fake documents,' they said, 'You will be shot as a spy.' They took me to Carl Carlovich Mitchell, a top army judge. He spoke perfect Russian, better than many Russians, and we talked for a long time until he was convinced that I was not a spy and not a commissar. From then on they kept me at that station as a prisoner, chopping wood, sweeping snow, even doing some electrical work for them. Although I was a prisoner I slept in the same room as the Germans and went with them to help at the bazaar where they did all their trading. It was from the bazaar that I eventually managed to escape and start the journey back to Kharkov. By then Nadia and Babushka had almost given up hope of seeing me again.

I wore the boots for many years and in the end couldn't even part with them completely when we came to Australia. I still have them here in the garage in Adelaide.

What can we do with all these stories that are told over and over again in Ukrainian and in all the other languages of the multitudes of people who have lost their homelands and their communal histories since the Second World War? First there is the obligation to record them and not to lose them in the way that so many have already been lost. Second, it seems clear that there is the double need to celebrate specific cultures and their particular experiences while at the same time joining a wider community of people with parallel histories. This is an essential part of the continuing postcolonial reshuffle, with all its radical redefinitions of groups, centres and margins, and its ongoing challenge to the dominant discourses of First and Second World official history. Beyond all this, for those of us who belong to later Fifth World generations, there is the immeasurable privilege of listening.

An earlier version of this chapter was presented at the Fifth Conference of the History of Ukranian Settlement in Australia, held at the Centre for Migrant and Intercultural Studies, Monash University, in February 1990.

4 Multicultural aesthetics: A preliminary definition

Manfred Jurgensen

For Gün Gencer and Nihat Ziyalan

Reviews of multicultural literature in Australia continue to suffer from the lack of a terminological consensus, indeed from a precise use of aesthetic concepts of any kind. Understandably, the social politics of multiculturalism has dominated the literary field, leaving a vacuum of critical vocabulary specifically aimed at the *art* of writing. Perhaps the time has come to attempt a few preliminary definitions of the nature and function of a multicultural imagination, if only to stimulate further discussion in the area of literary criticism.

Such preliminary work must of necessity be descriptive in character and it is important to try to keep the approach as free of ideological assumptions and constraints as possible. That is not to say that the attention directed at multicultural literature can ever be totally free from ideological considerations. However, it is possible to begin by accepting the existence of an Australian literature written by authors born elsewhere, mostly belonging to a non-Anglo culture. Whilst it remains true, for the time being, that most of these writers belong to a European culture, in the broadest sense, to which Anglo-Australian culture has demonstrated its commitment throughout its first 200 years, it is becoming increasingly evident that literary artists from non-European, especially Asian cultures, are beginning to find their voice in the context of a multicultural Australia. Dealing with such writing, then, is in the first instance an acknowledgment of facts. Until very recently, the existence of multicultural writers in this country had hardly been acknowledged.

It makes little sense to try to group migrants under one common class concept. The socioeconomic and hence political gulf separating Sir Peter Abeles from the Vietnamese boat people and other migrant workers in Australian factories and enterprises not infrequently owned by migrants needs no elaboration. Any attempt to construct an ideologically oriented aesthetics of migrant writing on the basis of class structure is

29

doomed to fail. Nor has it been helpful to 'integrate' migrant artists into the politics of racism or feminism or class definitions of a broader social philosophy—not because such categories do not overlap, but because their conception of multicultural aesthetics and migrant affairs is restricted by predefinition and ideology (of whatever kind).

What kind of imagination are we talking about? Specific examples may help make a few basic points. A Turkish poet who migrates to Australia and continues to write Turkish poetry, even if it is translated into English, is by definition not a multicultural writer. To determine what constitutes Turkish poetry presupposes a knowledge of Turkish literary history, the social and educational background of the author, as well as an appreciation of the writer's continued commitment to his or her native culture. Australia, like many other countries of active migration, harbours a large number of artists who consider themselves voices in a cultural exile or residents of a cultural ghetto. Some continue to publish in their native country or in Australia's ethnic press. The mere fact of a translation of their work into English does not articulate the expression of a multicultural imagination. Even where an Australian theme appears as the subject of a literary composition the native culture's sensibility is retained. It can prompt the Australian reader to adopt a multicultural response precisely because the imaginative text is recognised as 'different'. A Turkish (Vietnamese, Italian, Greek) author who, as a result of migration, begins to adopt some aspects of Australian (literary) culture will demonstrate paradigmatic features of imaginative transformation: the work will assume qualities of multicultural (or bicultural) aesthetics. It should be noted that *all* literary art, both in its creative and in its social realm, is multicultural whenever it extends beyond the boundaries of a national culture. In this sense, the classical works of world literature have conveyed to their diverse readership a multicultural imagination. A multicultural imagination is a transformational imagination, involving a transference of imaginative speech, in content and form, in semantics and grammar, in vocabulary and semiotics. It is recognisably 'open', volatile, incomplete, in a state of becoming. Often it amazes with an audacity inherent in the spectacular risks of a cultural *salto mortale*; frequently it collapses in mid air, occasionally it does not get off the ground. A multicultural work of literature is not carried by the safety of an established 'mainstream' literary culture. Instead, it is perceived by that culture as a threat to the canon, and so defined as a failure or as marginal.

At this stage there is a need for greater precision in the description of an author who chooses to continue using the native culture as a framework for writing. A distinction has to be drawn between someone who has left that culture a long time ago and is unfamiliar with its later and current developments, and an author who lives in Australia but has retained contacts with the contemporary culture of the mother tongue.

The former will write in the tradition of a bygone era, endorsing the aesthetics of an age long left behind by the native country. The latter is more likely to introduce into the writing more recent, even avant-garde poetics and other artistic developments. There is alienation in both cases: on the one hand the untimeliness of ahistorical decadence (often stylised into a claim of classical timelessness); on the other, the unrelatedness of current manifestations in a foreign culture (although it must be said that on the level of a multicultural world literature such isolation, estrangement or specificity is bound to be less of a problem). It is clear from what has been said so far that a valid, meaningful and responsible assessment of multicultural literature calls for considerable expertise in various national literary cultures, complemented by a thorough knowledge of world literature. Without such qualifications (and they remain relatively rare), the multicultural dimension of Australian literature will continue to be misread, misinterpreted and misunderstood. Judging migrant writing solely from the perspective of mainstream Oz Lit is at best like looking through the wrong end of the telescope. The traditional and still current canon of Australian literature, maintained by teaching at schools, colleges and universities, cannot explain or do justice to the importance of multicultural writing in this country.

It is time foreign language and literature departments at tertiary institutes addressed themselves to the existence of this body of literature and collaborated on the development of a theoretical and methodological substructure appropriate for the emergence of a new discipline. The first stage of properly coordinated research into multicultural literature is the gathering of bibliographic material covering so-called ethnic writers in Australia. Loló Houbein's bibliography 'Ethnic Writings in English from Australia' (1984) proved a vital initial, though by now necessarily incomplete, document for serious scholarship in this area. The second stage of national research into multicultural writing consists of a variety of monographs and critical studies of individual migrant authors, the publication of various anthologies of primary and secondary literature and further stocktaking in the form of surveys or histories of 'ethnic' literatures in Australia. Often such documentation forms part of a larger history of migration, usually the recording of one people's settlement and contribution to the host culture. There is evidence that this phase is currently asserting itself. The Bicentennial celebrations of 1988 have undoubtedly added to the momentum of such historical analyses. James Jupp's *The Australian People: An Encyclopaedia of the Nation, its People and their Origins* (1988) not only includes much analytical and historical discussion of migrant literature and multicultural arts but also offers an extensive bibliography of great significance to further research. No actual history of Australia's multicultural literature has as yet appeared.

Such a publication will prove a monumental task even when it is undertaken with the assistance of more histories of bicultural writing in this country. Before it can be attempted it is essential to develop the critical and theoretical tools, a conceptual framework and a properly derived aesthetics for the systematic study of multicultural literature.

Such a task can only be fulfilled by a multiplicity of critical analyses of individual authors and groups of ethnic Australian writers. By comparison and correlation certain methodological preoccupations will emerge, as will an appreciation of differences in specificity. Emphases may shift, the extent of first-culture dependency may vary, the very concept of literary art may change in accordance with the native tongue's aesthetic assumptions. A newly emerging discipline of scholarly studies in literary multiculturalism will have to prove more than the sum total of examinations of individual works, either of authors or of one group of shared cultural background. For it will no longer be a matter of relating to the writer's native culture only (although that will remain of vital importance), or of merely contrasting the author's first and second (adopted) culture. The unique contribution of the multicultural artist is more than a combination or rearrangement of native and second-language literature. A new quality of imagination asserts itself, realising visions which could not have been expressed in any other form. It may be termed a process of creative alienation, challenging both the original and the adopted culture. The attempt to superimpose a foreign logic of thought, emotion and imaginative expression on the language and art of an Anglo-Australian literary culture has not succeeded, linguistically or aesthetically. The inherent strength of a mainstream native culture cannot be destroyed so easily. There is a limit even in the verbal translatability of foreign literature. A truly multicultural aesthetics articulates new imaginative relations; it explores original concepts, ideas, images and experiences. Multicultural writing is the art of conveying a new consciousness; it is a different kind of imaginative thought. Unless it demonstrates this very quality, it does not deserve to lay claim to its own literary culture. Such demand asserts a first and basic value judgment of multicultural literary scholarship. The written work must possess a quality of originality capable of creating its own imaginative space in Australian literature; it does not aim for integration into a literary culture but strives to extend its range and concept. Attempts to marginalise it under headings such as 'migrant writing' are not only insensitive to the nature of multicultural literature, they are also doomed to fail because the quality of a multicultural imagination will not tolerate a fringe existence conceived as failure to achieve cultural integration.

While the inventory for a more embracing concept of Australian literature continues to grow, a number of individual writers have already demonstrated the specific quality a multicultural imagination has to offer. The Greek-Australian poet Dimitris Tsaloumas has developed his distinctive voice based on, but not confined to, Greek literary culture. The writings of David Martin have never been properly analysed as the work of a multicultural imagination. Walter Adamson's prose, especially his novel *The Institution*, deserves a detailed study as multicultural literature. So does the work of the Turkish-Australian poets Nihat Ziyalan and Gün Gencer. And there are many others. By contrast, some writers have offered little resistance to their integration into mainstream Australian literature. Although born overseas, they usually came to this country in childhood or early adolescence. Despite its title, Judah Waten's *Alien Son* became an Australian classic. Like many authors, the Russian-born Jewish migrant artist is shaped by an Australian education; there is no multicultural imagination at work in any of his writings. More recently, writers like Peter Skrzynecki and Cornelis Vleeskens have expressed amazement at being classified multicultural. In fact, publishers, journalists and critics have found it profitable or convenient to market authors as multicultural who, though often born in Australia, carry a migrant name. The treatment of migrant themes is equated with a multicultural imagination. David Malouf's family name is considered evidence enough by some academics to recruit his writings into a school of multiculturalism. Second and third generation Australians are contextualised in a migrant culture of which they frequently have little knowledge and to which they feel no sense of commitment. In each case it is not the quality of their writing which is the criterion of classification and judgment. Many authors who appear in anthologies of 'multicultural writing' or 'multicultural women's writing' do not display evidence of a multicultural imagination; most qualify for inclusion on the grounds that they write about aspects of migration.

It is the creative tension of living a double life which informs the sensibility of multicultural artists: they do not suffer from cultural alienation, they enjoy and celebrate it. There is freedom in the selection and transformation of inherited or adopted cultural values. Features generally accepted as Australian, such as anti-authoritarianism, understatement and larrikinism, may be absorbed into an initially Continental European literary intelligence with remarkable results. A productive clash of wits and sociocultural perspectives can eventuate which in turn is likely to produce its own brand of imagery and literary form. This is particularly apparent in recent writings by Australian authors born in Asia (Don'o Kim, Le van tai, Thien Do and others). A consciousness articulates itself which relates to more than one (literary) culture, expressing experiences, thoughts and emotions recognisable to Australian readers. Often there are critical conflicts in the use of language, even where translated; traditional syntax and orthodox semantics may be deliberately ignored or changed. Not surprisingly, many genuinely multicultural literary artists find poetry, with its inherently less rigid confines of language, their favourite genre. Others turn to theatre and its particular freedom of wordplay. It is in language that the imaginative transformation called multiculturalism takes place, and it is the imaginative quality of language which identifies the writer as multicultural, not the subject matter of the work or the birthplace of the author. 'We looked for writing conscious of crafting and making,' Sneja Gunew and Jan Mahyuddin write in the introduction to their anthology of multicultural women's writing (1988), 'of reconstructing image and experience in words'. Peter Skrzynecki, in the introduction to his anthology of multicultural writing (1985), argues differently when he says of the authors that 'many of them succeeded in communicating their art despite the absence of language'. These representative quotations demonstrate a symptomatic divergence in the assessment and interpretation of the role of language in multicultural literature. The publication of various anthologies of 'multicultural writing' (and of authors identified as 'multicultural') indicates an uncertainty in the assessment of the nature, quality and function of literary language. As yet, no detailed analysis of a collective multicultural imagination in Australian literature has been forthcoming. The need to demonstrate its existence increases with every new appearance of literary works identified as 'multicultural'. For if such a shared imaginative consciousness cannot be verified (which would have to be broad enough to accommodate a wide range of individual and group variation), all claims of a multicultural literature possessing its own imaginative character will necessarily collapse. Multicultural literary criticism will then prove to be no more than what it has already been in many instances: sociopolitical rhetoric.

The need to start work on the nature of multicultural aesthetics has become urgent. There can be no meaningful multicultural literary criticism without it. The challenge can be met only by scholarly collaboration between university departments of English, centres of Australian studies, foreign language departments, centres of migrant studies and institutes of multiculturalism, involving sociologists, philosophers and political scientists as well as literary critics. Fortunately, a number of academics, critics and writers have already begun this arduous task (Sneja Gunew, Con Castan, G.L. Rando, G. Kanarakis, Jacques Delaruelle and others). They would do well to include in their deliberations the sociological and aesthetic models set by Continental European migrant literature (Germany's *Gastarbeiterliteratur*, France's post-colonial migrant writing etc.) and England's Commonwealth's authors settled in the 'mother country', if only to accentuate specific features of multicultural literature in Australia. It would be highly revealing, for example, to compare Turkish-German with Turkish-Australian writers, especially in their respective relation to the host culture's national literature. Attempts to marginalise the new consciousness expressing itself in a truly multicultural imagination can only be countered by the development of specific aesthetic criteria, based on sociocultural considerations, which will form the basis of an authoritative criticism of multicultural literature. Enough work has now been done for this process to begin.

5   PMT (Post modernist tensions): Reading for (multi)cultural difference

Sneja Gunew

Once cultures are no longer prefigured visually—as objects, theaters, texts— it becomes possible to think of a cultural poetics that is an interplay of voices, of positioned utterances.(Clifford 1986: 12)

... and this is in fact the function of writing: to make ridiculous, to annul the power (the intimidation) of one language over another ... Only writing, by assuming the largest possible plural in its own task, can oppose without appeal to force the imperialism of each language. (Barthes 1974: 98, 206)

Given the recent so-called ethnic upheavals in Eastern Europe and else-where, the time has come to take stock of the debates around cultural difference, about how minority groups assert their specific claims in relation to a perceived national culture. I will approach this question from three different angles: first, by dealing briefly with the distinctions that have been constructed between modernism and postmodernism and their implications for so-called marginal writings, then by making a brief excursion into the debates around the term 'culture', and finally, by focusing on how post–1988 considerations of Australian literature are affected by the inclusion of multicultural writing.

MODERNISMS AND POSTMODERNISMS

The difference between modernism and postmodernism is a vexed question, and the debate is already set in certain directions depending on whether or not we pluralise each term. Each denotes a discursive formation that is refracted through particular cultures and histories. Furthermore, when modernism is seen as the precursor to postmodernism it takes on a shape which is necessarily biased and overly streamlined. Nonetheless, at a minimum we can say that the term 'postmodernism' usually conjures up the spectres of decentred subjects and of the non- or self-referentiality of language (Baudrillard 1984; 1988). Both have serious implications for those promoting the claims or the writings of any particular marginal group.

On the one hand, there are critics like Jameson (1983) who characterise the postmodern as a retreat from the political and argue that, through pastiche and schizophrenia, postmodernism replicates and reinforces the logic of consumer capitalism. Certainly those who are committed to emancipatory movements such as feminism or postcolonialism may have problems with postmodernist emphases on discursive as distinct from material reality and on the decentred subject, which apparently precludes notions of identity and agency. How can one argue for political change when there is no concept of material reality or of agency? On the other hand, many have wondered why these moves should suddenly emerge from high theory at this historical juncture when various minority groups are asserting their claims. Nancy Hartsock (1987), in her critique of Richard Rorty's work, refers to postmodernism's own universalising tendency to create a transcendent and omnipotent theoriser outside time, space and power relations. In other words, one needs to maintain due caution against over-simplifying these discursive fields as unified and noncontradictory.

When one asks whether the postmodern is necessarily either anti- or apolitical, it is important to note that postmodernism differs depending on where one is positioned. As Abdul R. JanMohamed and David Lloyd point out (1987: 16): 'The non-identity which the Western intellectual seeks to (re)produce discursively is for minorities a given of their social existence.' The implication here is that minorities seem always to have been within the condition of postmodernism if the fight for a provisional and strategically conceived identity is perceived as a necessary and intrinsic part of any engagement with postmodernist debates. For those positioned as minorities, identity has always been in a state of provisional and fragile construction, or, in Stuart Hall's terms, a place where 'the "unspeakable" stories of subjectivity meet the narratives of a history, of a culture' (Hall 1987:45). Within traditional academic discourse there is a distinct difference in register and rhetoric between, say, Jameson writing on postmodernism and the work of a Hall or a Homi Bhabha. Bhabha described his own hybrid position as that of 'an anglicised postcolonial migrant who happens to be a slightly Frenchified literary critic' (Bhabha 1987:5). It will be quite a victory when all academics feel the need to include such a positioning in their writings. One of the marks of a minority position is that it is always under pressure to define itself against an imagined, though invisible, 'universal' one. Some of us are not able to take this kind of universalism for granted, nor do we wish to do so. In his piece on identity, Bhabha (1987) theorises about the possibility of looking at the defining gaze (presumably Western and male) without being seen, and so imagining the *re*-defining gaze of the other from the other's position. This is related to, but must be distin-guished from, the position of the Orientalist who has been described as a 'knowing observer with a standpoint from which to see without being seen, to read without interruption' (Clifford 1986:12). In other words, we never really hear from the 'other' except in the terms already assigned it by the hegemonic culture. The play of visibility and invisibility, silence and speech is a complex one in relation to the discursive legitimation of power.

If one accepts Hal Foster's description of modernism as having a certain emphasis on formalism then, almost by default, the post-modernist does become political. Foster defines modernism as:

> Purity as an end and decorum as an effect; historicism as an operation and the museum as the context; the artist as original and the art work as unique—these are the terms which modernism privileges and against which postmodernism is articulated. (Foster 1984:191)

The centrality of the gallery and museum is emphasised by several postmodernist and postcolonial critics. Kum Kum Sangari reminds us that historical modernism was , significantly, accompanied by the endless documentation , classification and quarrying of the so-called primitive or incomplete cultures of the Third World (Sangari 1987:182). But again, it is in the interests of postmodernism, in its quest for difference and innovation, to characterise (and possibly caricature) modernism in such a limited way.

Against modernism's emphasis on aesthetic formalism, post-modernism defines itself as provisional and positional. For example, Deleuze and Guattari's theories about deterritorialisation, rhizomatic power networks and the concept of minority literatures have been very influential in the development of postcolonial theory (Deleuze and Guattari 1977; 1986; 1987; Guattari 1984). More recently, however, they have been accused of indulging in first-world theoretical tourism of the margins (Kaplan 1987:191). This again alerts us to the realisation that the conditions under which one enters the margins are crucial and change the terms of the debate. One also needs to consider, however, the way in which the very concept of positionality (as somehow stable, transparent, or able to be mapped) is undermined by a critic such as Jean Baudrillard (1984), who perceives the communicative act as an endlessly circular one in which sender and receiver assign power to each other, culminating in the formation of the silent majority, a central concept in his critique. I mention this here because, within the specific context of Australian literature, it might be productive to consider how the various minority groups assign certain powers to the centre and vice versa.

One can, at any rate, safely contend that the work of some feminists and some postcolonialists, with 'their profound suspicion of narratives of reconciliation and unification' (Lloyd 1987:173), has rescued aspects of postmodernism from being anti- or a-political. While using some of the elements of postmodernist theory, these critics have also been alert to its own propensity for universalising, notably as a master narrative of crisis and delegitimation, and to its continued purloining of minority cultures, particularly in its appropriation of the marginal position without the experience of material oppression (Sangari 1987:182).

WHY CULTURE?

The postcolonial position of cultural criticism functions in the main to deconstruct cultural hegemony. A critical focus upon culture is essential, because culture is often constructed as constraining and conservative. As JanMohamed and Lloyd put it (1987:6):

> Since cultural hegemony continues to play an invaluable role in the production of subjects who are compliant toward the economic and political domination of internal as well as external colonialism, and since it legitimates the acceptance of one mode of life and the exclusion—or extermination—of others, the function of cultural criticism and struggle is to contest continually the binary opposition on which such legitimation is founded.

In his seminal text S/Z, Roland Barthes (1974) characterises what he has termed the 'cultural code' as 'stupidity', comprising the inertia of commonsense wisdom. Echoing this, Baudrillard (1988) has designated the very concept of culture as an imperialist and centrist one. The validity of this statement depends on who is making what universalist claims in the name of culture. The use of the concept by marginal groups slides more characteristically into the microformations of ethnicity, a term which has a particular resonance within the Australian context. To speak of competing ethnicities is to eclipse the troubling identification of culture as simply comprising the contestatory expressions of various self-defined, autonomous nation states. In this context, ethnicity has understandably been a controversial concept for Australian analysts. Stuart Hall, in his analysis of the British scene, comments that: 'The slow contradictory movement from "nationalism" to "ethnicity" as a source of identities is part of a new politics ... part of ... that immense process of historical relativisation' which has accompanied the inevitable decline of the West (Hall 1987:46). In its traditional usage, culture is associated with the nation state; but since most such entities are now increasingly aware of their multicultural mix, the concept of cultural minorities, or the notion of ethnicities, is useful in undermining a centrist construction of culture as a privileged discourse concerned with the definition of core values.

According to the poetics of ethnicity developed by the US anthropologist Michael Fischer (1986), ethnicity is something reinvented for each generation. It is not necessarily a part of conscious, cognitive processes, but represents a type of excess to this. Fischer locates its machinations within the deeper psychoanalytic terrain of dreaming and transference. Ethnicity is predicated not on coherence but on the plural and the fragmentary, taking for granted the often contradictory components that comprise identity for the material subject caught up in a specific history. Thus ethnicity searches continuously for voices and not for a definitive stance. It seeks mutual illuminations in reading juxtaposed dialogic texts or utterances which swerve away from the binary structures that have traditionally been the model on which the ground of 'culture' is established. Perhaps most important of all, this particular way of conceiving culture replaces the notion of authenticity with one of irony—the latter being one of the most intractable areas of so-called marginal or minority discourse. The mainstream is extraordinarily reluctant to recognise the existence of irony among the marginal; irony is apparently reserved for (and a mark of) a dominant or privileged group. At its best, Fischer contends, ethnicity promotes play between cultures and emphasises a 'revelation of cultural artifice' that, by its very nature, deconstructs claims for cultural hegemony. As the noted critic of Black American literature Louis Gates Jr has put it: 'The hegemony implicit in the phrase, "the Western tradition", primarily reflects material relationships, and not so-called universal, transcendent, normative judgments' (Gates Jr 1987:32).

The recognition of 'ethnicity' as a category of difference thus serves as a safeguard against the development of imperialisms or 'nationalisms' in the worst sense. It is reminiscent of the argument that an admission of gender as a factor in human structures keeps us non-patriarchal, or at least makes the patriarchal structures more visible. Or, to put it another way, it is not merely a matter of telling stories but of legitimating these stories in the wider sphere and of allowing them to redefine discourses of nationalism and identity. We come now to a discussion of these stories in our present context.

OZ LIT POST-1988

In 1988 we were mightily busy inventing a tradition, in Hobsbawm's terms (1983). The recent development of studies in 'Englishness', and the rise of 'English studies',[1] provides a useful model for analysing the development of studies in 'Australianness', and 'Australian studies'. This, too, has traditionally been marked by a core curriculum in which nationalism has been synonymous with 'manliness' (Dodd 1986:5). As one manifestation of the myth, Australian literature, like its nineteenth-century English precursor, has been rooted in a pastoral or rural mode which came to be seen as the definitive expression of love of country (Brooker & Widdowson 1986). While the broad parameters of 'Englishness' and 'Australianness' are similar, the details are very different. The interest of pursuing such a study lies partly in defining these differences, which have to do with the fact that Australia was not an imperial centre, though there is some debate about the extent of its colonialism vis-a-vis Britain.

The process of constructing our own national literature has involved the creation of historical periods and canons of great writers; both have been characterised by Frank Kermode (1988: 125) as a matter of taste or fashion and personal desire, though these aspects remain covert ones. The whole purpose of a national literature is to convey the appearance of the self-evident, to parade as the 'best' that has grown out of a particular place. It is no coincidence that organic metaphors are often used in association with this process (Gunew 1990). The degree to which we can designate our literature as postcolonial is debatable (During 1988). Strictly speaking, only Aboriginal culture can be positioned in this way. More appropriate terms should be developed to describe the relations of Australia's non-Aboriginal citizens with Britain (or Ireland).

To trace a certain development in cultural appraisals post-1988, I will briefly comment on the *Oxford Companion to Australian Literature* and the Penguin *New Literary History of Australia*. The former contains entries on feminism and on Aborigines but nothing on migrant/ethnic/multicultural writing. The second gestures towards migrant writing, but does not draw the crucial distinction between migrant writing (by those who came here from somewhere else) and non-Anglo-Celtic writings (by those born here who have access to languages and cultures in addition to English). Laurie Hergenhan's introduction (1988) makes heart-warming statements about the provisional and competing nature of histories and the value-laden and political contexts of texts and readings, but we are still working with huge exclusions. On the one hand, certain universals are wielded. The terms 'Asian' and 'European' are unselfconsciously invoked throughout the volume and are the defining adjectives when migrant writing is mentioned—that is, migrants always seem to come from 'Europe' or 'Asia', whatever these terms may mean. Furthermore, migrant writers are simply seen as reinforcing the familiar, or as repeating the themes of the first settlers (Bennett 1988). This brings to mind the US critic Werner Sollors' contention that the primary function of ethnic literature is to remind all Americans of their codes of initiation and entry (Sollors 1986: 7). This also appears to be the exclusive function of 'migrant writing' in the Penguin volume.

I have argued in more detail elsewhere (Gunew 1990) that this kind of logic is often wheeled in to reinforce notions of the unified subject (usually seen as the necessary ground for a nationalist subject). Indeed, in Bruce Bennett's essay (1988), which is most consistent in its references to these new migrant writers, there lurks the shadow of the unified voice or subject of the migrant experience. In relation to Rosa Cappiello's novel, *Oh Lucky Country*, for example, Bennett comments that 'even here the migrant voice is denied its unity'. The point is awkwardly expressed; I think Bennett is referring to the manner in which the narrator differentiates herself from her fellow sufferers. But behind it seems to lie an evaluative assumption that a unified voice is the only possible manifestation for the migrant voice, its only conceivable and authentic representation. This approach is consistent with the little that has been written by reviewers and critics on this group: somehow a homogeneity is always implied (Inglis 1988; Gunew 1988a). Bennett also makes the point that immigrant writers have traditionally been more peripheral than expatriate ones, but he does not speculate about the reasons for this. If immigrant writers are seen as merely repeating the subjects of earlier settler literature then it is not surprising that their work is regarded as 'redundant' or tautological.

But we need to look more closely at the processes of homogenisation which underlie such claims. Chandra Mohanty has argued that a distinction should be made between the discursively constructed group 'women' and women as 'material subjects of their own history' (Mohanty 1988: 65). The use of universalist terms such as 'Asian' or 'European' to designate a whole spectrum of widely differing groups is part of the oppression of these material subjects. Something similar happens when it comes to applying analyses based on class. Time and again, particularly in sociological studies (including those on the sociology of literature), I have encountered the implicit assumption that all 'migrants' are working-class (factory fodder) and that this immediately positions them in particular ways in a cultural hierarchy. In other words, if you are dealing with the working class it is even easier to discount or delegitimate their previous cultures and languages. Thus it becomes not just a matter of writing nostalgically about the old countries and the dislocations of migration but of taking issue with prior representations of one's position, be they images of women, or Aborigines, or 'migrants'. And I do not simply mean 'images' in the superficial sense: we are contending with a whole tradition of representation here.

The deconstruction of the term 'migrant' is as crucial as the already achieved deconstruction of the term 'woman', and the political implications are similarly powerful and complex. As JanMohamed and Lloyd have argued (1987:10):

> ... minority individuals are always treated and forced to experience themselves generically. Coerced into a negative, generic subject position, the oppressed individual responds by transforming that position into a positive, collective one. And therein, precisely, lies the basis of a broad minority coalition: in spite of the enormous differences between various minority cultures ...

If we apply this to our own multicultural coalitions, its aptness becomes obvious. At the moment, very different ethnic groups are cooperating to achieve certain goals because they have been assigned a particular (often negative) place within the culture. But this is to be distinguished from the homogenisation which is imposed upon them by those who position themselves outside multiculturalism, those for whom the ethnicity of England or Ireland is invisible. Studies on Australian literature do not generally entertain the idea of 'migrant writing' as a dangerous supplement (in Derrida's sense) that redefines the whole domain. Perhaps they do not entertain it precisely because it has that potential power. I should reiterate here that the term 'migrant writing' is commonly used without any awareness of the differences it contains within itself, not simply those that exist amongst the various non-Anglophone groups but also the differences which have nothing to do with migration itself but everything to do with the fact that the writer is non-Anglo-Celtic. Anna Couani, for example, though a third-generation Australian, is consistently seen as a 'migrant writer' (Gunew 1988b).

What needs to be done? First the category 'migrant writing' needs to be broken down, at the very least to distinguish it from non-Anglo-Celtic writing. Once this happens, the old themes and figures no longer comprise the familiar narrative economies. What remains is to explore other landscapes (spatial representations) and literatures to rediscover the cultures and languages in which such concepts as the nomadic, displacement, identity, gender are figured differently.

As a quick example of what I mean, Bruce Clunies Ross's chapter (1988) in the Penguin *New Literary History of Australia*, which speaks of the familiar traditions of perceiving Australia as either paradise or exile, would look rather different were it not viewed through the prism of the Judaeo-Christian tradition. The seemingly familiar themes of 'exile', loss or displacement do not simply return as the same when produced by specific cultural groups. The naming process which Clunies Ross traces as a manifestation of taking imaginative possession of the place acquires a very different meaning when it has passed through the histories of migrant groups who were forced to suppress or relinquish their names and powers to name because their languages were not deemed legitimate currency in the hierarchy of international languages. In other words, what will happen (or has happened) when the next generation takes up that responsibility of 'naming'?

Speaking in terms of a model deriving from psychoanalytical criticism, everything we term Australian literature (a particular manifestation of the dominant culture) may be productively re-read—for example, by means of nostalgia (as the liberation of the uncanny)—from positions outside that literature, as constructed in non-'Anglo-Celtic' Australian writings. This renders uncanny the traditional renditions of the home/mother/land for which the referent is arguably an 'Australia' always mediated by somewhere else—the shadow of England, Ireland and so on. In the writings of these who adopt the cultural position of Anglo-Celts, 'Australia' is situated paternally, as the father or third term which disrupts the mother-child dyad. 'Australia' is never located in the pre-symbolic. Though there is a tradition of criticism which has always attempted to construct an organic link between writing and the land (for example, in the work of P.R. Stephensen), 'Australia' is always refracted by a particular cultural prism from elsewhere. In itself, this is hardly challenging or new. Writing is always mediated, and always exists in the symbolic order. But what has not been analysed in any detail is the nature of these mediations in relation to a 'home' culture and land. One could argue that the architecture of a collective memory is always bound to a particular place. My suggestion is that the fictions, or meanings, the allegories we have attached to the old landscape and the old language, as figured in a tradition of writing , have been transposed or transported to this place. Thus 'Australia' exists for us only through these allegories. The referent for home/mother/land need not inevitably be England or Ireland.

A further question might be, What does 'Australia' look like when these other motherlands and languages are acknowledged as constitutive repositories for these allegories? This would automatically involve one in considering the prevailing linguistic hierarchy of 'strong languages', and here the opening quotation from Barthes becomes relevant. One notes also the observation of the socio-anthropologist Talal Assad that: ' "Translations" of culture, however subtle or inventive in textual form, take place within relations of "weak" and "strong" languages that govern the international flow of knowledge' (Assad 1987:158). The metaphoric function of specific languages within Australia would make an interesting study here. One thinks in passing of the recently introduced convention of beginning anthologies of Oz Lit with a few poems in one of the Aboriginal languages, though why one language rather than another is not always clear. What is their figurative status?

Another implication is that we would need to grapple with the problem of irony (Fischer 1986:224). The use of irony by minority writers usually conveys an awareness of prior stereotyping. In another theoretical structure one thinks of Homi Bhabha's work on colonial mimicry (1984), or the writings of Ania Walwicz and her use of so-called broken English to parody certain stereotypes. Another instance is the work of Birimbir Wongar, which would be more productively analysed than hitherto as deriving from a central European legacy of irony and allegory, as well as evoking particular kinds of modernist engagements with the so-called primitive and oppressed. The question of Wongar's identity might then become instead an issue of the positioning of an implied author or narrator.

Within multicultural studies as they are often negotiated, it is necessary to guard against culturalism, that is, the reduction of everything to a matter of culture, narrowly conceived. As Arif Dirlik notes (1987:14), culture is a way not merely of describing the world but also of changing it. In other words, it needs to be on the agenda of those who are fighting for political change. It is also necessary to be alert to a certain kind of construction of a paradigmatic marginality, be it with regard to women or others. It is tempting to promote the claims of a particular marginal group as the privileged position from which there is an automatic dismantling of universalist or imperialist structures. As Nancy Hartsock asserts (1987:205): 'marginalised groups are far less likely to mistake themselves for the universal "man" '. There is some truth in this (Gunew 1989) but I do believe that there is a further danger of being perceived, or of perceiving oneself, as a representative paradigm of the marginal. I think that this is what has been happening with Aboriginal culture since 1988. In other words, there is often now an automatic gesturing towards Aboriginal Australians, but this is often left at a very general level and used as an alibi, a way of not having to engage seriously with the unsettling implications of this or any other marginal group. Women's writing used to serve this function, but has recently had to come to terms with a recognition of its own internal differences. Rather than seeking the 'core values' to which all Australians might be prepared to subscribe (Bennett 1988:443), we need to get away from this implicitly centrist model and think instead in terms of the mutual illuminations offered by juxtaposing various texts and reading for cultural difference in a non-binary manner. In other words, we need to leave behind that drearily familiar self-other distinction which always amounts to a reinforcement of the power of whoever is constructing the putative other. Craig Owens (1984:204) has suggested an alternative model of the allegorical palimpsest where texts are read through each other and none is particularly privileged. Here the primary impulse is not the hermeneutic one of recovering an original meaning. Instead each reading functions as supplement; but, as we know, supplements redefine the whole.

I agree with Simon During's contention that postmodernity 'wipes out the possibility of postcolonial identity' (During 1988:112), but it does not eliminate the possibility of writing from marginal locations, nor the need to legitimate and circulate these writings. How we then read them is another matter. Certainly it should not be simply a case of analysing multicultural texts in terms of not entirely appropriate postcolonial theories, though these theories may provide an initial way in, just as the emergence of black writing and culture was of help to the beginnings of second-wave feminism. Ultimately our readings of multicultural Australian texts will look very different from, say, our readings of Aboriginal texts and both will in turn generate very different re-readings of the familiar canon of Australian literature. It is useful to recall James Clifford's succinct formulation: 'Cultural poesis—and politics—is the constant reconstitution of selves and others through specific exclusions, conventions, and discursive practices' (Clifford 1986: 24). And to end with Antigone Kefala's poem 'Coming Home', from her latest collection, *European Notebook* (1988:47):

> What if
> getting out of the bus
> in these abandoned suburbs
> pale under the street lights,
> what if, as we stepped down
> we forgot who we are
> became lost in this absence
> emptied of memory
> we, the only witness of ourselves
> before whom
> shall the drama be enacted?

To me this last is an excellent example of how the decentred self is already an intrinsic part of this particular marginal position. The task before us is to re-read Australian literature from the positions of cultural difference.

Part II: Literary histories

6   Statement

Antigone Kefala

A migrant writer or an Australian writer? I feel that I am both, and that the positions are not mutually exclusive.The paradoxes under which a writer such as myself works are two-fold—on the one hand, to express a difference in either tone, assumptions, or approach, leads to constant rejections, and isolates one from a community of writers and readers, that place where people who are interested labour all the time to redefine their cultural reality. On the other hand, it is impossible to absorb rapidly, or take in wholesale, the local colouring because at the level at which a writer is working, one is dealing with inner forces that absorb things very slowly and take years to change and to effect that transformation into an evaluation, a language, a style.

So while on the one hand society resents the migrant's intrusion into its (assumed) safe, familiar world, on the other hand it would like, or confesses to wanting, to absorb the migrant totally, making him/her the same. Under what conditions would this total absorption take place? No one is certain, but what is constantly assumed is that such a transformation is simple, immediate, and possible and that it is the migrant's fault if it does not take place.

But this can only be wishful thinking. No one can give up one's past, however unacceptable it may be to the environment in which one lives. To do so will be to commit suicide. One lives, one writes out of a continuum—a past, a present, a landscape, family, cultural knowledge, languages or a language, changes and everything that cumulatively has happened to oneself, the family, the group. In this total interdependence from which personality, language and writing emerge, to apply such a brutal process of negation of the past and all its interconnections will kill everything else with it.

Nothing can be destroyed inwardly with impunity.

But as literature is supposed to reflect a given society in all its complexity, we are not looking for a uniform idea of what Australian society is nor Australian literature. Australian society has changed demographically and culturally in the last 50 years, maybe more rapidly and fundamentally because of the different waves of migration. Writers and analysts must come to grips with the change. Some of the accepted archetypes are no longer adequate and require a lot of modification— 'the pioneer on the land', 'the ocker in the pub' and so on.

However, the petulant conservatism at the core of a lot of current literary attitudes, analysis and criticism does not help. Yes, we need intellectual and imaginative structures, but these structures must be maintained as adventurous, open elements that will allow us to grasp the changing nature of Australian reality.

As Einstein has said: 'The Real is very subtle.' We must all sharpen our insights in order to see, and work at our tools, refine them so that we may be able to catch it stylistically in all its subtlety and force.

In this process our different experiences and backgrounds may provide a more open perspective from which to understand our lives and the powerful landscape in which we live.

7 Paradox of the empty socks (or, Slowing down to hurry up)

Peter Skrzynecki

WARSAW: TUESDAY, 25 JULY 1989, 8.30 A.M.

My last day in Poland!

After three weeks of non-stop travelling, sightseeing, attending official functions and visiting relatives, the time has come to leave. I have packed my bags and dressed, except for shoes and socks.

Mrs Dombrowicz, the lady who has billeted me, is moving around anxiously in the next room. She is in her eighties, a retired civil worker who has been most courteous and diligent in her duties. Even if we never communicate or see each other again, I know that we have become friends for life. While I have been in Poland, her own daughter has been visiting Australia. Several times during the last three weeks I have asked, 'What can I send you from Australia when I return?' Her reply is always the same: 'Send my daughter back.' She smiles lovingly and longingly.

A car is being sent by my host, Polonia Zagraniczna, the cultural arm of a government department, to pick me up and take me to the railway station. From there, I will travel across Poland and East Germany into West Germany and Frankfurt, then north into the mountains, to Westphalia, to the region known specifically as *Das Sauerland*. There, I hope to discover my birthplace.

It will be a warm day in Warsaw, dry and sunny. Plane trees grow outside my window in the courtyard of the block of flats where I have been living on the third floor. A pigeon struts and coos on the sill, as though expecting to be fed. A lace curtain hangs almost from the ceiling. The window is open and sometimes the curtain moves. A large desk and chair stand beneath the window, dark and wooden, heavy. Many times I have stood at the window in the evenings and listened to voices from the apartments carry across the courtyard, heard the laughter and swearing, the music and conversations—smelt the cooking that drifted out of rooms and mingled with the smell of the streets. I have heard the stumbling of feet on staircases and the turning of keys in doors. Lights have gone out, one by one, till only the moon and stars have filled the courtyard with a ghostly light, or a lamp has been left glowing eerily behind a curtain. I have sat at the desk and written poetry—or letters and postcards home to Australia, to friends in England and America, or ahead to Germany and Italy, where I will be completing the second stage of my journey to Europe.

All of a sudden—like a knee-jerk reaction or jolt to the arm—I react! I respond physically to my own departure.

I want to stay!

The awareness of seconds ticking by becomes unbearable. I hear time passing in my head and I hope that the car will be late. Yet, if it is, then I will miss my train. So much depends on being on time at the railway station.

I want to slow down, to commit that room to memory. Yet I must hurry up! I must put on my shoes and socks and say goodbye to my landlady. Of course it is not the shoes that are the hindrance, the cause of this inaction; it is the socks. They are the first step to be taken in effecting the exit. They must be put on first. The shoes part will be easy.

As I sit down and lean towards the socks a blur of names passes through my head: a conglomeration of z's and y's, of consonant combinations that I have identified with my own surname and which have caused the same question to be asked innumerable times in Australia: 'How d'yer pronounce that?' RZESZOW. KRAKOW. CZESTOHOWA. WARSZAWA TARNOW. Cities and towns that I have visited and inexplicably—desperately—want to glimpse again. Places that I have heard and dreamt about for decades suddenly come alive as images. If I delay in completing my dressing, maybe something magical will happen and I will not have to leave Poland. Maybe somehow I can exist here *and* in Australia simultaneously. *Fool!* a voice cries from a corner in my head. *Fool!* Even before the accusation is hurled into my face, I know that I do have an answer: that I am forestalling the inevitable, that which cannot be avoided.

Before I become conscious of what is happening, tears blur the vision I have of the open window, of the plane trees and the curtain. A clapping of wings betrays the pigeon's flight and I remember another incident in Krakow a week earlier. My namesake, Piotr Skrzynecki, cabaret director, is pleading with me not to return to Australia: 'You're one of us! Stay here!' I reply that I must return: that I have a wife and children in Australia. My parents are also still alive in Australia. 'Well, I can't do anything about the children,' he shrugs his shoulders casually, 'but I can find you a wife!' We both laugh until there are tears in our eyes. Krakow Square was full of people at that moment. It was raining and there were black umbrellas everywhere. Pigeons too. We were standing at the monument of Adam Mickiewicz, Poland's greatest poet. That was Wednesday, 19 July, the day General Jaruzelski was re-elected President of Poland. Students were demonstrating in long queues around us, carrying Solidarity banners. But we laughed and laughed, arms around each other's shoulders.

The recollection of that moment seems to coincide with rays of sunlight falling into the room and I see myself reaching for the empty socks; at the same time I hear my landlady announce that the driver is here to take me to the railway station. The incident of remembering placenames and the joke in Krakow Square must have taken several seconds—maybe two lots of several seconds, but the effect is one of jubilation: of knowing that the homesickness I have commenced to feel will be quelled and that soon I will be returning home, to Australia. But, also, that I am and always will be part of that part of Europe even though I have only explored the paternal side of my heritage, that my birthplace is still nestled under a green mountain, somewhere in northern Germany, waiting for my return.

When I stand up, I am fully dressed, socks and shoes included. The reactions of the last few moments have happened so quickly, so instinctively, I cannot even remember pulling on the socks. Did I really stop and think and wonder? Am I really a person about to step out of a room or just a person thinking he is a person about to step out of a room?

The paradox of the empty socks seems as important as the names on the map that I have already memorised and which the train will pass through in the next 24 hours ... Lodz, Kalisz, Wroclaw, Legnica, Gorlitz (on the border with East Germany) ... Dresden (Kurt Vonnegut Jr, *Slaughterhouse 5*, Billy Pilgrim, *So it goes* ...') The recollection of memory continues, the associations ...

I do not know that later in the day I will stand at the window of my compartment as the train rushes through rural Poland, that I will see produce like I have never seen in Australia: fields of rye, wheat, cabbages, silver beet, potatoes, apple orchards. That once again I will be trying to commit those images to memory even though I will have a camera.

What I cannot understand, but know that I must somehow accept in blind faith, is that not everything that appears logical is meant to make sense. To be ordered and understood. That it is quite possible for a pair of socks to suddenly stop one in one's tracks and for there to be a force, a compulsion from within, to stop and simply let oneself be: to become part of a room, a city square, a field of wheat, a foreign country. To be accepting of what is around oneself without judgment ... That one has to occasionally slow down for a moment in order for the next moment to be realised.

Before I know it, I have promised that I will write to my landlady and, yes, to send her daughter back to her from Australia. We have said goodbye so quickly that there seemed almost no point in saying goodbye at all. In the foyer of the third floor I can hear the lift arriving and see the driver carrying my luggage towards it.

As I turn towards my landlady for one last wave, I stumble and nearly fall. Mrs Dombrowicz laughs, pointing down at my shoes. 'You remember everything,' she says, 'but you forget to lace up your shoes.' We both laugh, breaking the tension created by the departure. So much for the start of my last day in Poland!

As I bend down to do up my shoelaces there is a fluttering sound in the room, a cooing. I look up. The pigeon has returned to the window sill.

The above story illustrates a momentary confusion I felt in having to leave Poland after visiting it for the first time in 40 years. How I felt strongly about wanting to stay, but knew as well that I must return to Australia. There are many *koans*, for example, in Zen Buddhism that teach how we are part of everything we have ever experienced. I think my visit to Krakow showed me that, almost to the point of absurdity, in what Piotr Skrzynecki was attempting to do for me (in all seriousness). So much so that all we could do was laugh about it in the rain.

I have always regarded myself as an Australian writer, but one with a background other than Anglo-Celtic. In my total output of nine publications there is more writing that deals with human relationships, with Australia, its landscape and wildlife, than there is about the immigrant experience. Indeed, until the multicultural debate flared up in the 1980s, I was included in anthologies and textbooks for writings other than those with an ethnic theme. Now it would appear otherwise. But I don't know who is right or who is wrong in these matters or who is really qualified to categorise any writer. I know that I write from intuition, always have, and that like the pigeon, I always return, drawn by an instinct that I never try to understand.

8 The Greek dimensions of Australian literature

Con Castan

Australian literature would, I believe, benefit enormously from a large scale multicultural project of re-evaluation and reconstruction, which would begin by posing the following questions. What kinds of cultural diversity are there within the dominant Anglophone writing which largely constitutes Australian literature? What roles do cultures and literatures other than the British and American play in the literature of this country? Are these roles of such a kind as to justify a description of Australian literature as multicultural? If not, do these literatures have the power to ensure some degree of openness in Australian literature to diverse contributions and influences in the same way that Australia's immigration policy has enabled us to receive people from all parts of the world and that our trade policy is no longer based on imperial preference? Does whatever openness exists assimilate other writings (force them to conform to the dominant pattern) or integrate them? How much work is hidden from sight?

These and the other questions that must be asked cannot be answered by one researcher, as the cultures and literatures that must be considered are many and diverse. The establishment of a multicultural perspective on Australian literature requires a joint undertaking by many researchers. The exciting possibility is that it could convert Australian literature into something more than a national literature, into a literature which is a field of comparative studies.

What I shall attempt here is to indicate in outline the position with regard to Greece, a country which has provided a large number of migrants for this country and which has a distinguished place in world literature, not only for the achievements of its classical past, which are one of the major points of reference for all European literatures, but also for its literary achievements in this century. I also hope to show that the 'ethnic' approach does not result in the separation of the nation into 'tribes'.

On the contrary, it can be more inclusive than any other approach. My own preliminary research indicates that modern Greek literature has had little influence on literature in Australia. It cannot even be assumed that all the Greeks writing in Australia have much familiarity with this literature, although there are some who clearly do. The influence of the great modernist Greek poet George Seferis, for example, can be seen in the work of Timoshenko Aslanides, Antigone Kefala and Dimitris Tsaloumas, particularly in his early (1975) volume *The House with the Eucalypts*. I would read the beautiful 'Introductory Note'—a sequence of six fifteen-line poems—in part as a dialogue with Seferis's 'Mythistorema'. Both are elegies on the loss of an unnamed homeland, Seferis's Asia Minor lost through defeat in war and Tsaloumas's island lost through migration. This dialogue is not a matter of imitation; Tsaloumas forged his own voice and his own meanings in the bitter loneliness and nostalgia of life in a Melbourne suburb in the 1960s and 1970s, and he imitates no one. Instead, his sequence challenges readers to bring it into relationship with Seferis's poem if they are to experience it to the full; this is a fruitful relationship which does not involve judgments of greater and lesser but enables 'intersupplementation'. Supporting my reading of the sequence is a comment made by the poet in his article (in Greek), 'My acquaintance with Nikos Kypraios' (1987). Speaking of *The House with the Eucalypts*, he says: 'These poems were like a distillation of a supra-personal sorrow—something like the very sorrow of our race, the torment of the Greek people.' This is also perfect description of the nature of Seferis's 'Mythistorema'.

Another great modern Greek poet, Constantine Cavafy, has played a part in the development of Tsaloumas as a poet. One type in particular of Tsaloumas's epigrams, a type that he favours, has its origins in Cavafy. This is the monologue in which an unnamed speaker relates querulously and chidingly to an unnamed listener. It involves both self-defence and attack, but stops short of complete hostility for the speaker is in need of the listener. As an example, I quote a part of 'To the Reader' from Tsaloumas in the Grundy translation (1985):

> But now you say I cheated you
> in the market-places of the years—I
> who every morning pore over the dregs of your dreams
> to let you see the traces of
> the nightmare. The way we're going my friend
> you won't prosper in this world
> and nor will I. Even the prayer they taught you,
> even that you had from me.

And here for comparison is a portion of Cavafy's 'Philhellene' in a translation by Keeley and Sherrard (1978):

Make sure the engraving is done skilfully.
The expression serious, majestic.
The diadem preferably somewhat narrow:
I don't like that broad kind the Parthians wear

Now don't try to be clever
with your 'where are the Greeks?' and 'what Hellenism
here behind Zagros, out beyond Phraata?'

Of course the comparison has nothing to do with the content of the two poems. It is rather a question of a definite tonal relationship between the two speaking voices.

Modern Greek literature, then, enters Australian literature through some, although not all, of our Greek-Australian writers. It enters it through very few others for, as Martin Johnston (1973:1) observed: 'modern Greek poetry is virtually *terra incognita* for most English-speaking readers'. He himself has given us an anthology of his own translations of a selection of modern Greek poetry and a scholarly study of his original work would require a knowledge of modern Greek literature. But Johnston is an exception because he spent his childhood in Greece and went to school there. The expatriation of his parents, George Johnston and Charmian Clift, to Greece in the 1950s did not bring much Greek literary influence into their own work but it certainly did into their son's. While further research may show that there is more knowledge of modern Greek literature among Australian authors than I am aware of, I feel confident in asserting that all in all it doesn't amount to a great deal.

This is not the case with Greece herself, as distinct from her modern literature. In the first place, migration from Greece to Australia has resulted in the presence in Australia of a number of writers of Greek birth or recent descent (parents born in Greece), some of whom write in Greek, some in English, with a few able to use both languages as a literary medium. In the main those who migrated in adulthood and did no schooling in Australia write in Greek only; those who were born in Australia or came here during childhood and thus did their schooling in Australia, and in general experienced their primary socialisation here, write only in English. Very few are bilingual at the level of literary creation. The major instance is Dimitris Tsaloumas. However, George Kanarakis includes in his *Greek Voices* (1988) work from Edward Parry, Andrew Fatseas, Costas Malaxos-Alexander, Thanos Nicolaides and James Galanis which shows that they too were bilingual writers. Hitherto unpublished work by these writers may show that some of them were substantial writers in both languages. At present not enough material is available in the public domain for this to be known.

The Polish-born writer Maria Lewitt made an interesting point about the ethnic writer and language:

> A migrant writer is faced with another [problem]. Problem No. 1—the language. Because we are so preoccupied with divisions and have managed to sort out fragments of literature into different slots, I would like to point out [an] anomaly. We are talking about ethnic writers without differentiating between those who went through the Australian education system and those who never had the chance to learn the language properly . . .
>
> So if an ethnic writer chooses to write in his or her native language—good luck to him/her, providing he/she realises that once published, he will limit his creative talent to a specific ethnic group. (Lewitt 1985: 125)

To the best of my knowledge none of the Greek-Australian authors who did their schooling in Greece turned their back on the Greek language as the medium of expression, although some, as I have already indicated, have written in both Greek and English. This makes translation a very important part of Greek-Australian literature, a matter I shall discuss later. I leave the question now with a fascinating poem, 'Things Never Regretted', by Timoshenko Aslanides (1990), who was born in Sydney but apparently started to write in Greek:

> Yes; though born this side of the world, I once wrote
> limericks in Greek (my cousins laughed and also
> thought them funny). Then one day a voice told me
> 'It's irrational to write in Greek of the Greece which
> only your mind inhabits; write about where your body is,
> then you'll grow as fast as these eucalypts
> you can't tell apart, or name.' But I don't regret the trying . . .
> I've since been to Barcaldine, seen the trees
> and skin of the far Barcoo . . .

Greek literary activity in Australia, both in a written and an oral form, can be found as early as the beginnings of this century. Until the 1970s, however, written literature had barely separated itself out from the public press. Very occasionally a book appeared, but the main outlets for literary publishing were the local Greek newspapers and magazines. It is interesting to note what happened when in 1957 the London-based magazine of the Greek diaspora, *The Krikos*, decided to devote the issue of July–August to the Greeks of Australia. Towards the end it included several short stories and poems but, although it had articles on a great variety of topics, it did not include one on Greek-Australian literature. It did, however, have one with the title, 'The Greek Press in Australia and its Mission' (Grivas 1957), and in very flowery language it ascribes to this press a mission which is at the higher reaches of any modern attempt to find an idealistic and nationalistic role for literature. I quote part of it in my own translation

> Within [the Greek migrant's] sensibilities, however, there always remains, deeply rooted and ineffaceable, his devotion to the ideals of our race and

the traditions of our ancestors. It is the Greek press abroad that suckles, nourishes, and develops these noble sentiments. The conscientious, honourable, sincere and enthusiastic journalist in foreign lands is the apostle of the nation, the educator, the protector and inseparable helper and comrade of the Greek Migrant. If overseas we have journalists who are idealistic, virtuous, and enthusiastic; and we have a press which ever preaches hope-giving and sustaining promises so that the Greek Migrant in foreign lands remains unpolluted from every harmful social influence, and thus can remain within the shelter of our noble ideals; and if we have a priesthood which is moral and conscientious; and both our journalists and priests are living examples of superior people; then there need be no fear that the Greek Race overseas will be lost.

Journalists are seen as 'the singers of the songs of Zion in a strange land', as the bards of a national consciousness in exile. And students of Greek literature in Australia before the 1970s found themselves constantly in contact with the press and journalists, as can be seen in Kanarakis's compendium of Greek-Australian writing, which has recently been republished in an all-English version. It is also clear from the Kanarakis volume (as well as from information I have gained directly from several writers) that there is a great deal of unpublished Greek-Australian writing both before and after 1970. While the publication of some of this material may add more significance to the pre-1970 period, I doubt very much that it will change its overall character.

In the 1970s three things began to happen. As a result of the huge influx of Greeks into Australia in the 1950s and 1960s, there was a considerable increase in the amount of literary activity. Greeks were now present in Australia on a scale far greater than before. By the 1970s they had, in the main, overcome their initial resettlement problems and had both the time and disposition for creativity. The case of Dimitris Tsaloumas provides a typical example. He arrived in Australia in 1952, having previously published two volumes of verse in Greece, did not start composing again till 1963, and did not publish again till 1974. On the other hand, the most creative period for Vasso Kalamaras was the first decade of her life in Australia: but that is unusual.

The second change that occurred was a separation, much greater than ever before, of creative writing from journalism. The Greek press in Australia became more of a scissors-and-paste activity, taking more and more of its material from the Athenian press. I cannot claim to understand the process that was at work here, but I believe that it was a highly significant one which had to do with the greater size of the Greek population in Australia, and a greater differentiation of the artists and intellectuals from the rest of the Greek-Australian community than had been the case when the community was much smaller. Whatever the process, a separate social institution of literary practice began to emerge.

The third change was the arrival of the ideology of multiculturalism.

This entails the concept of different kinds of Australianness; it posits the single Australian consciousness which all people who have committed themselves to Australia share, regardless of place of birth. It also posits a vast range of plural, 'hyphenated-Australian' consciousnesses, such as Greek-Australian, Italo-Australian, Anglo-Australian, Chinese-Australian and so on. Thus the idea that there was such an entity as Greek-Australian literature came into existence, an idea that is clearly absent from *The Krikos* of 1957. Furthemore, multiculturalism entails the use of the term 'Australian literature' in both the singular and the plural. In the singular it applies to the literary work of all Australians, regardless of the languages it is written in, the place of birth of the writers, or their cultural ideology. In the plural it refers to such parts of Australian literary work as Greek-Australian literature. These are understood as both distinctive within Australian literature and essential to it: distinctive in that each one has its own qualities and characteristics deriving from its own inheritance; essential in the name of both social justice and the common core of experiences which inform all Australian literatures and about which I will have more to say.

It is important to distinguish between individual recognition by the social institution of Australian literature—in its singular aspect—and the firm establishment of Greek-Australian literature. A few writers who belong within this literature have received such recognition. Most are authors whose literary language is English: Antigone Kefala, Angelo Loukakis, George Papaellinas, Tony Maniaty, Timoshenko Aslanides, and, as a significant part of its avant-garde fringe, Π.O. Dimitris Tsaloumas received amazingly strong recognition—before he had written a single poem in English—with the publication in 1983 of *The Observatory*, a bilingual selection of his poetry with translations by Philip Grundy. He has since published a volume of poems (in English), *Falcon Drinking*, and further such volumes are likely in the future. Other writers in Greek who have received some individual recognition are Vasso Kalamaras, John Vasilakakos, and Dimitris Tzoumakas. All three have received Australia Council grants; Tzoumakas's work has appeared in *Meanjin*, and Vasso Kalamaras's work has been published recently by Fremantle Arts Centre Press and won a major Western Australian literary award.

However, it is important to distinguish such individual recognition from the critical and theoretical recognition of Greek-Australian literature as an entity; for the former can be, and has been, given exclusively on the basis of current ideas of literary merit quite separately from (and even in opposition to) the question of social justice that the latter entails. Greek-Australian literature is a category that includes all authors who are Greek-Australians and all their writings, independent of questions of merit or of theme. It exists as one of the manifestations of the multicultural and multilingual nature of Australian literature. At this stage it is clear that this critical and theoretical battle has not yet been won, that the notion of the plural 'hyphenated-Australian literatures' has not gained general acceptance. To the best of my knowledge it has not been attacked but it has largely been skirted round, both from within by some successful authors who fear that it might place them in a ghetto and from without by those who feel they have more important matters to concern themselves with.

I would like to return now to the question of the languages of Greek-Australian literature. Because it is a literature in which two languages operate, translation is an integral part of it, not something which lies on its margins. For the last decade or so bilingual volumes have been a common feature, although there are signs that the economics of book production and pricing are making this a luxury that can less and less be afforded. The number of book buyers who can read both English and Greek is severely limited, and buyers who can't are often unwilling to buy 'half a book for a full book's price'. In this connection M. A. Sophocleous's comments from the preface to *The Endless Journey* (Kastamonitis 1987) are interesting and perhaps indicative of a future trend:

> [These] personal recollections were originally recorded in his first language, Greek, but we have produced this English translation in order to make his experiences accessible to a wider public. In order to retain the flavour of the original, we have provided a fairly literal translation which adheres as closely as possible to the syntax and the cadence of the original Greek and which will, therefore, sometimes come across as stilted or 'foreign' to the native speaker of English.

Translation, then, is a central activity of Greek-Australian literature and has been since that concept came into existence. However, the translation traffic from Greek into English has been very much greater than in the opposite direction. What this indicates is that the pull on the Greek portion of this literature by Australia is almost infinitely stronger than the pull on the Anglophone portion by Greek society. Furthermore, the proportion of texts appearing in English increases as time passes. Because of a program of Greek language teaching which is stronger than ever before, it is unlikely that the production of texts in Greek will cease in the foreseeable future; but it will continue to decline.

The Greek connection with Australian literature does not end with Greek-Australian literature. It will be necessary at this point to introduce another concept, which I will call, for lack of a more suitable word, the Greek 'genre' of Australian literature. This is a much larger field than Greek-Australian literature, for it includes most of it but also much else. In this 'genre' are to be placed all works in which a Greece–Australia dialectic operates. This is not just a thematic matter, for this dialectic can also work its way into any and every aspect of a literary text. And the criterion here is, in contrast to the case with Greek-Australian literature, the presence in a literary text of the dialectic. In some of the texts of Greek-Australian literature it is not present at all, an example being Timoshenko Aslanides's third volume of verse, *One Hundred Riddles*. (It is, however, strongly present in the earlier volume significantly titled *The Greek Connection*, and in *Passacaglia and Fugue*.) On the other hand, in much Greek-Australian literature this dialectic involves the conflicts between and within the two homelands, that of birth and that of adoption. This places Greek-Australian literature in what I have called the settler tradition of Australian literature. I shall limit myself here to one fascinating example from Dimitris Tsoumakas's narrative sequence *Merry Sydney* (1987). This work has much in common with what has been called the Australian New Novel, 'in which the centre of gravity is outside the self, in time and space and the field-relations among things, in the laws of large numbers and in the incoherence of things' (Daniel 1988: 5). Consider the following passage:

> It snowed in Sydney. The city was dressed like a bride. Armies of unemployed are now busy on snow-clearing projects in the suburbs of Turramurra and Woolloomooloo.

> The German SS assault battalions are retreating, leaving boot prints in the snow.

> Slender first-years from the exclusive Bilingual Christian School of Virginity are skating about on the ice, scattering crumbs to the birds, reciting cancerous verses of the monk Ambrosius, talking about cabbalistic letters.

> Every face glows with merriment under the jagged light of alcohol and the moon. I am not—I don't exist. I have no meaning, no outlet, no ally, no company. Apathy and bitter cold exist. So does the pipe of a melted snowman.

The aspect of this most fascinating piece of writing to which I want to draw attention is the way in which Europe has been superimposed on Australia as in a palimpsest. Both places are governed by 'the laws of large numbers and . . . the incoherence of things'; but the point I wish to highlight is the way they are jostling one another. This quality of the palimpsest exists throughout and indicates that Europe and Australia are not so much in dialectical antithesis but exist as two poles of the same 'disease'. Nikos Papastergiadis (1987) is right to draw this contrast between Tzoumakas and Tsaloumas: 'One might suspect', he says, 'that the essential difference between the two is their conflicting attitude to the past and history . . . Tsaloumas seems to write from and with the past, while Tzoumakas seems to be against the past . . . [For Tzoumakas] memories of Greece which are stained by the ubiquitous horror of the junta are contrasted with the condition of being a foreigner where the horizon is similarly filled with threat and madness.' The contrast with

Tsaloumas is important and indicates that the Greece–Australia dialectic takes multifarious forms in Greek-Australian literature.

The genre, however, is not limited to Greek-Australian literature because there are texts outside it in which forms of the Greece–Australia dialectic are operative. In addition to the migration of Greeks to Australia, this dialectic can be set up through the centrality of ancient Greece in Australia's European heritage, the joint struggle of Greece and Australia during the Second World War, the expatriation of Australian writers, the effects on others of the presence of Greeks in Australia, and the lure of Greece to Australian tourists. This dialectic is present in texts by Richard Beilby, Rosemary Dobson, John Hetherington, James Aldridge, John Manifold, Henry Gullett, Kenneth Slessor, Patrick White, George Johnston, Charmian Clift, Martin Johnston, Beverly Farmer, Gillian Bouras, and Mark O'Connor (Castan 1988). It is an impressive list and one that can be extended. What it reveals is that the Greek presence in Australian literature since 1940 is substantial. However, this fact has so far received very little critical attention. Some little attention has been given to the Greek influence on Patrick White, two Greek scholars (Raisis 1983; Lambadaridou 1986) and one Australian (English 1982) having written on the subject. There are, indeed, many opportunities here for critics.

To conclude I shall say a few words about the opening section of Charmian Clift's *Peel Me a Lotus* (1987), a very beautiful book, a diary transformed into narratives of nine months of the life of Clift, her husband, George Johnston, and their children on the Greek island of Hydra.

The opening section concerns the couple's purchase of a house on Hydra. Buying a house is for most Australians an important, not to say momentous occasion, especially when it is their first home. This underlies the whole section and is the opposite pole of the vivid descriptions of island people, customs, and scenery. The bipolarity surfaces most strongly at the following point:

> I must say George flung down the money with quite an air, just as if it was truly one hundred and twenty glittering golden sovereigns he was scattering across the notary public's table. I think that at that moment his courage, which had been flagging a bit during the last weeks of these negotiations, was warmed by the fine brave glow of his own audacity. When one has had a lifetime's conditioning in terms of building societies, insurance policies, and second mortgages, it *does* seem to be a reckless romantic thing that the first piece of earth one has ever owned in all the world should be Greek earth.

There is one form of the polarity: building societies etc. on the one hand, and 'a reckless romantic thing' on the other. It surfaces in a different manifestation earlier in the section. Five people are present at the formal purchasing ceremonies, three Greeks and the two purchasers, Charmian and George. The islanders, as befits the occasion, have put on their best clothes; the Australian purchasers were 'both smoking rather nervously and conscious that [they] looked a ragged and scruffy pair.' What makes the contrast even stronger is that none of the Greeks is a principal in the business, none of them is the seller.

The final paragraph of the section reads as follows:

> 'Kalo riziko!' George whispered to me as we trooped after Creon down the stairs and into the glittering white well of the monastery courtyard and the cold dazzle of the early spring sunshine and the red splashes of hibiscus burning away against a cool procession of columns white under the blue balconies. 'Welcome home at last.'

'Kalo riziko' is what the Greeks have been saying to them, wishing them well for their life in the house. But the 'welcome home at last' does not refer only to the house, for they have not yet reached it, but to the island, Greece, the adopted homeland. Throughout the book it is stressed that the Johnston family are most unusual among the expatriate colony of the island because they have children and behave in part as if they intend to become settlers. Are they migrants, settlers, or are they simply members of the expatriate artistic colonies which were to be found at that time in the Greek islands and who were nothing but romantic outsiders, often in reality 'destitute bums', to borrow the phrase George Johnston used in the same connection in Clean Straw for Nothing (1970)? This unresolved dualism is a powerful motor in all the books that Clift and Johnston wrote about Greece.

As I have indicated, the links between Greece and Australian literature are numerous. A literature, however, is created jointly by authors, readers, and those specialised readers we call critics. Australian authors, I contend, have been much more open to Greece than have the readers and the critics. It remains to be seen how willing critics and readers are to construct a multicultural literature; in this particular case, to construct firmly the categories of Greek-Australian literature and the Greek genre out of the texts the authors are producing. Detailed study of the Greece–Australia dialectic in texts of both Greek Australians and others, as well as illuminating features that are purely textual, will throw much light on that deepest preoccupation of Australian literature: our identity and our relationship to the rest of the world.

9 About multicultural writing

Walter Adamson

Who is a multicultural writer? One answer might be: one who writes in more than one language. Although I have learned to speak and read in several languages I can only write in two: English and German. As German is my mother tongue it stands to reason that I should do a better job in German than in English, which I began to speak only at the age of 28 on my arrival in this country. However, experience has taught me that my German has dated and that the German I write, and even speak, is no longer identical with the language written and spoken in Germany now. When I was in Berlin promoting a book of mine I was given to understand that I speak a 'better' German than those who have continued to live in Germany. I could not take this remark as flattery, as I realised that one might as well have told me that my German is out of date.

I believe there are not many *truly* bicultural or multicultural people. More often than not they have only one predominant language no matter how well they know other tongues. In retrospect I might have said of myself in my early migrant days what Heinrich Böll said in Stockholm on receiving the Nobel Prize for Literature in 1973: 'My only valid passport is the German language.'

But language is not only a means of communication. It is also a means of self-expression. Here we have the weird situation where a writer's 'Self' continues to develop using for its expression a language which has ceased to develop. Are we at an impasse? One's native language becomes a kind of 'Latin' and that is, I'm afraid, how many migrants in Australia communicate with each other when they *think* they are speaking in their native tongue.

Even so, communication goes on. Language, I submit, is *not* the problem. Our problem, and our enemy, is silence. It is silence which divides and it is silence which ultimately destroys.

I think that most multicultural writers would welcome a better

65

understanding by the 'monoculturals', and that we may have to strive to overcome misunderstandings of our position. The fact that Australia has become our permanent domicile means that Australia has become *our* country and *our* place of work. Our writing constitutes part of the mainstream of Australian literature and this country is now our home. We have—*nolens volens*—brought multiculturalism to Australia and there are indications that multiculturalism is beginning to be welcome in this country. Whilst we can contribute something that we have experienced in the past outside Australia, we must not limit ourselves to that experience. Many of us have lived in this country longer than people born here, and our experience in this country might in many cases be more important and more alive than what we have experienced outside Australia. Whilst we cannot and should not try to escape from our past, we should not and must not try to escape from our present, which is as truly Australian as that of Australian writers born here.

It is, therefore, wrong to put multicultural people into a separate category and treat them as foreign bodies in a homogeneous society. Australia is by now, like it or not, a multicultural society and multiculturals are as Australian as monoculturals.

There is no divisive difference, and this should express itself in present-day Australian literature. We are in the best position to achieve that end. Instead of lamenting what we have lost (e.g. a home country) we should welcome what we have found (a home in Australia). Too much has been expressed in prose and poetry of what has been lost. Multicultural writers must emancipate, must integrate, and I have the feeling that this country is ready to accept us.

This is a condensed version of a paper given at a seminar in Melbourne in 1984 and printed in Delaruelle and Karakostas-Seda 1985.

10 Teething pains

Maria Lewitt

I have been living in Australia for over 40 years and have observed many changes which have made this country the way it is today. No one could have foreseen that during this period Australians would find a new cultural identity: the Australian arts would thrive and universities would establish chairs in Australian literature; schools would teach Australian history; the attitudes towards Aborigines would change; the white Australia policy would be dropped; the human rights of migrants would be recognised; and the concept of instant assimilation would be replaced by that of multiculturalism.

I had belonged to a minority group in the country of my birth and, having exchanged my status for that of minority in the country of my migration, I have reached the conclusion that if one was destined to be placed into a minority slot, then there is no better country to live in than Australia.

The debate around multiculturalism and Australian literature should have been as stimulating as *glasnost*, but has proven to cause as many problems as *perestroika*. The consequences, though not threatening the stability of the world, are causing a lot of confusion and unrest in literary circles.

I see literature not only as 'books and written composition especially of the kind valued for form and style of a country, or period' (*Oxford Dictionary*), but also as an eye-opener. I have always held it in high esteem and have been grateful to writers, regardless of their origin, for sharpening my perception, for offering me glimpses into multitudes of human problems and cultures.

Literature is one of the few elements which can be seen as a unifying force leading to better understanding among communities and nations. Writers' ethnic backgrounds may find reflection in their writing, thus contributing to this important process. Writing can be judged by its capacity to encourage cross-cultural understanding.

Multiculturalism is one of the most positive concepts adopted in Australia since the end of the Second World War. The present ethnographic composition of Australian society should not only nourish and accelerate the economic growth of the country, but also leave its mark on the arts, including literature. The diversity of cultural backgrounds should awaken artistic curiosity and stimulate an upsurge of creative work amongst both Australians and newcomers.

Initially, there seemed to be openness and plenty of curiosity, concentrating rather on the culinary traditions of the migrants than on any other aspect of multiculturalism.

Once migrants accepted multiculturalism and recovered their voice, they began putting various demands, sometimes valid, sometimes not, often ones which they themselves had denied to minorities in the countries of their birth. In the process, Australian society managed to form artificial divisions, thus missing the rare opportunity of forming a symbiotic coexistence.

In the literary field, the new term 'ethnic' writer took root, though the definition became more and more muddled; it embraced not only writers who were born overseas, but also the offspring of migrant parents, or even those whose grandparents were migrants. To confuse the term even further, knowledge of the English language had nothing to do with it; quite a number of writers went through the Australian education system and would have liked to be seen as Australian writers but remained branded as 'ethnic' because of their background. The irony of the situation is that the foreign-born writers themselves would voluntarily form separate writers' groups as though they were excluded from already-existing writers' organisations.

In an ideal world, a literary work should be assessed according to its particular merits and no concession should be given, or discrimination inflicted, because of a writer's background. In an ideal world, literature should thrive on multiculturalism, with all the diversities it has to offer. In a normal situation certain facts would come to the surface sooner or later. Plenty of goodwill still exists towards migrant writers, contaminated now and again by patronising attitudes, but the fact remains that, though all writers ought to be equal, some are more equal than others. Namely, a migrant writer is not as easily accepted as one who was native born.

Writers in Australia are not classed according to chronological order, or the category of their work, but rather according to their origin. Instead of allowing new voices into our literature, we often strangle new talents by putting them into a special, second-class category.

Government-backed literary organisations have devised separate departments for writers of non-English-speaking backgrounds. Special grants have been offered to assist foreign writers, though they are entitled to apply for general grants alongside their Australian counterparts.

This division is contrary to the spirit of literature and multiculturalism and should be discontinued.

If we have writers' festivals open to all, there is little need to run separate ones for migrants only, where 'ethnic' writers read works in their native languages, and where literary papers of general interest are delivered to the predominantly non-Australian-born audience. If there are any important issues to be brought to the attention of literary bodies, it is central that all writers should participate in a given debate, otherwise the whole exercise doesn't make sense.

We need more dialogue between the groups, from which both parties will benefit.

If it is necessary to seek assistance from the literary organisations, ethnic writers should concentrate on valid points and ask for support where it is really needed. I think that editorial services would be important for those with difficulties in English, as well as translation facilities for those who write in their first language. But we have to remember that assistance ought to be given only to writers and not to people who write; the aim of the whole exercise is to enrich Australian literature, not to fulfil the ambition and pander to the vanity of individuals.

I have never looked for any concession on the grounds of my background; no one forced me to become a writer and I alone am responsible for this decision. I have been aware that any kind of apartheid, even its intellectual form, is disabling and suffocating.

I have only one wish, to be accepted as a writer, and not to be treated as a freak who writes in a language which is not hers. After all, writers who have grown up in different cultures, who have had particular life experiences, would be able to bring into their writing new elements which could become a part of Australian literature. Without their contribution, Australian literature would miss an opportunity to represent its present generation.

11 The literary and paraliterary expression of the Italo-Australian migrant experience

Gaetano Rando

Writing by Italian-born immigrants to Australia can, to a large extent, be correlated with the patterns of migration from Italy to this country. The period 1840–80 was characterised by the migration of individuals who were educated, articulate and had left Italy for other than economic reasons. They were either missionaries (Confalonieri, Mazzucconi, Salvado), political exiles (Carandini, Carboni, Cilento), individual professionals (Cattani, Fiaschi, Zelman) or businessmen (Gagliardi, Meyer, Maggi) who landed in Australia through curiosity or the spirit of adventure. Chain migration of fishermen and *contadini* (peasants) from the Isole Eolie began in the 1850s, although it did not become significant until the final years of the century, and the first coherent group of some 200 farmers from the Veneto arrived in 1881. In 1891 the Queensland government recruited 335 Italians as cane-cutters to replace the kanaka labourers in the sugar plantations of the north.

From 1880 to 1930 (and particularly after 1921 when the United States placed severe restrictions on immigration), Italian labourers and *contadini* reached Australia in ever-increasing numbers. At the outbreak of the Second World War there were some 30 000 Italian-born in the country.

The Australian Government's 1946 immigration policy, which initiated an immigration program of unprecedented proportions, saw nearly 357 000 Italians enter the country between 1947 and 1978. Although the initial arrivals possessed little education, successive waves were in general better schooled and oriented towards skilled and semi-skilled occupations. In fact, according to Ware's (1981) analysis of the 1976 census data, some 21 per cent of the men and 15 per cent of the women had completed secondary school. More than four out of five qualifications held by Italian-born men, and two out of five held by Italian-born women, were trade qualifications.

Italian immigrants have made substantial contributions to the Australian economy, not only as workers (a stereotype perpetuated in O'Grady's novel *They're a Weird Mob* (1957)) but also in the entrepreneurial field. Their contributions, however, have also been other than economic. The most obvious are perhaps gastronomic, through the change brought about in Australian eating habits, and sporting, through the development, with other 'migrant' groups, of soccer. Sporting activities, in fact, were largely responsible for the growth of the Italian clubs such as APIA (*Associazione Polisportiva Italo-Australiana*), Marconi and the Fraternity Bowling and Recreation Club, which through their social, sporting and recreational activities provide substantial grassroots links between the Italo-Australian and the wider Australian communities. The strengthening links between the two communities have led to the establishment of closer ties between the two countries through official visits of heads of state, the increase in trade, the 1975 cultural agreement and the 1986 social security agreement.

The presence of large numbers of Italian immigrants in Australia has led to the formation of a complex community structure with aspects which cover not only social and sporting activities but also religion (with religious orders such as the Cappuccini and Scalabrini), welfare, culture, education and language. As well as the above-mentioned big clubs there are, in New South Wales alone, some 110 Italian clubs and associations, of which about 80 are in the Sydney metropolitan area, which cater to the religious, social, cultural, welfare and educational needs of the Italo-Australian community. The various clubs and associations constitute perhaps the more formal and visible element of the non-economic aspects of the Italo-Australian community. The fact that they exist is an articulation of the desire on the part of immigrants not to lose their unique social, cultural and linguistic identity and perhaps a confirmation that the aspirations of the immigrant group do not run to bread alone. Among these aspirations may be noted that of giving literary and artistic expression to the migrant experience. It is an activity which is undertaken by a very small minority but nevertheless one which has its place and importance in the totality of endeavour by the community.

In some respects, the development of Italian writing in Australia follows a pattern analogous to that of the development of writing in English: an initial concentration on the description of the physical and social environment followed by creative writing. However, some element of creative literature was present in English writing in Australia almost from the beginning (if we accept the early songs and ballads as part of this category). In the case of Italian writers there is a time lag (the first recorded instances date from the 1840s) and a relatively long period (to the late 1920s) during which several accounts about various aspects of Australia (travel, environment, history, commerce) were produced but creative writing was very much in the minority. If, during those 70 odd years, Italian immigrants produced ballads, poems or other creative writing, nothing is known about it today.

An attempt to quantify this phenomenon is presented in Tables 1, 2 and 3, which provide statistical data on the production of works of pure and applied literature by Italian-born residents in or visitors to Australia.

Table 1: Numbers of works in volume form published by Italians in Australia (long- or short- term residents)

	1851–1914[a]	1928–38	1946–66	1967–87
Narrative (novels & short stories)	1[b] (1)[b]	1 (1)	1 (1)	18 (11)
Theatre	3 (1)	1 (1)		4 (3)
Poetry		1 (1)	15 (9)	34 (21)
Memoirs and chronicles	3 (3)		3 (3)	3 (3)
Biography	1 (1)		5 (5)	
History/society, travel and geography	4 (3)	2 (2)	2 (2)	17 (16)
Other[c]	1 (1)	1 (1)	2 (2)	22 (23)
Anthologies[d]		2 (2)		16 (17)

[a] As far as can be ascertained, no works in volume form were published between 1788–1850, 1915–27 and 1939–45.

[b] Number of volumes on left of column; number of authors on right (in parentheses). In some cases a book is by more than one author.

[c] Includes religious and philosophical treatises, studies, grammars and dictionaries, collections of correspondence and essays, translations.

[d] Includes anthologies of Italian literature (1928–38) and anthologies of Italian and Italo-Australian literature (1967–87).

Table 2: Books published by Italians resident in Australia

	1851–1914	1928–38	1946–66	1967–87
Total no. of books	12	7	23	119
Av. books per year	0.190	0.700	1.150	5.950
Census figures at mid period	1880	26 756	119 325	280 154

Table 2 (continued)

Books per year per 100 000 Italian-born residents	10.1063	2.6162	0.9637	2.1238

Table 3: Works in volume form published by Italian visitors to Australia

	1851–1914	1928–38	1946–66	1967–87
Narrative (novels)		1[a] (1)[a]		1 (1)
History/society, travel and geography[b]	12 (7)	2 (2)	4 (2)	9 (8)

[a] Number of volumes on left of column; number of authors on right (in parentheses). In some cases a book is by more than one author.

[b] Includes government reports, trade relations, the Italian community in Australia, emigration, accounts by explorers and missionaries.

Most works produced between 1851 and 1914, with the exception of Raffaello Carboni's poetry and theatrical pieces, dealt with personal memoirs, the social, historical and physical aspects of Australia, the possibilities of trade with Italy and the question of Italian migration to Australia. Migration was particularly important to the Italian government of the day, which saw migration abroad as a panacea to the country's social and economic ills. This period also coincided with the publication of the greatest number of books per capita by Italian migrants, most books being published in Italy. While none could be classed as a best-seller, they must certainly have provided information on the new land and aroused some interest in it among the emerging Italian middle class. There may perhaps be some correlation between the number of books published, the presence of some 50 Italian companies at the Sydney exhibition of 1879 and the migration of Italian businessmen such as Oscar Meyer. As far as the Italian community in Australia was concerned, its major publishing effort during this period lay in the production of Italian-language newspapers (the first one, *L'Italo-Australiano*, was launched in Sydney in January 1885), which had a significant role both in dealing with issues of interest to the community and in keeping it in touch with events in Italy.

For Australia, the most important publication in this period was Carboni's *The Eureka Stockade*. Initially suspected of being an inaccurate and partisan chronicle, Carboni's account of the Eureka incident has now been fully vindicated. Carboni's competency as a writer in English has, however, continued to be the centre of some controversy. In his introduction to the 1942 Sunnybrook edition of *The Eureka Stock-ade* (the first since the original one!), H.V. Evatt enthusiastically compares Carboni to Conrad, although one wonders whether a comparison with Joyce might also have been appropriate. Evatt's judgment was obviously swayed by current trends in political nationalism but there would nevertheless seem to be some genuine sincerity in Evatt's appraisal of Carboni as a writer. H.M. Green, in his history of Anglo-Australian literature, finds himself somewhat at a loss as to how to classify *The Eureka Stockade* for the purpose of literature and, although remarking favourably on Carboni's gift of sarcasm, claims that much of what he wrote was broken English. In his introduction to the Melbourne University Press edition, Geoffrey Serle (1975) also finds difficulty in appraising Carboni as a writer, claiming that the book is 'so unusual and so little susceptible to most canons of criticism, that only a small part of any judgment can be objective', although 'Raffaello does, in his agony, rise here and there to great narrative heights'. The text, while drawing on various registers of the English language as well as incorporating elements from other languages (Latin, Italian, French, Spanish and German) does, on the whole, constitute a polyglot mosaic which is effective for its purpose and genre.

Some of Carboni's literary works written after his return from Australia contain references and themes related to his Australian experiences. The melodrama *La Santola* (Carboni 1861) presents the theme of Australia as a fabled land of faraway riches which, however, does not live up to its promise. *Gilburnia*, a ballet–pantomime in eight scenes complete with an 'antarctic vocabulary', relates the story of the love of two white men for an Aboriginal girl and contains references to the Eureka Stockade episode. The protagonist of *Schiantapalmi* (Carboni 1867) is Professor Nazzareno Schiantapalmi, forced into exile because of his participation in the Roman insurrection of 1848–49 and lately returned to Italy from the Australian goldfields where he had managed to accumulate a modest fortune. The account of Nazzareno's Australian experiences provides one of the central themes of the play. The characters compare Italy's past glories and present plight with an idealistic Carbonian vision of Rousseau's noble savage living a simple life down under.

The first book on Australia to be published in Italy is probably Salvado's *Memorie Storiche dell'Australia*. Nearly 400 pages in length, it provides an exhaustive and encyclopaedic account of Australia in the late 1840s, an account which must have proved fascinating to European readers of the time with its extensive description of people, places and things so alien to their experience. To the modern reader, parts of the book (omitted in Father Stormon's eminently readable English version, 1977) may now seem uninteresting and dated, but the description of the flora, fauna and people of the New Norcia area (Salvado even includes an Italian glossary of the local Aboriginal dialect) is both effective and accurate as well as a valuable source of information on those aspects of the natural habitat which are today extinct. Perhaps the most fascinating aspects of the *Memorie* are Salvado's account of his voyage out to Western Australia, the founding and early years of the New Norcia mission, his impressions of Perth and his experiences in the bush—where he initially shared the nomadic life of the natives, thus gaining an intimate knowledge and understanding of their customs and outlook.

After Salvado's *Memorie* a number of diaries and memoirs were produced by visitors to the country, such as the report of the visit by the Italian naval ship *Magenta* in 1867 or the Australian section of the account of the circumnavigation of the naval vessel *Caracciolo* (de Amezaga 1885–86). These voyages, sponsored by the government of a recently unified Italy, were undertaken partly though scientific curiosity and the desire to show the flag, partly because of the Italian power elite's expansionist ambitions, in terms both of finding somewhere to dump its outcasts and of opening up new markets for Italian products. In fact, during the nineteenth century eleven Italian naval ships visited Australia and their captains all wrote reports on the country. Journals such as the *Gazzetta d'Italia*, the *Bollettino della Società Geografica* and the *Giornale delle Colonie* published many accounts of travel and exploration in Australia, New Zealand, New Guinea and Polynesia.

Ferdinando Gagliardi, for many years resident in Melbourne, was an enthusiastic promoter of trade and other links between the two countries. A significant proportion of his promotional efforts went into the production of reports and letters, many of which appeared in the *Gazzetta d'Italia* (Florence), with a collection subsequently published in volume form (1881). In some of these letters, Gagliardi presents his views and impressions of life in the colonies (including a long description of the Melbourne Cup!). In others he depicts the small Italian community which had begun to form in Melbourne and which counted among its members persons who had become prominent in the cultural life of the city (the musician Zelman, the opera singer Majeroni) and in the professions (the engineer Checchi).

There are no publications in volume form between 1915 and 1927. This is probably due in part to the war, in part to the nature of Italian immigration to Australia in the first 30 years of the century. With one exception (Giliberto 1939), books published between 1928 and 1938 were all published in Italy. Books on Australia published by either residents or visitors provided the Italian reader with a detailed and fascinating picture of Australia and particularly the Italo-Australian community in the 1920s and 1930s. They did not, however, appear to enjoy wide circulation, although a collection of short stories and factual accounts (Nibbi 1937) was well received by Italian critics.

This collection, *Il Volto degli emigranti,* presents a wide panorama of

Italians and Australians in the 1930s. Each of the nine stories and three brief travelogues is set in a different location—eight in North Queensland. Nibbi does not hide his dislike for certain aspects of Australian life, especially its pragmatism, its materialism, its rough-and-ready attitudes and its anticultural outlook, a dislike which is carried over in the consideration of similar aspects of the Italo-Australian community which Nibbi observes somewhat sardonically from on high. Nibbi's main concern is with his observations and comments on Australia and the Australians. Perhaps to the modern reader these stories may seem somewhat dated in both language and content. Yet they present a rare view from the periphery of Australia in the 1930s. What interests Nibbi are the unusual, prurient, complicated aspects of life 'down under'. Hence we are provided with a series of reflections on a society which prudishly bans the display of nudity in art and the circulation of erotic literature, leading to the question of what cultural values such a society can have. For Nibbi, Australians are also a race lacking in sentiment or emotion, to the point that they consider Italians 'too emotional'. Theirs is a society which segregates: old people having to live separately, sick people being sent straight to hospital, landladies not bothering to inform their lodgers' friends even when the lodger is on the point of death, as happens to the Swiss Italian Roberti. The death of a Yugoslav miner and the disappearance and probable death of another in the rugged mining country of south-western Tasmania cause no interruption to the work, which is carried out in all weather and is not accompanied by song as it is in Italy and other southern European countries. In this story, 'Tasmania', which is tinged at times with melodramatic tones but is, nevertheless, effectively told, Nibbi expounds the theme of the sad and tragic fate of the immigrant worker who has no one to mourn him when he dies far from home. His case demonstrates the absence of humanitarianism in Australians and their relentless pursuit of material gain.

Factual accounts of Australia were produced not by the immigrants but by visitors. *La Terra dei Fossilli Viventi* (De Scalzo 1938), an unmemorable and overly journalistic account of the author's travels in Australia over a brief period in the mid 1930s, gives an overview of the physical characteristics of the country and its political and social climate as well as the Italo-Australian community, its history, its relations with the wider Australian community and its contributions to Australian cultural life. A more lively but schematically comprehensive account is provided in *Il mio viaggio in Oceania* (Cipolla 1928).

After 1945 the production of books seems in part to be correlated with the progressive urbanisation of Italian immigrants. Few books were published in the period of peak migration, partly due to the relatively low education levels of most immigrants but also because in their initial years in the new country these new arrivals had little time to devote to writing. The numbers of books published increased substantially between 1967 and 1987, particularly in the latter part of this period and despite a decline in the total number of the Italian-born population since 1971. In the four years between 1984 and 1987, seventeen volumes of creative writing (poetry, narrative, theatre) alone were published as well as three anthologies. Until 1973 creative literature in volume form was published solely in Italian, but since that date works have also been published in English. Six authors have published solely in English, 24 in Italian only and three in both languages. The most significant book to date in terms of reaching the non-Italian reader is perhaps Rosa Cappiello's novel *Oh Lucky Country*, which was published in English translation in 1984. It is also the contemporary Italo-Australian literary work most favourably received by critics in Italy.

As in the inter-war period, poetry has continued to be the mainstay of creative writing by Italian immigrants in Australia. Since 1947, 27 writers have published 58 volumes of poetry, while many others have seen their works published in anthologies or in Italian-language newspapers. Most volumes have been published at the expense of the writer, although in the last few years some writers have been able to publish with the assistance of grants from the Australia Council and other bodies. Unlike narrative, poetry produced by Italian writers in Australia is not necessarily tied to migration-related themes. Indeed much of it is preoccupied with 'universal' issues. Some poetry, however, does deal with social realities and this gives it perhaps its most distinctive characteristics.

In this poetry the migration experience is internalised, rendered partial and subjective and subject to alteration over time. A common starting point is that of nostalgia for one's place of origin (Sardinia, in the case of Concas 1977) or the feelings of isolation and exile which such thoughts provoke (Coreno 1980; Di Stefano 1978). Forced to live away from his native land, the poet can only find happiness in memories of a time before his confined isolation as an exile in Australia, something which does not represent a new life but which is destructive, fatal, and heraldic of melancholy. As time progresses there is a critical re-evaluation of this position. The native land is seen not only through the nostalgic eyes of the exile but in terms of the conditions which had instigated the poet to leave it. Australia is seen as less alien, particularly because of its acceptance of the various manifestations of the Italo-Australian community (Concas 1988). Other aspects explored are: the dislocation in time and space caused by the journey, both material and spiritual, from Italy to Australia; the strangeness of the new land, both in a physical and in a spiritual sense; the cultural and age gaps between the immigrants and their Australian-born children; the reaching back towards pre-migration places and experiences. In her latest volume, Di Stefano (1988) reaches the conclusion that while time has tended to weaken the ties with the native land, the reality of the adopted country does not completely fulfil all the immigrants' spiritual needs, despite its positive and satisfying aspects.

The most prolific and best known poet, Luigi Strano, who between 1959 and 1989 published twelve volumes of poems written over a 50-year period, provides some continuity between pre- and postwar production. Initially emanating from a classical, humanistic context closely linked to his pre-emigration cultural experience, Strano's poetry underwent a significant structural and stylistic transformation in 1934 with 'Giardini Bui' (Rando 1983: 124–125), a metaphysical image of Sydney in the grips of the Great Depression. Acclaimed for its ring of sincerity, its anti-sentimentalism and its ability to transpose the many facets of the migrant experience into poetic terms, his poetry tells the personal 'inner' story of the migrant experience universalised to embrace that of all those who have undergone a similar process. It also succeeds in externalising the migrant experience by presenting portraits and comments related to specific cases. There is the poignant lament of the grandfather from Calabria who cannot adapt to his new environment and bitterly regrets ever having left his native village ('Un pappu a l'Australia', Strano 1964: 39—the poem is, significantly, written in dialect), 'Vivenzi' (Strano 1970: 3), who cannot understand why he is charged with vagrancy when he does not conform to local norms (the poem is written in a spoken variety of Italian), or the comment on the poignantly ironic fate of Fortunato La Rosa, who dies during a trip back to Italy, the first after many years' residence in Australia ('A Fortunato La Rosa—Buonanima', Strano 1984: 11).

Of the more recent Italo-Australian poets a few may be mentioned: Rosa Cappiello, whose poetry reflects the savage irony and the linguistic disruption evident in her prose works; Cristiana Maria Sebastiani, who, while appreciating the social and physical aspects of the Australian scene, nevertheless accuses the host society of rejecting the cultural contribution of the non-Anglo-Saxon immigrant; Emilio Gabbrielli, who has so far concerned himself with his reaction to the cultural and the physical contrasts between the old country and the new; Walter Cerquetti's prose poems of subjective introspection; Valerio Borghese, whose poetry presents hermetic fragments of existential introspection; and Paolo Totaro's finely written poems—many of the most recent in a multilingual mode—with their deep sense of anguish and irony, of linguistic and cultural disruption.

Although numerically fewer than the poets—some nine narrative writers in the postwar period have published sixteen volumes of novels and short stories, while a further 22 have seen their works printed in anthologies—prose writers seem more directly concerned with the migrant experience. The preference for poetry seems due in part to a cultural concept, reinforced by the traditional Italian education system, that poetry is the highest form of creative writing; in part to the fact that for these spare-time writers it is usually more satisfying to produce the relatively shorter poetic text than to engage in the longer-term enterprise of writing a short story or a novel. Further, it is easier to have poetry published than it is prose. Narrative writing has been as diverse as Pino Bosi's facile and somewhat commonplace novel of the arrival and settlement experience of an Italian worker in the 1950s (Bosi 1971) and Cappiello's complex and powerful account of the experiences of a single woman migrant (Cappiello 1984). Two Italo-Australian prose writers, Nibbi and Cappiello, have been distinguished by a modicum of success in Italy and also, in the case of Cappiello, by some recognition from the Anglo-Australian literary establishment. Both writers are critical, ironic and incisive but vastly different in style and technique. Nibbi is a detached observer, traditional if not slightly old-fashioned in style, whereas Cappiello's approach is highly subjective and her language charged, impetuous and aggressive. With few exceptions, Italo-Australian fiction concerns characters and situations connected with migration and its consequences. It comments directly or implicitly on Australian society and the migrant's relation to it, concentrating on five broad themes: the Italo-Australian community, Italy, bush and outback, personal reactions to migration, and multiculturalism. Attitudes to migration range from qualified optimism (Abiuso 1984) to bleak pessimism (Borghese 1984). Some writers, like Bosi, have de-emphasised the problems it causes; others, like Cappiello, have given full recognition to its painful implications, the disappointments, losses, loneliness, despair. Autobiographical elements are strongly present, though Cappiello manages to go beyond her immediate personal experience to universal aspects. There is a widespread tendency to overwrite, a flaw not shared by Cappiello, and structure and technique are sometimes shaky, almost always conservative. Many works comment favourably on the natural features of the new country (the harbour, the beaches), but few venture in writing beyond the city limits. Even fewer (Andreoni 1982) attempt to theorise about a multicultural Australia.

The staging of Italian plays (particularly those by Verga, Pirandello, De Filippo and Dario Fo) has been a regular feature of Italian cultural activities for at least the last 30 years. Only in the last ten years or so have Italian community amateur and semiprofessional groups included in their repertoires texts by local authors. Most of such activity seems so far to have taken place in Melbourne. Although playwrights such as Nino Randazzo and Osvaldo Maione have been quite prolific, few Italo-Australian plays are available in published texts. Usually conceived as comedies or farces, they share the overriding theme of the cultural, social and linguistic contrast between the world of the Italo-Australian immigrant on the one hand and the host society on the other.

In the postwar period, the first book-length works in prose which began to emerge at the end of the 1950s are non-fiction works which narrate the writer's experiences as an immigrant or, in one case, experiences before coming to Australia. Curiously enough this represents the revival of a genre which was particularly in vogue among Italian writers in Australia in the mid 1800s (who were intent on describing the new environment) but subsequently died out. The new wave of memoirs are the personal accounts of immigrants, such as *Italians as They Are* (Luciano 1959), *A Migrant's Story* (Bonutto 1963), *Amelia: a Long Journey* (Triaca 1985). Having lived for 30 or so years in Australia, they have felt the need to write about their experiences. Initially such works are written by persons who have achieved material success; it is not until many years later, for example in *With Courage in their Cases* (Loh 1980), that it is possible to obtain a direct, albeit mediated, account of the immigrant worker experience.

12 Neither here nor there, left nor right nor centre: Functioning as a multicultural writer in Australia

Loló Houbein

As a multicultural writer, the things that appear to set me apart from mainstream writers have on the face of it little to do with migration or being an immigrant.

As soon as i could express myself in my first language, at age two or three, i realised i was being misunderstood and that the reality out of which i was already living was an unknown quantity to the adults who nurtured me. The fact that i could not as yet use such words as 'reality', in Dutch or any other language, did not mean that i could not perceive concepts (which seemed to take the shape of unmet expectations), nor did it alleviate the frustration of the situation in which i found myself.

Having at last trained my adults to understand my speech—after all, i had addressed them for years without getting through to them—i now found they disagreed with my opinions and wanted to change them.

Wisely, i learned to keep my thoughts more and more to myself and at eight I became a writer. At the same time i sought the company of other writers through reading their books. I always marvel when proud parents tell me their ten-year-old is reading *Lord of the Rings*. But on reflection i marvel more at the fact that, unprompted and unguided, i was reading Zola, Sartre and Dostoyevsky at eleven, twelve and thirteen. I found Zola a bore, disagreed with Sartre and found truth in Dostoyevsky.

My alienation from the adult world i grew up in—a household without books or religion—increased quite naturally to the point where migration seemed the only way to achieve some space for personal pursuits.

I had already left home at eleven, because of war circumstances, but returned four months later. I left home again at sixteen, but returned within the year. I finally left home at eighteen to marry and left the country at 24 to migrate to Australia.

It was this physical removal from the place of my birth that gradually revealed to me that more than two cultures—Dutch and Australian—vied for acknowledgment inside me. And by now, almost half a century after i became a writer, five cultural streams flow through all my thinking and the one that most often appears to have the casting vote does not reside in the place where i reside.

This has never really been otherwise. Hence, to me, to feel somewhat alien in the place where i am is to feel normal. Why then should i write about alienation, as a migrant writer is more or less expected to do? I don't, of course. Alienation is the normal state of affairs, the unmentioned given condition. Some claim it is basic to the human condition and i would not disagree.

So it is from this perspective, calling on any part of my cultural baggage, that i approach areas of conflict as life presents them.

This no doubt has made me difficult to classify as a writer, as much as it has eased my path in life. Yet classifications there must be. I myself invented ethnic writers as a classification in order to present to Australia at large a species of writers hitherto not acknowledged, because they were already classified as migrants. Those were the days when simplicity reigned supreme.

There is presently a great longing for truth among readers. 'Did that really happen to you?' people want to know after reading one's novel or short fictions. And you have to say that indeed some of it did, though not quite in that way, but that most of it is fiction grown on the compost heap of experience. So, yes, it is true, in a sense, but . . . not to be taken too literally.

Somewhere along the line i quite consciously decided not to change, not to adjust to 'the market'. I was content to just write for myself for a while. I hoped, suspected, that the wheel might come around. Meanwhile, there were literary competitions.

The main difference between publishing houses and literary competitions is that publishers' editors reject what they like if they think it won't sell, whereas judges of competitions are under no such constraints and give prizes to what they like. Evidence of this is that a great number of literary works which have won prizes do not immediately, sometimes never, get into print. Because i talk a lot with readers, i have a feeling publishers are short-changing readers, writers and themselves. Readers read far more imported books than they would if so much of Australian literature didn't seem to be 'more on the same theme in the same tone', as one put it.

My first book, *Everything is Real*, a collection of short stories, collected a number of very respectable rejections in the form of two-page letters of appreciation and helpful advice. I am still grateful for these. They kept me going. Eventually the book was published by Phoenix Publications in Brisbane, which in the mid 1980s was aiming to become an important publishing house for ethnic literature in English. Problems with distribution apparently gave the death knell to that hope and i ended up selling hundreds of copies of my book at a give-away price to 'get known'. I am grateful for the Phoenix publication. It was physical evidence that i was a writer.

My novels (only one has been published, *Walk a Barefoot Road*) contain migrants, as do some of my stories. But their status of migrant is taken for granted as they battle with one or another of life's problems. It is not central to their lives. And my autobiography, *Wrong Face in the Mirror*, which is a search for identity, does not seek that identity from a recognition of loss, but from a knowing of multiple strains that have been repressed and denied existence by cruel whims of history. Being a migrant has been of marginal importance in my life, even though i could not speak English when i arrived here. I would even dare to suggest that being a migrant is marginal to the lives of most migrants. They sought space for their pursuits and only if the pursuits do not work out does being a migrant take a central place in their perception of themselves.

Yet in another sense i am much more a migrant writer than seems to be appreciated. For what i write about is what has occurred to me because of my confrontations with all Australia does and does not stand for. This has shaped my adult life. In not revealing the bare bones of my experience as a migrant i am in fact taking my readers through the garden of my experiences. But instead of saying: 'I dug a tonne of rocks out of this bed before it became soil and i'm forever weeding here and pruning over there,' i invite them to come and see my flowers.

I like to use similes like these because life is, among other things, a journey towards experiencing a oneness with nature, of which we are an aspect. 'Oho-ho-ho!' i hear some say, 'Here comes the monkey out of her sleeve!' This is an old Dutch proverb (challenging us to guess how the monkey got into the act) and i want to contribute it to the body of Australian English. But no, the monkey is not just my pagan view of nature. It is, more so, my Buddhist philosophy (adopted at an early age) which has made speaking with forked tongue a necessity for the sake of social expediency. For, when someone says: 'Ah, well, we live only once . . .' you can't just butt in with: 'Oh, no, we live numerous lives and you and i are far enough from enlightenment to have a few more coming to us,' without losing a new acquaintance or offending a deeply entrenched philosophy. When people say so glibly: 'You can't choose your parents,' and you retort with: 'But you do, you know! You chose them quite deliberately,' you are bound to appear troublesome. And when you counteract cop-outs of how unfairly fate or the government has treated a deserving soul with a reference to karma, you are not on the road to making friends and being successful. So, out of compassion and cowardice, you hold your peace a lot of the time, as must all people who hold opinions not concurrent with orthodox Christianity. At least, you hold your peace in conversation.

Such self-inflicted conscious suppression makes a writer. And in writing there is no holding back. The stories themselves may be more fiction than truth, but the sources out of which i write are no longer hidden. They are my inspiration and motivation and i declare them as such. But they get me reviews that talk of romantic nonsense, or a blend of fantasy and a glorified reality. As these reviewers don't take my sources seriously, i cannot take their opinions seriously either. It is the reviewer in that case who has wasted her time reading my work and writing about it.

My philosophy has also settled me with a different view of time. This is an advantage when the break in your career comes at age 54. But it also means i am not going overboard in a mad scramble to hammer the iron while it is hot. What i don't manage to write in this life, i'll write in the next. There's a marvellous example of a writer taking up his writing career at exactly the point where he left off in his last life, in that classic autobiography of transculturalism *The Way of the White Clouds* (Govinda 1970); the story of how an educated German growing up in the early part of this century followed his instincts and found his true identity.

To date my published works are a bibliography, a collection of short stories, a novel and an autobiography. It will come as no surprise that i am now working on a cookbook. This covers up a multitude of writing that is taking place, being filed and being reassembled, without as yet adding up to a recognised literary form. I am also steadily chipping away at a biography of 73-year-old environmentalist whose exciting life inspires others. After every book—not just the writing of it, but seeing it through the publishing process and having it launched—there is some living to be done to get the next one to declare itself for what it is.

I have drifted far from my proposed outline of what being a multicultural writer in Australia means in my existence. I don't know that i really know. What else can one be in Australia but multicultural? One doesn't have to be born overseas any more to become multicultural, it's now a matter of choice: of friends, partners, food, work and leisure pursuits. Who wants to be pure Anglo or whatever anyway? When i travel overseas i often feel the pressure of a monocultural population as stifling and long for the diversity of Australia.

One of my deepest concerns has become the spurious debates that keep surfacing about race, racism and which differences between people are cultural and which genetic, etc. For me, much of the meaning of life comes from the diversity of humanity and i find attempts—scientific or otherwise—to show we are really all the same, as suspect as earlier attempts to show there were superhumans and less than human humans. It is quite obvious that humanity is what unites all people and also that there are some large subdivisions that so far have been called 'race'. Whether or not 'race' is a good word to use or not depends much on how it is used, as with New Australian, Aboriginal, migrant, etc. But it will be a sorry day when we have to amend our language to avoid referring to the differences between groups of people because some deem these to be reason to feel superior—and be robbed of the delights to which our differences give rise.

As for writing . . . ? About the present past and future present? I will continue. But i'd prefer to sit under a banyan tree and tell you stories. Next life, maybe.

13 Multicultural Australian literature and me

Jim Kable

When I studied for my matriculation a quarter of a century ago in the New England region of northern New South Wales, I was quite fortunate in studying some Australian poets. In this my own memories are unlike those which Shirley Hazzard incorporates in her novel *The Transit of Venus*, where the literature Caro recalls studying at school denies the Australian landscape and experience in favour of what seems natural: 'hedgerows, hawthorn, skylarks, the chaffinch on the orchard bough'. And what writers did I study then, a boy of Anglo-Scottish Australian ethnicity, growing up surrounded by neighbours whose cultural and ethnic diversity was as great as any to be found in a Carlton–Fitzroy Cabramatta–Marrickville setting today, amongst them Hollanders and Friesians, those of German and Chinese descent, Scottish and English immigrants, an Italian, others of Irish background, a Koori family. We studied Douglas Stewart's 'The Fire on the Snow', A.D. Hope's pessimistic 'Australia' and Judith Wright's 'South of My Days'. Judith Wright was writing about the countryside where I grew up. Tamworth, 'Thunderbolt' and other local features rated mentions. I can't recall that these obvious connections with my experience were ever discussed in class. We rarely discussed things in class in those days, treating literature as something removed from both the writer and our own experience, concentrating more on a critical analysis I never really understood and reading the notes handed out by our teacher. It was a terrible waste. There was still a gulf between the literature and reality even though the literature was written in Australia. I know why Judith Wright finally protested about the way her poetry was distorted in the classroom.

It took me many more years to discover Australian literature for myself. Interestingly, it was my involvement with immigrants which opened this door, as well as an accumulation of life's experiences, not only in Australia but overseas as well. How could I best present images of this country to those to whom I was teaching English? Colin Thiele

(1961), with his stories of rural South Australia liberally sprinkled with characters of German origin, certainly drew a response, for here were reflections of the experiences of my students, not only of their lives as strangers in a new land, but also drawing connections between an older rural Australia and rural South-East Asia. Ronald McKie in *The Mango Tree* presented images of a culturally diverse Australia in the years surrounding the Great War. In close connection with each other were the German farmers, the Chinatown inhabitants befriended by Jamie's grandmother, the remittance man from England known as the Professor, whose presence reminded us of the original Koori inhabitants, the Italian musicians, the Greek-born Georgi Comino, the Gaelic-speaking Bandy Mac, and the three principal churches facing each other, reflecting other ethnicities: 'The Catholic church with its white Virgin outside, the Church of England with its green spire and leadlight windows, the Presbyterian Church of plain God-fearing board, and all in a group lowering suspiciously at each other like family enemies at a wake.' (McKie 1974: 30)

Suddenly I was seeing Australia anew, through the eyes and via the experiences of those who were newly here, illuminated by some close literary observations made by other writers. I sought images in writing which drew upon the experience of those who had come to Australia from other countries. Initially I focused my search on writers of non-English-speaking background, although it wasn't such a leap to discover that many Anglo-Australian writers had also, like Ronald McKie, painted the society which lay around them. Rex Ingamells (1951) introduced me to Cheng Ho from *The Great South Land*, immediately recognised, though, by my students of Chinese background. In his Jindyworobak poetry he also drew attention to Koori Australia, a shadowy spotlight whose focus was sharpened with the writing of Jack Davis (1978; 1983) and Oodgeroo Noonuccal (1970). I was beginning to learn that the writers who best presented particular experiences were those who had lived them. I was also discovering for the first time that many writers did indeed draw fairly directly from their observations of life. Both Hal Porter and Judah Waten pointed this out in connection with some of their writing (Walshe 1975). Judah Waten suggested it was 'life turned into literature which bears the ring of life.' While the writers did not necessarily reflect the experiences of everybody in similar situations, there was an essential truth in their portrayal of character and event in the Australian landscape. Peter Skrzynecki was another whose poetry was measured against the lives of my students and deepened the sense of awareness we were beginning to uncover.

About this time I first listened to Angelo Loukakis. He confirmed for me that the real (as distinct from bowdlerised) .terature I was exploring with my students was the best. He defined Australian literature as: 'anything written in English in the way of prose or poetry by any persons who care to call themselves Australian, whether they are in residence or expatriated.' (Loukakis 1983) This description was quite liberating for me, seeking as I was then some all-encompassing definition which would answer to my interest and tentative discoveries. It allowed a broader vision than the traditional view which tended to throw up only Lawson, Paterson and Patrick White. At that time I really did find it difficult to get any names outside those three as a first response when I would ask for the names of Australian writers. Sometimes women like Henry Handel Richardson or Miles Franklin or Christina Stead might make an appearance. This has radically changed, I'm happy to say. Nowadays the names mentioned might well include Kate Grenville, Helen Garner, George Papaellinas, Brian Castro, Thomas Keneally, Tim Winton, Zeny Giles, Gabrielle Lord, Jim Sakkas, Gillian Bouras, Paul Radley, Gwen Kelly, Victor Kelleher, Uyen Loewald, David Malouf, Olga Masters, Trevor Shearston, Les A. Murray, Anna Couani, Ania Walwicz, Elizabeth Jolley, and many more. I do not mean to dismiss any of the canonical Australian writers. In fact a further stage in my appreciation for writing which reflects our cultural diversity in one way or another has been a re-examination of the earlier writers in particular. A period spent living and working in the Mudgee–Eurunderee–Gulgong area where Henry Lawson grew up certainly makes me appreciate his stories set around Pipeclay Creek with characters of German origin. Ted Noffs 1983 (of The Wayside Chapel) recalls his own origins, which sprang from German roots in that region:

> In his cups, intoxicated by
> The grapes of Roth,
> Henry would stand on our vineyard's corner (near the cellar)
> And sing his songs,
> To ease the poet's burden. The inland night,
> Stunned and star-strewn,
> Would listen to his ecstasy,
> But German neighbours in their homesteads
> Shut their windows with a groan, intolerant of the intrusion
> Of anyone who toiled with pen
> And did not work the soil.

And Henry Lawson himself would have been quite at home in Australia today, where he would have figured in the 40 per cent of our population who are either overseas-born or the child of a parent born overseas (as was his father, Henry Larsen, of Norway). Patrick White's writing, too, details much suggesting our connections with other parts of the globe. Hearing Ivor Indyk's analysis of the panorama of characters in Xavier Herbert's *Capricornia*, when I studied Australian literature at Sydney University in 1984, furthered this process for me. It was then, too, that Leonie Kramer's lectures introduced me to Martin Boyd's *The*

Cardboard Crown, essentially the story of an Anglo-Australian family never quite at home whether in the England of their origins or in the Australia in which they had settled, even after four generations! This provides an archetypal Australian experience. Brenda Niall's (1988) recent biography of Boyd also draws out this restlessness, which was indeed a part of his personal experience.

In measuring the authenticity of books from the past, in particular where the writer of one cultural background speaks through culturally different characters, I have to admit that my sceptical filter immediately comes into operation, even for books published relatively recently, though more so for books which are older. Stories where Koori characters are described in simplistic or 'primitive' terms, such as *Walkabout* by James Vance Marshall, tell us much more about the writer's paucity of perception of cultural differences than about the characters. They tell a lie, in fact. As far as possible, I read all such literature with the mental reservation that it is part of a range of writing by writers of that particular cultural background. If I want to read literature expressing aspects of the Koori experience I can read Archie Weller and Sally Morgan, Obed Raggett and Paddy Roe, Mudrooroo Narogin and Elsie Roughsey, Ella Simon, Ruby Langford and Eric Willmot, Glenyse Ward, Robert Merritt and Lionel George Fogarty. I can also read from a growing body of works relating aspects of the various Koori cultures in Australia, ranging from traditional public stories in bilingual publications to personal tales in Aboriginal English as well as autobiographies, novels, plays, poetry and short stories dealing with historical and contemporary issues. And if I want to read how other Australians see Kooris then I can look to Billy Marshall-Stoneking, Sreten Bozic (B. Wongar), Katharine Susannah Prichard, Catherine Martin, Margaret Sharpe and Robert Drewe.

In the context of Greek-Australian writing, it was Angelo Loukakis who drew a parallel between George Johnston and Morris Lurie, two Melbourne writers with a Greek connection (Garry Kinnane's sensitive biography of George Johnston explores his Greek experiences). Johnston's *My Brother Jack* is a book of harsh self-judgment set in the immediate post-Second World War period. It was a stroke of insight to range it against Lurie's *Flying Home*, a novel which explores the very Australian theme of finding one's origins (Greece just happens to be on the way).

While I used to be satisfied with the original Loukakis definition of Australian writing, it seems now that the more I read, and, particularly, the more I read about Australian literature, the more I am forced to modify my view of what it is. András Dezséry (1979), pioneer multilingual publisher of Adelaide, first alerted me to the many Australian writers who do not write in English. His own writing is done in Hungarian, then translated into English. Hanna Foks of Melbourne also depends upon translation to bring her often ironic insights to the general Australian reading public. Her important memories of Egon E. Kisch should soon make their translated appearance by courtesy of Margaret Diesendorf, a Sydney writer, poet and translator whose images of this country come from an artistic vision rich in allusion to the European traditions.

It is clear, then, that Australian writing is not necessarily only in English. Further, if writers from other countries describe this place and its people, may we not also include their works within the canon of Australian writing? D.H. Lawrence's *Kangaroo* seems to have uncovered much more about us than we have wanted to admit, despite his being here for only three months in 1922. Andrew Moore's (1990) recent *Overland* article appears to connect Lawrence's visit with characters forming the King and Empire Alliance, a secret army of the extreme Right. But what of Michiko Yamomoto's *Betty-san*, written out of her experiences of three years living in Darwin (1958–61). When Betty-san, married to an Australian stationed in Japan following the Second World War, finds mandarins in the local fruit store in her Australian town, memories of her childhood discomfort her, but this discomfort worsens when she meets other Japanese people whose work has brought them to Australia. Her world is upside down, the landscape is too big and separated from the people. By way of contrast, the Australian character Linda in Ross Davy's *Kenzo: A Tokyo Story* looks to the landscape for a way of describing the differences she feels in her alien setting. In her story the scale is smaller, the landscape unthreatening, with people and land complementing and modifying each other: 'The vista is not so breathtaking but the sea and sky seem very soothing in their drowsy closeness and warmth. All is calm and quiet, the horizon soft and hazy.' (Davy 1985: 22)

At the beginning of 1986 at Writers' Week in Sydney, Sneja Gunew suggested that the cultural perspective would become the key issue for reading and analysing literature. Clearly, this perspective must also be central to our judgment of literature in a world where we increasingly acknowledge cultural diversity. All writing, whether it can be defined as multicultural or not, is open to *readings* which take cultural diversity as a starting point. And so I am still an avid reader of Australian writing, still exploring what it can tell me about the multicultural society in which I live: whether it is through the work of children's writers and social historians such as Morag Loh, or Junko Morimoto or Barbara Ker Wilson's *Jane Austen in Australia*; or Nadia Wheatley's *The House that was Eureka*; or Loló Houbein's short story collection *Everything is Real*, with its extraordinary awareness of our environmental and human options; or her novel *Walk a Barefoot Road*. Also important in enforcing new cultural awareness in the Australian literary scene are the anthologies: Manfred Jurgensen's *Ethnic Australia*; Ron Holt's *The Strength of*

Tradition; Peter Skryznecki's *Joseph's Coat*; Gunew and Mahyuddin's *Beyond the Echo*; Spilias and Messinis' *Reflections*, George Kanarakis's *Greek Voices in Australia*; Π. O.'s *9 2 5 The Works*; and so on.

Australian writing is rich and diverse. It may originate here or it may be written beyond our shores. Usually it is in English, but often it is not, and sometimes it is written in a hybrid form which does not conform to standard English. Most is written by Australians, but there are occasional pieces from others. It tells us about ourselves and our environment and it is best when it folds itself around those cultural features which unite us and yet also outlines the differences of our varied ethnic origins.

14 Life makes some strange connections

Lidija Simkus-Pocius

As I was pondering the issue of multicultural writing in Australia, I came across an article by John Berger (1985), exploring aesthetics and the role of beauty in an ugly world, in which he took as symbol the wooden White Bird. Some time after reading this article I attended a literary translators' conference in Lithuania and, to my amazement, I set eyes on the White Bird. This strange connection helped me address this issue on my return, as I will explain.

I was caught up in what I could not have expected—the great and stirring demonstrations for reform following Gorbachev's *glasnost* policy. I not only witnessed the crowds and confrontations in the streets, the revival of the Lithuanian national anthem and national flag, but, as an exiled Lithuanian poet, was a speaker at many important events. In addition, I gave talks on Australia and many poetry readings (my collected verse is to be published by Vaga publishers in Lithuania, whereas my earlier books were published in the USA). The return of the national flag, freedom of speech, the possibility of the autonomy of a nation which was always culturally distinct from its neighbours are things which are taken for granted in the West but they were excitingly new to the people of my original homeland. They meant the resurrection of their cultural vitality.

Having been so caught up in all the excitement and optimism, I can only say I was uplifted beyond words. It was another world. I had opportunities to meet people with extraordinary backgrounds, among them former political prisoners whose strength and dignity, considering what they had been through, left me in awe.

In all this—the wooden White Bird!

For one of my many visits was to the home of Veronika Povilioniene, a much-loved folk singer. There, hanging in her house among her collection of folk carvings, I saw the wooden White Bird. It is a popular motif with Lithuanian carvers. The White Bird is a simple, homemade object, made according to a traditional pattern, yet its very simplicity allows it to be pleasing, mysterious and evocative to anyone who looks at it. Seeing it, I recalled Berger's observation: 'The problem is that you can't talk about aesthetics without talking about the principle of hope and the existence of evil.' Berger (1985) asks what it is about the White Bird which evokes an aesthetic reaction, reducing aesthetics to art, which he admits says nothing about the long-argued relationship between art and nature:

> Nature is energy and struggle. It is what exists without promise. It can be thought of by man as an arena, a setting, it has to be thought of as one which lends itself as much to evil as to good. Its energy is fearsomely indifferent. The first necessity of life is shelter. Shelter against nature. The first prayer is for protection. The first sign of life is pain. If the Creation was purposeful, its purpose is a hidden one which can only be discovered intangibly within signs, never by the evidence of what happens. It is within this bleak natural context that beauty is encountered, and the encounter is by its nature sudden and unpredictable . . . . However it is encountered, and beauty is always an exception, always *in despite of itself.* This is why it moves us. (p. 7)

Later in the essay, Berger says:

> In any case, we live in a world of suffering in which evil is rampant, a world whose events do not confirm our Being, a world that has to be resisted. It is in this situation that the aesthetic moment offers hope. (p. 8)

The happenings I witnessed in Lithuania gave me hope and triggered off trains of thought leading into the mysterious, the coincidental, the unpredictable, the marvellous workings of the imagination and the possible connections between things. The White Bird, along with Berger's statements, became a symbol, a connection between the macrocosm of events in Lithuania on a national scale, and the microcosm of my writing and the way I see my position in relation to multicultural writing and to mainstream Australian literature.

As I write in Lithuanian, I am naturally isolated to a large extent from my Australian environment and the people in it. And yet I have had all my formal education in the English language and have spent the greater part of my life in this vast and very different continent. These two things have formed me to a very large extent. And yet, in my innermost spirit, I need to belong to the Eastern European tradition from which I come, rather than to the external reality I have had to struggle with for the greater part of my life.

But as I have said:

Australia has formed me . . .

Australia has given me bread and water . . .

Australia has inhibited my development; as as child I was afraid to speak out since I expected to be greeted with intolerance. . .

Australia has absorbed me into its wide open spaces . . .
Australia has been restrictive, narrowing and critical . . .
Yet Australia is my land; it has given me shelter . . .

Perhaps out of these contradictions comes the reason why I turned to the Lithuanian language, hoping that it would express my feelings more appropriately and help me protect myself from the environment where my body had learned to cope but my mind was neither confident nor at home. For there were many people who, I found, did not want to understand, and whom I could not understand.

It was reassuring to come across writings I could identify with, such as those of Czeslaw Milosz, a Nobel Prize-winner for literature in the 1980s. He says that although he is a Polish writer, he does not forget that he was born in Lithuania, and that in his works are to be found traces of a typically Lithuanian, if not pagan, mysticism. (Lithuania is, according to Milosz, the most poetic country in Europe, next to Ireland.)

The mystical–sacral existence which mattered to Milosz, and which matters to me, is found in his novel *The Issa Valley*, which is an almost Proustian revivification of a long-lost and longed-for Eastern European childhood. Similarly, it was rewarding to come across the writings of Oscar Milosz, who lived in France and was a Lithuanian ambassador during his country's period of independence (1918–40). This Milosz, by the way, is a distant cousin of Czeslaw the laureate. Because of a complex family history and the once Grand Duchy of Lithuania and Poland, Czeslaw chose to be Polish. Oscar, although writing in French, chose to be Lithuanian. Together with Oscar Milosz, I believe that one can get used to everything. The important thing is to live as little as possible in what is called the world of reality—a world ruled by the absurd cult of domination and of matter.

Oscar Milosz, then, turned to his roots, to Lithuania, which he called the mother of the Indo-European race, the spiritual homeland of the Aryan world.

I came to the conclusion that I am a Lithuanian-Australian poet. And that is not an easy thing to be. I made an independent choice to write in Lithuanian. It was a choice which would have been easier to make now, when 'multiculturalism' is public policy and widely accepted. Earlier, it was a costly choice, for Australia was uncompromising in expecting conformity to its Anglo-Celtic perceptions. But to have conformed would have obliterated what I see as my essential identity.

Recently I came across an article in a Lithuanian periodical by Jonas Mekas, who writes poetry in Lithuanian and makes avant-garde films in New York. He was attempting to define the characteristics that differentiate Lithuanians from others. He stresses the importance of listening to our inner selves; of pondering on the things that touch us personally. He says that we can never be Brazilian or Australian: for the things that lie deepest in us are from the homeland—the fields of flowers, the smell of pine branches, the colour of linen . . . And he says that we are like bees, finding honey and wanting to take it home. Wherever we are, we are still part of our mother country, Lithuania.

So poetry for me, expressed in the Lithuanian language, is like forming a prayer to broken roots. I write because of an inner need. I write because I am at once a Lithuanian and a resident of Australia. I write to express my self—my part of the primordial eternity, of which we are all a part in the collective unconscious; but my roots are deep in Lithuanian soil, and it is in the language of that land that I can make the meanings I want.

I could be seen as a cosmopolitan choosing as a tool the language closest to my heart; but as a poet I feel myself destined to be a lifelong seeker for a place, in both the physical and the metaphysical sense.

I said that the reality of feeling that I am 'the other' in Australia has made me experience alienation; and yet this very alienation has been intrinsically involved with my need to write poetry. I *need* exile, homelessness perhaps, to drive my interior journey, the exploration of the mind and soul.

My lot in life, like that of many culturally displaced writers, is to have been a kind of Ulysses, destined to wander through challenging seas of the mind which are even more daunting than the Baltic or Mediterranean in their worst aspects.

I am a long way from the village of Samogitia.

In brief, then, my destiny as a displaced person, a Balt, a New Australian, an ethnic, a bilingual or an element in Australia's multicultural mosaic, has been a test of identity and endurance. It has been a journey into the unknown from an absurd war and insane genocide to a land of ignorance and indifference. All this has understandably been a continuing upheaval.

Many years ago I came across a book of translations of Czeslaw Milosz's poetry into Lithuanian. In the foreword he wrote that all that was presently being written in Lithuanian or in Polish was like messages put in bottles and thrown in the sea. He admitted that this was hard to accept, for we humans hate emptiness, and like to imagine the eyes and faces of those taking up and opening our works. And yet Milosz, in time, came to be awarded the Nobel Prize for literature. In reading his work and that of others, I have gained strength to persist, to say as the Beckett (1965) character says:

> I can't go on
> I'll go on.

15 Writing from a non-Anglo perspective

Anna Couani

The piece of writing I am about to write is about writing from a non-Anglo perspective from the point of view of a fiction writer who is a non-Anglo Australian. That is the brief I have been given but it puts me in a quandary because I have never written from this position about this field. I think it is an area which has been dealt with best by cultural theorists anyway. I do not have the appropriate specialist language and experience to do the field justice. It is a situation where I am positioned by the context as a fiction writer trying to write a kind of academic prose about myself, academic prose in the sense that it is neither fiction nor journalism nor autobiography. But academic prose is not written about yourself, it is written about something external to yourself, and it is written usually by people who have expertise in the field; authority. By definition you cannot write about yourself with authority. I am positioned here in the anecdotal sphere. So the way I choose to proceed is to write about being positioned and taking up positions because it seems the most possible and least platitudinous path.

THE WRITING SUBJECT POSITIONS HERSELF

My family were migrants to Australia like all non-Aboriginals, but from Greece and Poland and therefore non-Anglo. The first family member came about 1880, and since then more came and some went back, some changed countries a few times—and so on up to the present.

When I write fiction I often refer to cultural identity and the situation of migrants:

> Through your eyes I see a city. I look through you to the city. As you walk you echo the footsteps on that city's streets. Behind you a city lies in ruins. Your eyes look past me at that city you carry with you. Behind your eyes and in your movements the city is intact, it lives and breathes. The streets are crowded with people. Your solitude suggests the crowds, your

movements are the street life. I walk into your city hesitantly when everything is still, walking through a city of two-dimensional buildings, frozen people. (Couani & Lyssiotis 1989)

The reason I wrote this piece was because I am and have always been surrounded by migrants to Australia in a host of different private and public settings and sometimes I have tried to imagine people in their other contexts, other countries. But to say this simply restates the passage above in a less evocative way.

Generally, I regard newly arrived migrants, or any migrants to Australia, as rather different from myself and I think this is obvious in my fiction. I talk about migrants, I hope sympathetically, but I never speak as a migrant writer. This makes me very curious about the fact that I am often regarded as a migrant writer.

When I write about education (being a teacher of migrants), I write about second-language learning, language teaching, attitudes of the host community to new arrivals etc.:

The demonstration of the students' approximation to genre takes place on two levels. On one level, particularly initially when the activities are more programmed, more scaffolded, the activities specifically direct the students towards the operations necessary to develop aspects of the text genre and the register appropriate for it. So analysing the students' dialogues in these activities will be more a reflection of the success of the curriculum genre. (Couani 1989)

I write like this as a teacher researching ways of teaching English to migrant students who are under my gaze and I wrote the following piece within a paper about the attitudes of school teachers to Arabic-speaking students:

As Mukherjee (1986) points out, there are many disadvantages and problems in the host community which are being projected onto new arrivals. One could argue that in Australia, which is a country where the original people were very badly dealt with by the colonizers, whose white community was founded as a penal colony, which has never been truly self-governing, which consists of older migrant communities which have deep-seated identity problems (are they British, Irish, Scots, Welsh or Australian?), which is patriarchal and sexist, where most of the wealth is in the hands of very few people, which is being and has always been manipulated by foreign powers ... there are many crises and profound problems gnawing at people and it could be that the very fact of migrancy can disturb this nation of migrants. (Couani 1988)

For me, as a fiction writer and poet (but not as an education writer), the marginal position is a desirable one, one which escapes confines inasmuch as that is possible. I know that to a certain extent this is impossible: you cannot invent new literary conventions for yourself. However, if you are prepared to publish your own work and write for a fairly small audience, as I am prepared to do, then you can maybe avoid the problem which so much big press literature has—that of being bland, conservative and already-seen.

But although I accept the marginal position so fully, I suspect there was never another one open to me. The history of my life as an artist is one of multiple exclusions. It is only now in retrospect that I am grateful for the absence of an accepting peer group to which I would have had to conform.

THE WRITING SUBJECT IS POSITIONED

My writing is variously labelled feminist, experimental, and migrant. I am described in *Buongiorno Australia* (Pascoe 1987), a book about Italo-Australians, as an Italo-Australian feminist writer and I have often been asked to speak on panels about being a migrant writer, to contribute to anthologies of migrant writing.

Whilst I was thinking of myself as someone who was making efforts in the public writing arena to support people from disadvantaged sections of the community in a more or less altruistic way and was trying to give my fiction significant social content, the Anglo writing community perceived my work as the efforts of a self-promoting migrant and even promoted my work themselves because they believed they should foster migrant writers. My Anglo patrons are unable to see me as a patron like them, even though I am a small-press publisher and have, in fact, published a number of books by Anglo-Australian women writers.

So, regardless of my attempts to position myself, my work—like that of all writers—is positioned by the literary community in which I operate in a way I cannot control. I suspect that the experimental nature of my work, its non-narrative structure and collaging effects, is the trajectory along which I must travel in order to avoid the armoury of literary stereotypes which can be used to describe my work.

The term 'non-Anglo perspective' remains a difficult one for me to write about. It tends to simplify the idea of a perspective from which to write because the perspectives we all write from are informed by so many factors. It presumes that the perspective which we are positioned in by the literary establishment is the only one we have. When I refer to the marginal position I take up, I have in mind a chosen ideological position informed by a number of different threads, more complex than Anglo or non-Anglo.

Part III: Author studies

16 Before the migrant writer: Judah Waten and the shaping of a literary career

David Carter

To begin, a word about my title. It does not refer to a time before there were 'migrant writers' in Australia. Whether we mean by this term writers born outside Australia, writers whose first language is other than English, or writers whose cultural formation was other than Anglo-Australian, it is highly doubtful whether there was ever a time 'before' the migrant writer in Australia.

What it does refer to is a time before the concept of the migrant writer existed, before it was available to the writer in Australia as a category through which a literary career could be conceived; or, again, before 'migrant writer' was available as a speaking position from which a writer could intervene in what we might call the cultural economy. More directly, we need to examine the time before the category of the migrant writer became possible *within* the field of Australian literature, and this will mean looking at what happens among the critics as well.

I will use the term 'migrant writer' here as a shorthand which condenses all the possible alternatives: ethnic writer, multicultural writer, non Anglo-Celtic writer. Such a procedure has its dangers, for it means ignoring the slippage and the politics that exist across the different terms. In one sense, though, the point of my argument is to draw attention precisely to the operation of such concepts and the discursive fields they describe. 'Migrant writer' was the only possible term before multiculturalism, and the period I will be discussing, after the Second World War, is still to be found under the sign of assimilation. That fact is itself a significant one for the shapes a writing career, a career as a migrant writer, could then take. Although the distinction might only be a matter of shades of emphasis, I think it is true to say that Judah Waten's writings in this period were received in terms of migration (the passage towards assimilation) rather than ethnicity.

My particular subject, then, is Judah Waten—who, it could be argued, made the category of migrant writer a site of meaning and value within the local cultural economy. Waten's *Alien Son* (1952) is widely known and has become, as they say, both a popular favourite and a 'classic' (it featured as one of 'Australia's greatest books' in Geoffrey Dutton's (1985) anthology *The Australian Collection*).[1] That the book has nevertheless received very little sustained attention from literary critics and commentators is a subject to which I will return.

Waten was born in 1911 in Odessa, of Jewish parents. However, the family was already established in Palestine, then under Turkish rule, and he spent his first few years there. In 1914 they migrated to Australia, to Perth initially, then to Melbourne. *Alien Son*, in 1952, was Waten's first published book—a series of connected short stories set around a Russian-Jewish family in Western Australia and then in Melbourne.

I want to understand the writing of *Alien Son*, not as autobiographical, but in terms of what we can call its 'literary occasion'. By 'the writing' I mean both the process of composition and the composed text. By the 'literary occasion' I mean the moment of the writing defined in terms of a network of ideas, styles and alliances, and of publishing or career possibilities, all of which help to determine what literary options are open to the writer at a given time and in a given place—to Judah Waten in Australia, in Melbourne, in the 1940s and 1950s. My concern is thus with a specific 'case study', but the very specificity of the study will be part of a larger argument about the way literary careers, or writing selves, are constructed within a given literary history (which is of course not really given at all).

Such an understanding of the literary occasion can be explored by asking such questions as: what sorts of fiction were being written and read in Australia in the late 1940s? What groupings of writers existed? (Who knew whom and who read whom?) What kind of audience could a writer support? (Whom did you write for?) What kinds of literary or writing careers were available, both practically (getting published and getting paid) and conceptually (how was a 'career as a writer' conceived)? With each question focused on the writing of *Alien Son* I want to trace the formation of Judah Waten's writing career in a situation defined (in the sense outlined earlier) as 'before' the migrant writer.

To write is to conceive oneself as a writer, to construct a writing self which must also be conceived as a point of entry into a particular 'writing scene' or cultural economy. This means taking a position among a varied but delimited range of possible positions; taking a position, that is, within the network of current notions of writer, novelist, journalist, intellectual, Australian writer, Jewish writer, communist writer, migrant writer, female writer and so on. The positions are never equal, never equally present, and my argument begins with the point that in the mid 1940s the position of migrant writer was scarcely available, especially in a field dominated by the category of the Australian writer. This is perhaps even more the case when the category of the Australian writer could itself be the mode of a politically motivated intervention from the cultural margins in the figure of the radical nationalist, democratic or working-class writer. But we will also need to examine the possibility that the categories of migrant writer and Australian writer could thus be conceived as complementary, the former as a unique kind of qualification for entry into the latter.

The forms of a career are shaped within a specific 'field of possibility', a set of options and constraints which operate intellectually, publicly, and at the level of the text. For Judah Waten, writing himself a writing career in postwar Australia, the field of possibility is defined by prevailing debates about realism, modernity, democracy and propaganda, Australian literary traditions, and the intellectual's responsibility to the national culture; it is defined also by a limited range of publishing outlets and organs of criticism, and quite tightly defined formal and informal groups of writers (grouped around different institutional sites and different attitudes of possession towards literature and Australian literature). This is the field of possibility which defines both the writing of *Alien Son* and the absence of the migrant writer as a category within Australian literature.

The stories that make up *Alien Son* were being written and revised over a period extending from the mid 1940s to the early 1950s. Judah Waten himself has spoken of this moment as the beginning of his 'second literary career' (Waten 1971: 87). The nature of the first literary career would probably surprise those who know of him only as the author of *Alien Son*. In the late 1920s, still a teenager but already a member of the Communist Party, Waten began as a writer in a mode best described as 'left-wing avant-garde'. He wrote a novel called *Hunger*, influenced by John Dos Passos and the early James Joyce, and edited a radical magazine called *Strife*. The novel was never published, though excerpts from it appeared in little magazines in Paris (when Waten was overseas in the early 1930s), published alongside work by William Carlos Williams, Louis Zukovsky, Ezra Pound and others (Waten 1971: 83).

Although a number of Waten's artistic and political friends in Australia in this period were Jewish and immigrant, the prevailing discourses in the circles in which he moved were not those of ethnicity (or 'foreignness'). Instead they were internationalist, whether of the international avant-garde, the international proletariat, or, as in Waten's case, some combination of the two. If there was an ethnicity that figured locally in bohemian and radical political circles, its inflections were Irish-Australian. Although ethnist and nationalist, the Irish-Australian discourse positioned itself as displaced and oppositional—and it could be seen as a *kind* of proletarian internationalism. (Interestingly, much later in his life as a novelist, when Waten's characters are not Jewish they're likely to be Irish-Australian.)

Both the avant-garde and the proletarian sides of this early period provide only *anti*-models for a career—or models for an anti-career. That might be why Waten seems to have abandoned this first attempt at a literary career in the early 1930s, abandoned it for two other careers which he pursued in fits and starts: a career as a communist journalist and a career as a bohemian (which after all has its own career structure and which no doubt you have to work at).

The beginning of Waten's second literary career can be dated roughly 1945. What is most interesting for us is that this new attempt at a literary career appears to depend upon an increasing investment both in the forms of a national culture—an Australian literary tradition—and in contemporary Jewish–Yiddish culture. This dual interest in both a democratic Australian tradition and a modern Jewish cultural tradition can no doubt be understood in the context of the war (Waten was later to become secretary of the Jewish Council to Combat Fascism and Anti-Semitism). But what does the intensification of *both simultaneously* mean for the formation of a literary career? What space was available for the 'Jewish-Australian' or 'Australian-Jewish' writer?

In the mid 1940s we can find evidence of a range of writing, editing and publishing activities in which Judah Waten was involved, activities which reveal a literary career in the process of formation across both Jewish and Australian cultural fields. In 1945 he published an essay called 'Reflections on Literature and Painting' and a (pseudonymous) story in a magazine edited by the nationalist historian Brian Fitzpatrick. Waten's essay argued for a militant, democratic tradition of Western art, and ended by placing contemporary Australian literature within this tradition. The magazine, *Southern Stories*, also carried an essay by Fitzpatrick called 'The Australian Tradition'.

Southern Stories was the first product of Dolphin Publications, an enterprise established by Waten and the painter Vic O'Connor to publish cheap editions of Australian works. Waten and O'Connor together edited Dolphin's second publication, *Twenty Great Australian Stories*, an anthology of short fiction from Marcus Clarke to Alan Marshall. Critical in all of this work is the sense of an Australian literary tradition; above all, a literary tradition felt to be a contemporary (and political) force – *the* literary tradition for any writer wanting to address (and to politicise) a contemporary Australian audience.

At the same time, *Southern Stories* contained two stories, translated by Waten from Yiddish into English, by the immigrant Yiddish writers Pinchas Goldhar and Herz Bergner. In addition, in 1946 Dolphin published Waten's translation of Bergner's novel *Between Sky and Sea*, excerpts from which also appeared in a magazine called *Jewish Youth*, from the Jewish cultural group the Kadimah. Waten was on the magazine's editorial board. The published novel carried an introduction by

Vance Palmer; and in 1947 Nettie Palmer was to write an obituary notice on Goldhar for *Meanjin*.

We can find evidence, then, of two sets of influences or models (models both for writing and for a literary career) available to Judah Waten in the mid 1940s. And we can see the complexity of the literary occasion of the writing of *Alien Son*. Waten was already, consciously, a writer and his literary career was already a diverse and public (if marginal) one. His writing was neither an unstructured activity nor simply the result of direct experience (that is, the 'migrant experience'), as many later critics would have it.

On one side, we can see the influence of the Yiddish writers Goldhar and Bergner (and the painter Yosl Bergner as well). On the other, we can see the influence of a group of 'Australian' writers in Melbourne: Nettie and Vance Palmer, Frank Dalby Davison, Alan Marshall (plus Fitzpatrick, and painters O'Connor and Noel Counihan). Through the former, we can imagine the active presence of a Jewish–Yiddish literary tradition— not as a matter of nostalgia or mere cultural birthright but as an immediate and political presence. Waten repeatedly told the story of how it was Goldhar who suggested to him that he write stories about his own Russian-Jewish immigrant experience, rather than the stories about Aussie battlers and Aborigines which he had been attempting. The Aboriginal stories appear to be lost, except for one ('Black Girl') that appears in *Alien Son*; but it is interesting to speculate on links between these stories and Yosl Bergner's 1940s paintings of urban Aborigines as figures parallel to the dispossessed Jews of Europe.

Through the second group of fellow writers and artists, we can imagine the presence of an Australian literary tradition, as suggested before—a tradition also felt to be an immediate and political force, a contemporary intervention, not merely an inheritance. As is suggested by the involvement of the Palmers with Bergner and Goldhar, the two sources of possible influence could be complementary as well as potentially contradictory. The Palmers' nationalism was also a cosmopolitanism; they welcomed migrant writers as signs of 'national' and democratic or populist cultural activity all over the world, even as they welcomed them also as part of the developing project of Australian literature.[2]

In terms more directly of the writing, from both sets of models we can also note a pressure towards the short story. The Australian work will be more or less familiar to readers. Palmer, Marshall and Davison, Waten's closest contacts, all wrote realist stories with identifiably Australian settings; the first-person narrative voice is common; and the stories, while clearly literary, are also popular in address.

What of the Yiddish writers? The modern European Yiddish writers such as Sholem Aleichem wrote stories which can be understood in part as literary imitations of the traditional folktale. Their literary trick is to re-create a strong sense of orality, of oral narratives produced and received communally, but also to give their stories a modern ironic edge (Waten described Aleichem as 'the funniest and the saddest' of these writers). The stories typically create the illusion of orality and community by using such techniques as a talkative style of narration or a child narrator within a family (aspects I've emphasised for the way they can also be made to bear on our reading of *Alien Son*).

The Yiddish writers in Melbourne gave more emphasis to the contemporary experiences of migration and displacement. If their stories still create a sense of community, the primary communal experience is now that of marginalisation or alienation. In *Alien Son*, too, migration is clearly a central theme: the stories are full of journeys and dreams of journeys. And the title alerts us to the theme of alienation. But the interesting thing is Waten's difference from these writers—writers whose works he was in the process of translating even as he was writing the *Alien Son* stories. The position of immigrant Yiddish writer was one that was not available to Waten, or not attractive as a cultural politics, not just because of the different experience of migration but because of his different relation to the community of Australian literature. If there is a sense in which Waten wants to speak from the position of the Jewish immigrant community, he also wants to speak to an Australian literary community (and through it to an *Australian* public).

We could say that the stories themselves are thus written under the sign of assimilation, enacting their own 'merging into the life of this country' (to paraphrase Vance Palmer's review). But we can also say that their position of mediation, of being both inside and outside, is precisely what defines the effective cultural intervention of *Alien Son*. It is the quality suggested by the perfectly judged title of the collection (given to Waten by Davison or Palmer—depending on the anecdote): the son shares the alienation of his parents but is also alien to them. On a larger scale, it is this doubleness which 'invents' a position for the migrant writer within, or at least provisionally within, the field of Australian literature.

To put this in another way, I would want to argue that what enabled *Alien Son* to be written, and what has kept it in print ever since, is not so much its discovery of original subject matter but its discovery of a *point of view*. In some ways it harks back to the European, rather than the local, Yiddish writers as Waten discovers his own means of imitating the oral and communal tale, but with a distanced ironic or comic edge. For example, the language is frequently proverbial in quality, both in dialogue and subtly in narration:

> It so happened that on a number of occasions someone Father trusted acted on the plans he had talked about so freely before he even had time to leave the tea-house. Then there were fiery scenes with his faithless friends. But Father's rage passed away quickly and he would often laugh

and make jokes over the table about it the very same day . . .

'How should I know that people have such long memories for hate? I've only a cat's memory,' he would explain innocently.

'If you spit upwards, you're bound to get it back in the face,' Mother irritably upbraided him. ('Mother')

But the point is that this proverbial speech isn't the main kind of language in the stories. The proverbial qualities are worked into a stricter, less idiomatic language of literary realism, and so the stories are not folksy or vernacular or, even more remarkably, nostalgic. They are more about alienation than authenticity, as much about asymmetry as adaptation. The asymmetries in what I called above their position of mediation are caught in the double negatives of the difficult final sentence of 'Neighbours': '. . . we did not speak to one another as we walked on, but neither of us knew that there could be no reconciliation with the ways of our fathers'; and again in the final sentence of 'Looking for a Husband', which allows no resolution: 'Tomorrow morning we would land and go on for ever our different ways—Mother to beat her wings against an enclosing wall and Mrs Hankin to go on relentlessly upholding the old ways in the new land.'

In describing the stories in this way I am also describing my own reading position. I am reading the stories from a position, however tenuous or self-knowing, within the contemporary field or structure of 'Australian literature'; and yet from a position which seeks to make a difference, to open up a distance, within that field by resisting its habitual modes of assimilation (still). In positioning the text, then, I am positioning myself: there is something the text enables me to do, something which I enable it to do (for me). In either case the question of point of view becomes central and does so by way of an argument with the book's critical history.

The 'simplicity' of *Alien Son*, a quality on which all the critics comment, is the result of a complex manipulation of distancing in the stories, of a point of view that is at once distance and intimacy. The narrator as the child-within-the-family, for example, means intimacy and community. But the child is also distanced from the Mother and Father (the words are thus capitalised, and we never learn their names or the narrator's); and so distanced from their tenuous community as well. More accurately, the narrator is not a child at all. These are stories of recall from an adult perspective, and this further doubleness adds another level of intimacy within distance or distance within intimacy.

The composite child-narrator figure throughout the stories is both observer and observed, both innocent and implicated, and both inside and outside any possible community. This is nicely suggested in an episode in the opening story, 'To a Country Town'. Playing with a group of Australian boys (their Australianness is underlined—he takes off his shoes and socks to join them), the child sees and is seen by an old Jewish man. They recognise—suspiciously—each other's foreignness; and the narrator comments, 'It was as though he had caught me out.'

Indeed it seems to me that what *Alien Son* discovers as central to the—to *this*—experience of migration and alienation is the experience of *self-consciousness*. The stories are full of moments of embarrassment, of being caught out in public or in private, moments of shame and of guilt (often incommensurate with its cause). Again the position of the child as observer and observed is crucial—we are most conscious of him when he is being looked at or is caught out looking. Even the horses have a role to play in the narrative, counterpointing the perspective of child and migrant: '. . . as soon as he ran out of the house he began shouting ugly and hateful words at the inoffensive horses who looked at him with grateful eyes' ('Uncle Isaac'). The varieties of self-consciousness are also related to a theatrical quality of the stories. The characters tend to be real *characters*: they perform and they are all full of talk, overflowing with talk (contrasting with the spare realist style of the writing itself). The migrant story, for Waten, comes to us *as* story. It is full of stories, full of mismatched stories, and full of misreadings too, both within and beyond the community. For these reasons the story 'The Theatre' is for me one of the keynotes of *Alien Son*, for it links all these themes around the central 'scene' of theatrical performance itself.

We could try out the hypothesis that the theme of self-consciousness and self-conscious performance in the stories is itself a sign of this migrant writing occurring under the gaze of Australian literature. But the self-consciousness is dramatised rather than being a quality that disturbs the writing itself—unless we read its spare realism as just such a self-conscious response. In fact the critical gaze of Australian literature has looked elsewhere when regarding these stories, and we can take a moment to review how the category of the migrant writer was taken up into the field of Australian literature. It is revealing, I think, that critics often fail to notice that these are stories of recall, failing to see the distancing this implies. *Alien Son* has been read in rather simple ways as autobiographical or, loosely speaking, sociological. That is, it has been read as the simple expression of the author's own childhood experiences, which are understood in terms either of the individual or of the migrant group. Both these readings are invited by the stories themselves: they're designed, we might say, to appeal to us with the veracity of actual experiences recalled and as fragment stories within the larger story of the migrant experience.

The trouble is that the very success of the stories in estabishing their veracity, their illusion of simple recall, has meant that their art has been mistaken for artlessness. Though the book has long been regarded as an Australian classic, the critics actually find very little to say about it. The book's qualities are put down to 'experience' or 'background', and the commentaries are full of phrases such as 'unforced simplicity', 'simple flat recounting', 'unvarnished social realism' and so on.[3] It is as if all Judah Waten had to do was to open his mouth . . .

My argument is that the migrant writer is not born but made, and made within a specific and uneven literary context or literary occasion. The critical reception of *Alien Son* exemplifies something noted in an article by Sneja Gunew (1985), which points out how migrant writers are accommodated within the literary regime by the ways their work is read as simply autobiographical or as endless repetitions of the migrant story. What Judah Waten manages with *Alien Son*, it seems to me, is to discover a speaking position, a point of view, which invites these readings in terms of autobiography and the migrant story and yet refuses to be contained wholly and simply within them. It is both inside and outside the immigrant Jewish cultural sphere, both inside and outside the field of Australian literature as then constituted. To put it another way, and so as not to be caught out romancing the margins, the position of migrant writer, if it were not to be perpetually in translation, perpetually foreign, was only possible via an accommodation within that Australian literary field.

We can draw these points together by looking at the question of audience or address. The *Alien Son* stories do ask to be read in part as 'Jewish' stories, for example via a range of references they contain to Jewish writers, songs and folktales. Their address, however, is not primarily to a Jewish or migrant community of readers but to a broader 'Australian' readership (which might indeed assimilate the Jewish-migrant communities). Thus the stories also ask to be read in the light of literary realism and local traditions of the short story: that is, as *Australian* stories. Their intimate sense of audience, I think, is less the product of a limited address to a Jewish–migrant community than something Waten shares with and has learnt from the community of his fellow writers such as Vance Palmer and Alan Marshall (and given the institutional position of Australian writing at this time, this might also be an intimacy within marginality).

The shape of Waten's literary career, then, is less a product of the migrant experience than of the particular field of possibility that was Australian literature. In this light I find it useful to understand Waten's position through the concept of a minority literature as defined by Deleuze and Guattari. By a minority literature they mean a literature 'which a minority constructs within a major language' (Deleuze & Guattari 1986: 17). Their subject is Frank Kafka, a Czech Jew writing in German; but there are some interesting parallels with Judah Waten, a Russian Jew writing in English. The differences, though, are equally illuminating.

Deleuze and Guattari argue that the condition of a minority literature is defined by 'linguistic deterritorialisation'. The consequences of this deterritorialisation are that, within the 'cramped space' of a minority literature, each individual or family story takes on a collective value, becomes the story of the whole community or culture (of its marginalisation), and thus becomes political: 'each individual intrigue [is forced] to connect to politics . . . a whole other story is vibrating within it. In this way, the family triangle connects to other triangles— commercial, economic, bureaucratic, juridical—that determine its values.' As Sneja Gunew has noted, Deleuze and Guattari have 'been accused of indulging in first-world theoretical tourism of the margins' (Gunew 1990: 23) and there is a liberationist (indeed theological) excess in their arguments in which 'minority' seems to disappear into 'revolutionary' or 'avant-garde'. What can be redeemed is not their sense of liberation but their articulation of limits, of the cramped field of possibility of a minority literature *within a major language*.[4] This is what draws out the similarities and differences between the linguistic and cultural situations of Kafka and Waten.

The rhetorics of marginality are much less extreme in Waten's writing than in Kafka's. The sense of belonging to a minority is tempered in Waten by that of belonging also to a local literary tradition and community, and to the larger traditions of European realism. We need to remember that, in the literary culture in which Waten was involved, the 1940s and 1950s in Australia (and in Melbourne above all) saw a vast investment of signifying activity going into the business of creating something to belong to, a tradition that was always and already there. Nevertheless, or rather therefore, the conditions of a minority literature leave their imprint on the text of *Alien Son*—in the aspects of point of view and language, and in the overall structure of the book as a series of short stories, often sketchlike and seemingly insufficient in themselves, the whole adding up to what Waten called 'a novel without architecture'.

From the perspective of the narrator's recall in *Alien Son*, Australia is no longer a foreign place. And yet the stories are still pervaded by an apprehension that, in Waten's own phrase, 'in the twentieth century the Jewish migrant has been the symbol of the oppressed and the migratory person'.[5] This political and symbolic dimension is why, far from being nostalgic recollection or quaint family anecdote, *Alien Son* can still seem to be the text that separates us from the time 'before the migrant writer'. And in more than one sense it is the text that made Judah Waten's literary career possible.

17 Letter in response to a questionnaire

Margaret Coombs

In response to your comments, I feel I'd like to make some attempt to explain why I don't mention my 'non-Anglo-Celtic' background in the information I supply to publishers for use in 'biography of the author' pieces. It's for the same reasons I don't supply them with the information that I am the mother of two children—another fairly significant fact of which there's not a trace of a mention in most of my biogs. I find the homogenising assumptions people make on the basis of facts supplied—or not supplied—in biographies very disturbing and threatening: no matter what you say or what you leave out, people jump to all sorts of bizarre conclusions on the strength of it and this often severely distorts their reading of your work. With bitter experience I have learnt (fast) to give as little information as possible unless I have the space (as here) to give enough information to make my doubts about the whole genre 'author's biog' clear. I don't mind supplying all and sundry with the information that I live in Petersham, Sydney, for instance, because I feel that if people are stupid enough to assume there is such as thing as 'a typical Petersham resident' and that I am one, then I just don't care. But I *do* care if people assume there is such a thing as 'a typical non-100-per-cent Anglo-Celt' or 'a typical mother' and that I am one. *Why* I care is precisely because my cultural background and my motherhood are so much more important to me—important in making me the particular individual that I am—than is (say) the suburb in which I now live.

My father was an Australian-born Jew. His parents, my grandparents, were both Jews: both my grandfather's parents emigrated here from Prussia, but my grandmother was born in Woolwich, England, emigrating to Australia in 1878, aged three. Does the accident of her having been born in Woolwich, though a 'Jewess', make her a sort of honorary Anglo-Celt? Her daughter (my father's sister) says she (my grandmother) was of German Jewish background. (I would guess she was no more an 'Anglo-Celt' than a child born to 'Anglo-Celtic' diplomats in China and raised within the Western enclave is 'Chinese'.) Her father was born in Kurnick, Posen, 'Germany' (a part that's now Poland), and her mother's father was also a German Jew.

I'm surprised at how upset I feel at the idea of being excluded from the bibliography and collection of multicultural writers. Like people accused of being 'whites who think (or like to pretend) they're Aborigines', I feel resentful that I'm being deprived of the right to define myself—even though I understand the problems you face in undertaking the task you're undertaking, and I don't have any better selection criteria to suggest. All the same, I feel hurt enough to bother to raise some questions about the selection criteria. Please remember I speak from the position of somebody who feels she has had to put up with some of the negative aspects of having a 'non-Anglo-Celtic' background without enjoying any of the positive aspects—like support from fellow 'outsiders'. I feel that a bona-fide Anglo-Celt can recognise at 1000 paces that I'm *not* 'one of them' and, if at all prejudiced, will treat me and my writing accordingly. So it rankles when I find 'non-Anglo-Celts' regard me as 'not one of them' either.

The project seems to accept unquestioningly the idea that 'the family' (and of the biological parents at that!) is *the* important shaper of the human subject—that and the place of birth. To assume these things is to reinforce the idea that they *should* be. Life is, or can be, a lot more complex than that—as a lot of the people accused of being 'whites who like to pretend they're Aborigines' could, I believe, attest. Let's get hypothetical: what if I were the genetically Anglo-Celtic daughter of an Anglo-Celtic woman who, three months after my birth, had gone to live in a lesbian relationship with an impeccably non-Anglo-Celtic woman and who had herself lovingly adopted that woman's language, customs etc. and brought me up in the household accordingly? By your criteria, I would be excluded from your bibliography—but should I be? Isn't this business of attaching so much importance to the family tree, and the accompanying assumption that each of us has important relationships on only two sides, a bit conservative/out-of-date/limited to specific *kinds* of people? Let me speak for myself and say I feel my relationships with two friends have been at least as important in making me what I am as any relationships with relatives—and yet your project takes no interest in their places of birth etc. (Likewise books have been important!)

It also seems to me that class enters into all this. Isn't it only 'respectable' people who know things like where their grandparents were born? And yet a writer's psyche and work can, I believe, be very much shaped by a 'non-Anglo-Celtic' background without that person's even being conscious of that 'non-Anglo-Celtic' background, e.g. for many years I quite sincerely believed my father's 'not liking' pork, ham, etc. was just a personal eccentricity! It's predominantly the middle-class writer (isn't it?)

who is conscious (*self*-conscious) of the position from which s/he writes and who knows who her/his parents and grandparents were and where they were born.

In other words, your selection criteria seem to me to take for granted a stability and continuity that are not a reality for many people (except, paradoxically, those in nineteenth-century Anglo-Celtic novels!). Anyway, stability and continuity are especially alien to refugees of various kinds who are/were/always have been busy covering their tracks and pasts, not celebrating them. My parents—one a Jew, one a Gentile— were, after their marriage, the victims of both Jewish and Gentile prejudice/ostracism that seems fairly shocking from where I sit looking back, so no wonder they tried to teach me to take no interest in my 'roots'. Doesn't that make me very much the product of a non-Anglo-Celtic background? (Hope it's not presumptuous if I suggest some comparison with Sally Morgan's *My Place*). It has taken some money and effort for me to find out where my grandparents were born because such matters were never talked about in our household. (The stereotype of the cosy, non-Anglo-Celtic family bites the dust!) Someone in my shoes but with less education and less money and less energy would never have found out—and yet their 'selves' and their writing may be very much shaped by their non-Anglo-Celtic background!

Something prompts me to add: what sort of evidence are you asking writers to give regarding their background? Do you simply believe what writers *say*? Very unreliable! Don't many people who feel themselves to be misfits concoct myths about their origins to 'explain' their feelings of 'differentness' and come to believe them themselves, e.g. Charlie Chaplin, Edgar Allan Poe? And I know of one Australian writer of impeccably Anglo-Celtic origins who is quite frequently published (and reviewed) as a non-Anglo-Celtic writer because she has taken her husband's conspicuously non-Anglo-Celtic name. I'm sensitive about this, being stuck with a painfully Anglo-Celtic name myself. I married a Coombs at 19 (before feminism) and did not revert to being Margaret Harris after my divorce partly because my children found the idea of a name change too disturbing and partly because I knew of two other 'literary' Margaret Harrises and didn't want to be confused with them. I guess, judging from my memory of an old document, that 'Harris' was originally 'Hirsch' (or maybe Hirschl? Hirschel?) but nobody remembers our being called that.

Perhaps what I'm getting at is this: OK, consciousness is a cultural construct. So, for that matter, is unconsciousness. I just don't think the key to any writer's psyche necessarily resides in the birthplace of their biological/legal grandparents, especially if their biological/legal grandparents were (as two of mine were) wanderers.

And what *do* you do about people like an acquaintance of mine who feels herself to be of an altogether different ethnic background and skin colour from what she is? What gives *your* yardstick for judging non-Anglo-Celticness its authority? Well, maybe I am misconstruing what you say and maybe your parameters are flexible enough to include me and other 'doubtfuls' in the bibliography and collection. If so, I would be delighted to complete the questionnaire you sent me, so please let me know if you'd still like me to. In the meantime, I will visit my aunt and try to find out from her at least the correct spelling of 'Hirsch' (I don't think I've got it quite right) and you'll be welcome to list me as Margaret Coombs/Harris/Hirsch (or whatever it is) if you want to.

Anyway, I'm glad to have been prompted to think about how much the assumption that a person's blood ties (or legal ties) and place of birth tell 'the story of her life' (regardless of class, race, etc) bothers me.

By the way, I'm well aware that some writers in a similar position to mine react in the opposite way: I'm told David Malouf is constantly resisting efforts to appropriate him as a non-Anglo-Celtic writer and insisting on his fifth-generation Australianness. Perhaps, paradoxically, if I'd had a more foreign name than either Coombs or Harris, I would have reacted in this way too. But, because of my name, I'm sometimes assumed to be as Anglo-Celtic as any Smith or Jones and I suppose that helps make me want to insist on my non-Anglo-Celtic-ness!

The questionnaire was sent by Jan Mahyuddin and Sneja Gunew, who are compiling a bibliography of multicultural writers based on the earlier work by Loló Houbein (1984) and Alexandra Karakostas-Seda (unpub.) The response is dated 24 July 1990.

18 Mena Abdullah, Australian writer

Yasmine Gooneratne

Mena Abdullah is a writer of Punjabi background, all of whose stories were first published in the *Bulletin*, with the exception of 'The Babu from Bengal' and 'A Long Way', which appeared in *Quadrant* and *Hemisphere* respectively. They were published by Angus & Robertson as a collection under the title *The Time of the Peacock* (1965; reprinted in paperback 1973, 1974, 1989).[1] 'Because of the Rusilla', a moving account (apparently based on personal experience) of a young Indian family's first encounter with the world of white Australia, is included in the anthology *Best Australian Short Stories* (Stewart & Davis 1971), and 'Grandfather Tiger' is included in a more recent anthology of Australian women's writing.

In writing the twelve stories which make up *The Time of the Peacock*, Abdullah collaborated with Ray Mathew, a high-school contemporary, writer and friend to whom, when discussing her work, she gives the position of equal co-author. The stories, says Abdullah, would not be what they are without his contribution.

Critical responses to her stories when they first appeared were warmly appreciative, both in Britain (where a *Times Literary Supplement* reviewer found them 'a joy to read') and in Australia. The *West Australian*'s review of *The Time of the Peacock* said: 'Never has the other fellow's point of view been put forward with more gentle suavity than in this tale of Indian children growing up in rural Australia ... The style throughout has a simplicity and purity of language that is a delight to read.' The *Australian* congratulated Abdullah and Mathew on their sensitive depiction of 'a beautiful new world in Australia: the gay, touching and agonising life of an immigrant Indian family as seen by their young daughter'. Maurice Shadbolt, writing in the *Bulletin*, called the book 'a small miracle', adding: 'I don't think I will find *The Time of the Peacock* easy to forget, and I don't think—when they come to read it—that my children will either. It is that kind of book: to be passed on within a family, with love.'

Although Abdullah is one of the very few authors of Asian background who have achieved substantial publication in Australia, her finely crafted stories have not yet received the attention from critics that they deserve. This is possibly because, although she is Australian-born, the experiences she writes about place her inevitably on the 'periphery', and beyond the line that has hitherto lovingly enclosed Australia's 'traditional' authors in an enclave that is deemed 'central' to the nation's literary and cultural development.

Abdullah's father arrived in Australia in the 1880s, at the age of fifteen, from the Punjab in northern India. He spent his early days as an itinerant hawker around the country. Eventually he took up land at Bundarra in the New England district of New South Wales and became a successful grazier. Mena was born in 1930. Her early days were spent in Bundarra where, with her family, she lived 'an almost enclosed existence' on her father's sheep property, experiencing little contact with other children.[2] The birth of a son to the family highlighted the children's need of an education. The sheep property was sold and the proceeds invested in Sydney real estate in the suburbs of Gladesville and Hunters Hill.

Autobiographical to a large extent, some of the stories are based on Abdullah's experiences as a child growing up in New England; others, such as 'Grandfather Tiger', have connections with the years in which the family moved from New England to Sydney. There is a brief reference to her father's life as a hawker in the story 'Because of the Rusilla':

> Uncle Seyed came the next day with the wagon. It was always used on town days, but it was very old. It belonged to the time when father first came to Australia. He had nothing but the clothes he wore and the Koran tied up in a red handkerchief which he used as a prayer mat. With the money from his first jobs he bought the wagon. Faded, but still proud, the letters on the side said: MUHUMMAD DIN—LICENSED HAWKER. (p.14)

The word 'proud' is significant. The poverty (in its early days) of the Indian family Abdullah describes in her stories does not make them humble or ingratiating, and the security and comforts they find in Australia do not make them materialistic or self-satisfied. The tradition passed on to the children by their parents, who have made the crossing from one society to another, is twofold: Nimmi, Abdullah's child narrator, calls the Indian part of that tradition 'gentle and strange, stories of the time when magic people walked through Hindustan, and everything they touched was right and good' (p.42). The Indian tradition of family and community story-telling which still shapes Indian fiction from Rao to Rushdie was evidently able to survive the crossing. Nimmi and her brother and sister absorb from their mother both the fantasy of India's myths and legends ('magic people walked through Hindustan') and its essentially moral significance ('everything they touched was right and good').

The other strand in Nimmi's experience is her Australian inheritance; and this, according to her, was the 'true and real' one (p.42). She grasps its various meanings through her father's stories of his early experiences as a hawker and later as a farmer and grazier in the land of his adoption. The two strands merge in Abdullah's story, 'The Outlaws', in which Nimmi's 'Uncle Seyed' (no blood relation, but a friend of the family who shares both its Indian and Australian experience) tells her a tale which links the two traditions and locks them as a unit into her memory for evermore.

Uncle Seyed's story comes to Nimmi at a moment in her childhood when she is feeling rather lost and disoriented. Indian family traditions are strong in her home, and this young 'new Australian' feels out of place and unwanted. Her elder sister Rashida and her younger brother Lal have each their traditional niche. Nimmi alone, caught in the middle, is unsure of her role and uncertain where she belongs. Rashida is her mother's helper, given the grown-up tasks of preparing fruit for the making of chutney, and is quick to point out to Nimmi that she is 'Stupid! . . . She had chilli on her hand and she rubbed it in her eyes. She's too young to be in the kitchen.' Even young Lal knows what he must do: longing to go with Nimmi and Uncle Seyed to explore the Outlaw's Cave, he still accepts the call of duty:

> 'Lal-baba,' said Uncle Seyed, 'your father is in paddock. I must mend fence. What man stay to look after Ama, Rashida, the baby?'
> 'I am afraid,' said Ama, 'when there is no man here.'
> Lal looked at her and her downcast head. He looked at Uncle Seyed. 'I must stay,' he said. 'Men must look after women.'
> So Uncle Seyed and I went alone to the Outlaw's Cave, and the story that day was given to me. (p.45)

Seyed's story about an Indian bandit-hero, 'the eagle that struck from the mountains . . . the great dacoit' (p.48) comes naturally out of their visit to the cave where, in earlier times, a bushranger named Thunderbolt had hidden:

> . . . 'They caught him?'
> 'They kill him,' said Uncle Seyed. 'They shoot him in water. He have no chance. Grave in Uralla. I show you one day.'
> I gaped at the cave. 'But he was a bad man,' I said.
> 'People here like him, sorry he killed. I sorry. He like horses.'
> I stared at him. Uncle Seyed was devout and embarrassingly honest. 'But he was a thief,' I said.
> Uncle Seyed stopped banging the post. 'Are thieves that are thieves,' he said. 'Are thieves that are men. Some men steal and die, but they not crawl

street with begging-bowl. Better to steal and die. A man ... a man can be a thief,' he said. Without noticing, he had begun to speak in Punjabi. 'A man can steal and still have honour. He can be a great dacoit, great. Like Malik Khan.' (p.46)

Hearing the tale of Malik Khan, who refused to take the path of lawful obedience yet gave his life to save that of his old tutor, Nimmi learns of the code of honour that binds together the outlaws of the Punjab: 'Sanctuary, hospitality, safe-conduct—are part of the law of the Pathans. A man who breaks them, a man who refuses them, is no Pathan, and all his people are dishonoured' (p.48). The moral standard that she draws from Seyed's story-telling is especially valuable to Nimmi in her disoriented state because it is not exclusive to one of the two strands of her inheritance, but weaves them together. The story as a whole gives expression to a distinctively Asian-Australian sensibility that is part of Australia's cultural history.

It is a similar weaving together of disparate traditions and experiences that Abdullah achieves in her stories, which are 'true' in a sense that transcends the merely historical: for though the details of Australian life in both country and town in the 1930s are accurately recorded, the fiction built upon them is remarkable for the fineness of its author's observation and the delicacy with which she notes the significance of what her child characters see and hear.

Nimmi notices, for instance, that as her 'Uncle Seyed' begins to speak his inmost thoughts and convictions, he slips unconsciously from the acquired language, English, to his native Punjabi. She notes the different ways in which the members of her Indian family attempt to live within the alien environment. Her mother, for instance, has never accepted the change; instead, she tries to make her new life tenable by re-creating the memories and observing the familiar rituals of an India she has left behind:

[Ama] was standing there, in her own garden, the one with the Indian flowers, her own little walled-in country. Her hands were joined together in front of her face, and her lips were moving. On the ground, in front of the Kashmiri rose bush, in front of the tuberoses, in front of the pomegranate tree, she had placed little bowls of shining milk. (p.2)

The bowls of milk are intended, in Nimmi's Ama's imagination, for the friendly cobra that often makes its home among the roots of a tree in an Indian village centre, around which people gather for an evening smoke and gossip. But, as her practical father tells Nimmi in a private, 'secret' conversation which helps her grow up, and grow in understanding, there are no friendly cobras in Australia. Her mother's sentimental memories of 'the old ways' would, if allowed to rule unchecked, destroy the family:

'There is no honour in snakes. They would strike you or Rashida or little Lal or even Ama. So . . . I go to the garden in the night and empty the dishes of milk. And this way I have no worry and you have no harm and Ama's faith is not hurt. But you must never tell.' (p.6)

The secret of survival seems to lie, in fact, in intelligent and sensitive compromise. This is the 'secret' Nimmi learns from her father, whose energy, humour, and sense of adventure direct the family's fortunes and sustain their happiness and unity. It is no accident that 'The Time of the Peacock', the story in which this little incident occurs, begins Abdullah's book and gives it its title, for one aspect of her intention as a writer is to inform new migrants of ways in which the unavoidable trauma of expatriation can be minimised and borne, especially by children. In story after story she probes areas of real or potential social and racial conflict, indicating how they have been or can be resolved.

In 'Because of the Rusilla' and 'Grandfather Tiger', little Indian children who have known only the safety, happiness and acceptance of the family within their own homes are brought into contact, for the first time, with ignorance and insularity. Sometimes the pain of an experience is needlessly sharpened by adult ignorance, as when Joti's Australian teacher, though seriously concerned about the new Indian child in her class, unconsciously robs her of her identity as a person by mispronouncing and Anglicising her name from the very start:

'Hullo, Josie,' she said. She had thought about this new girl, off and on, ever since she had interviewed her mother. She was a difficult case, and her enrolment card was going to be a worry. The cards had a space to tick for 'Australian' and another space to tick for 'new Australian'. What was to be done with a dark-faced Indian child who was a second-generation Australian? (p.95)

It is a situation which immigrant writers everywhere can parallel in many different areas: the individual presents a vexing problem and a 'worry' to the host community because s/he does not fit into existing categories. The individual must either change the shape of his or her worrying name or even sensibility, or a new slot must be created into which the 'worrying' individual can fit with reasonable comfort. Unfortunately, little children are not usually in a position to create new slots or to adjust official shortsightedness, so they usually pay a hurtful (if hidden) price. In 'Grandfather Tiger', Joti's own good sense (operating through her imagination as the voice of her late grandfather) tells her where and how to draw the line:

'I *cannot* go back!'
'You have to go back,' said the tiger. 'You are the eldest. You are not the only one; there's your brother and sister. And your mother and father

had the same trouble and pain, but your mother was patient and your father was brave—the bravest in the school. It is for you to be patient like your mother and brave like your father, little one.'

Joti looked at the ground and said nothing.

'It is hard,' said the tiger. 'But when they accept you they will accept you for always.'

Joti stared at her feet and noticed for the first time how dark they were.

'The lessons are good,' said the tiger. 'Your teacher is good.'

'Oh yes,' said Joti. 'I like the lessons. The teacher is nice. But she calls me Josie.'

The tiger banged his paw on the ground so that Joti jumped. 'That is a different matter,' he said. 'You'll have to stop that or it will last you all your life. Your mother's name is Premilla and they call her Milly. Your Aunt Halima was called Alma. And your Uncle Shamshir'—the tiger shuddered—'they called him Sam!'

Joti giggled and the tiger glanced at her sourly.

'You may think it funny now,' he said. 'And another thing, I would not wear that dress again. Wear your own name and your own clothes and they will understand you better.' (p.97)

This sage advice works. Joti becomes 'herself' again, and makes a friend on her own terms. She finds that the tiger waits for her no longer in the darkening garden, and realises that 'he had gone away because she did not need him; she was a schoolgirl now' (p.100).

'Because of the Rusilla' is a story that presents this core situation at greater length and in greater depth, but resolves it in a different way: by placing beside the hurtful, hostile incident another that contrasts with it and might, one day, even blot it out altogether. The opening sentence gives the reader the story's essential elements:

The whole day—the trip to town, the nigger word, the singing kettle—was because of the Rusilla. It had flown away. (p.11)

The rosella, which Nimmi, Rashida and Lal call the 'rusilla', had been found trapped in long grass and brought home to the farmhouse, where Lal had made it his special pet. To Lal, Nimmi's delicate only brother, the rosella had been 'a friend, from heaven' (p.13). When it flew away, Lal had been inconsolable, and it is in order to make him feel better that Uncle Seyed takes the children, for the first time in their lives, out of the safe, known world of their farm and into the neighbouring town. There, two things happen. The first, a chance meeting with three white Australian children at a street corner, brings anger and hatred into their experience for the first time:

Suddenly they were there, white children—a big boy, a middle-sized girl, and a little boy. We stared at them. They stared at us.

'What y' wearing y' pyjamas in the street f'r?' said the big boy.

'What y' wearing y' pyjamas in the street f'r?' said the girl. (p.16)

It is a good and reasonable question, but it indicates to Nimmi that she and her family are being assessed according to unfamiliar standards. While she is still trying to reason out the implications of the question (she does not regard her everyday clothes as sleepwear) the incident takes a regrettable turn. Prejudice gets the better of curiosity, and the white children mockingly echo the racist humour bred into their family life by the early Australian–Aboriginal experience. Since it is Nimmi who describes the incident, her pain and bewilderment come through vividly in Mena Abdullah's choice of language:

> Why were they pointing, and singing, and saying such sharp pointy words?
> 'Nigger,' sang the big boy. 'Nigger, nigger, pull the trigger.'
> 'Nigger, nigger, pull the trigger,' said the others. They were all saying it, singing it, like a game. (p.16)

Since the story has already established for the reader the Indian children's sense of their own individuality as Indians, the reader grasps through Nimmi's response ('such sharp *pointy* words') the shock of her realisation that they have apparently been mistaken for 'black people', Aborigines, with whom they are not aware of any special kinship ties: their own identity has been somehow obliterated. At the same time, the playful hostility of 'Pull the trigger', in association with the rhyme-word 'nigger', erases Nimmi's sense of happy security. Without being able to analyse the experience, she senses that she has entered a superficial, hostile world in which she has no place.

Nimmi's little brother Lal is, however, too young to react in this way. Ignorant of the message the voices carry, he responds enthusiastically to their song, and to the presence of boys whom he takes to be like him and naturally, therefore, his friends:

> 'Game!' cried Lal. He ran forward. He lived in a world of women, an only son, and here were boys. He ran to meet them. (p.16)

Predictably, he is tripped up and bullied. Rashida and Nimmi promptly forget all they have been taught about the gentle good manners appropriate to Indian girls. Defending Lal, they do violence to their enemies and to their own Muslim traditions, using language that 'is a terrible phrase to us', and actions which shock Uncle Seyed when he sees them at it. Violence has indeed been done, and the story might have ended there.

But it does not. Seyed takes the children to visit an Australian friend's house. Here the children meet with a range of new experiences, as unfamiliar as their encounter with the children at the street corner, but pleasant and rewarding in that they provide material on which the imagination can heal itself and grow. Rashida discovers a 'miracle' when she finds she can pick out her mother's songs on the living-room piano.

Nimmi discovers the fascination of shining pages and the smell of print-er's ink in a magazine. And Lal rediscovers his lost 'Rusilla' in the singing kettle their friend has put on the stove in order to make tea. By the time they go home in the twilight to the familiar scents and sounds of the farm, the second experience has crowded out the first. The girls descend, laughing, from the wagon, eager to show their mother the roses their Australian friend has given them:

> But Lal pushed between us.
> 'Look, Ama,' he said, holding up his kettle. 'Rusilla.' (p.20)

The themes of displacement and the need to belong somewhere are taken up again and again in Mena Abdullah's stories. It would be a mistake, however, to see her only, or even largely, as a 'writer with a message'. Other stories span the generations and the miles that separate Australia and India. 'The Dragon of Kashmir' describes 'old Grandfather Shah and the days when he trained camel-drivers for the long rides through Australia, stories of Kashmir and the jewels that the Indian Maharanis wore' (p.78). Characters from Australia's rural past, like 'Paddy the Singing Man' and the crafty 'Babu from Bengal' who writes business letters for his employers in English, 'the language for business and rudeness' (p.87), are developed as vignettes. Her best stories are about what Henry Handel Richardson called 'the getting of wisdom'. They focus on the experience of growing up, and in their human truth and artistic skill transcend a purely local context.

Mena Abdullah was at high school when the Second World War erupted, and at business college preparing for the public service adminis-trative examination when Singapore fell. She has written of that time, and what it meant to her and her fellow Australians:

> I couldn't believe it. I remember the morning after—an early morning in February 1942—walking down George Street and looking at the shops draped in black cloth and purple ribbons. An eerie quiet hung over the city—an air of dread. Dame Mary Gilmore cried out our rage in her poem 'Singapore', she rallied us with 'No Foe Shall Gather Our Harvest', and comforted us with 'This Too Shall Pass'. In the months that followed the casualty lists seemed quite unreal. Familiar names popped out. So many from this one small suburb! Our neighbour's son, 'Malcolm . . . Killed in action'.

The 'small suburb' was Gladesville in Sydney, to which Abdullah had moved with her family in the 1930s, when running his country property in New England had become increasingly difficult for her father (then in his sixties). The reader of this passage might ask why an Australian writer who had found her deepest feelings expressed in Dame Mary Gilmore's poetry in 1942 should have felt called upon in 1988 to end this paragraph on her memories of a wartime adolescence with the words:

122

Throughout that terrible year I never felt more Australian. And since then, I have never felt the need to question it. I am Australian, and that is all there is to it.

For some Australians 1988, Australia's Bicentenary, unexpectedly became another 'terrible year' of ideological and psychological trauma, when what was euphemistically called 'the debate' on Asian immigration caused controversy in the nation at large and stirred feelings of deep distress and bewilderment among the people who make up Australia's tiny proportion of 'Asian Australians'. Readers who encountered Abdullah's work for the first time in that year would have found that it quietly confounds, in its quality and cultural wholeness, the assertions of politicians (and of at least one misguided academic) regarding the nature of 'One Australia': *'I am Australian, and that is all there is to it.'*

Mena (her name means 'woman') was educated at Gladesville Primary School and at Sydney High School, finding the stimulation of books 'an absolute joy' after the years of isolation and intellectual deprivation: 'We could not get enough.' Learning with delight to read, she read anything and everything that came in sight—street signs, placards, notices in shop windows. Brought up in a traditional Indian home, the Abdullah children had more responsibilities than other children of their age, and even when very young they wrote business letters for their father, shared in family business discussions, and helped in every way they could. Although her parents called themselves Australians and her father had by then lived in Australia for over 40 years, Abdullah believes that sharing with their suburban neighbours the privations of the Depression, suffering with them the epidemics of scarlet fever and diphtheria that followed in its wake, and treating as their own the tragic losses suffered by other Gladesville families during the Second World War 'transformed our family, and made us Australians and not foreigners in the eyes of the community'. She recalls this period of her life as 'a hard, hard time', but believes 'it was also a great time for a child to grow up in':

> It was a time of great courage, perseverance and faith. People worried about each other, cared for each other—there were no foreigners, we were all in this together and we all had to pull together to get ourselves out. And under all the hardship the unquenchable spirit of the people which said 'Hang on. We'll ride this out together. Just hang on.' Well, we did come through, most of us. We were bruised and battered, but we survived. Our family were now fully-fledged Australian but ... in a few short years [as] refugees were pouring into Australia from all over troubled Europe, suddenly, it seemed, we became old established Australians and these newcomers were the foreigners.

Mena Abdullah recently retired from the Commonwealth government service, and from the CSIRO, which she has served as an administrative officer for 46 years. Since 1973, *The Time of the Peacock* has been regularly included in the text list for Macquarie University's third-year English Literature course on Modern Asian Writing in English. Here Abdullah is read side by side with writers of such international stature as V.S. Naipaul, R.K. Narayan, Pramoedya Ananta Toer, Ruth Prawer Jhabvala and Salman Rushdie, assisting students' understanding through literature of the cultures that surround Australia and contribute to its richly multicultural society.

19 Instead of a statement

Aina Vāvere

When as a writer I am asked to make a statement on my craft I find it difficult to come up with anything remotely like a statement. I prefer to give the questioner one of my few books or literary works, hoping that a statement will emerge from these. However, on this particular occasion I cannot do it. Ninety-nine per cent of my 'statements' are written in a language in which about 20 000 Australian Latvians converse, and barely two million people in the whole world. My 'statements' in the form of a literary work would be of little use to my other fellow Australians. Unless one day they might (just might) be translated into our lingua franca, English.

There is the story about an intruder who walked into a room full of people. Later those people were questioned and asked to tell their impressions of the intruder. The big man said the intruder was small and nondescript; the small man recalled him as being big and threatening; the do-gooder felt the intruder had got lost and was in need of help; the young matron found him exotic and attractive in a repulsive way; the intellectual had formed no opinion as the intruder did not speak the intellectual's language.

We need no psychologist to tell us that people's own make-up and inclinations guide them in the perception of others.

If Australian society—meaning Australian society as it was 40 years ago, Anglo-Saxon to the hilt—was the room, then the waves of post Second World War immigrants were the intruders. Consequently they were perceived as all of the above and more, depending on the point of view of those assembled.

The big man found it relatively easy to come to terms with his views. Although at first glance the immigrant seemed to be small and nondescript, he soon turned out to fill a very useful place at the conveyor belt, the sewing machine, the hospital kitchen and the laundry; the small man, after a period of unease, found him less threatening as the immigrant generally was law-abiding and seldom married outside his own circle. The lady, who was accustomed to organising dinners in aid of the world's starving, transferred her energies to being a good neighbour, and wondered why there was so little good-neighbourly work to be done. The immigrant seemed to fend for himself very well indeed. The young matron found it hard to sustain her view of the 'noble savage'. Although some shops started to offer 'exotic' fare and some hall in some neighbourhood would occasionally be taken over by dancers in colourful costumes and nostalgic and lilting tunes, she somehow could not find her way into it. It was hard to get an introduction. The intellectual ignored the immigrant as he did not seem to fit into any pre-existing cultural category.

The immigrant was accommodated in a corner of the room and the consciousness of those present and he seemed to be reasonably happy with this arrangement—an arrangement lasting almost two generations.

But migration all over the world during the last 40 years has occurred on such a scale that it could not be ignored for long. Nor could the immigrants live forever without trying to express their common experiences in literary form in order to come to terms with them, to sublimate them, for is that not the purpose and the meaning of all art forms? Nor can it as successfully be done in any other language as in the one in which your mother sang her lullaby.

Sociologists claim to have enough data on hand to say that the colonial cultures which developed during the last 200 years (the American, the South African, the Australian) did so in four fairly well-defined stages: first, a period when the colonists import the parent culture; then a period of modification of the imported forms in order to accommodate the new environment and novel experiences; next, a period of revolt and rejection of imported forms as inadequate for the expression of these experiences; and finally, a period when an indigenous culture asserts itself as a part of a wider civilisation. According to H.G. Kippax (1965), Australian literature offers Harpur and Kendall as figures of the period of adaptation, Lawson and Furphy as figures of revolt and Patrick White as the representative of the fourth period, the coming of age of Australian literature.

On scanning the various Australian ethnic literatures, one cannot but conclude that the development of the ethnic cultures follows the colonial model, all immigrants in many ways being also colonists. First, the maintenance of the traditions brought to the new land, then dissatisfaction with these forms as inadequate for the expression of new experiences, then attempts by each ethnic culture to assert itself against the traditions which, separated from the source of renewal, are becoming ossified.

The only additional observation that would have to be made is that an ethnic literature, such as we know it at present in Australia, has to assert itself on two fronts. First, towards the parent in a distant country where the experiences of the migrants arouse little interest. Second, towards the Australian Anglo-Saxon culture as the pre-existing and thus the ruling form. In many countries from which migrants come—Italy, for example—there has been hardly any interest in the phenomenon of migration. There the creators of literary works do not belong to the migrating masses; they are members of the class which does not emigrate. The emigrants belong to the working class and have no time or skills to turn their experiences into art. A generation or two have to pass before new talents in a new country find their voices. Or else, if the waves of immigrants brought intellectuals, artists and writers with them, as from Eastern Europe where under Stalin they had become personae non gratae, by and large they were ignored by the establishment. Neither the *Oxford History of Australian Literature* (Kramer 1981), nor the *History of Australian Literature, Pure and Applied* (Green 1985), mentions a work which deals with the theme of being an immigrant beyond David Martin's *Young Wife* (1962) and Judah Waten's *Alien Son* (1952). They hardly signify an effort on the compilers' part to take a broader view of the meaning of 'Australian'. In Candida Baker's three books (1986; 1987;1989) no Australian writers writing in a language other than English talk about their work.

Yet man must create art in order to express his own particular pain, joy, love, hatred: in this case the pain, joy, love, hatred of being an immigrant, a dago, a Balt, a wog. And not only that; just as important is the fact that these expressions are nourished by the Australian environment, its climate, the reversed seasons, scents of eucalypts, hot north winds, cold southerlies, coastal cities and the Australian social setting. That is what Australianness is about, rather than the mere fact that something is said/written in the English language. That is why, I am told, the Greek Australians produce on average three literary volumes a year, the Latvians one or two volumes, the Italians stage theatrical works dealing with social problems of migration, and so on. In a chapter on non-English-speaking writers, Ken Goodwin (1986) acknowledges the existence of Dimitris Tsaloumas, Pino Bosi, Rosa Cappiello and a few others. Likewise in Hergenhan's *New Literary History of Australia* (1988), Rosa Cappiello and Angelo Loukakis are mentioned. This may be a sign of a changing awareness, belated but nevertheless a welcome sign.

It would be easy to say: let each of us express our joy, love, pain, hatred in our particular style and language as long as certain values and tastes are promulgated as the only desirable ones. But it won't work. In too large a section of the Australian community the stiff upper lip is not the most desirable attitude; nor is the understatement—the ultimate in good taste. From among the early immigrant nostalgia and first-person accounts which the oral historians and the sociologists sometimes like to accept as literature, new and powerful voices are emerging, asserting themselves as truly artistic and as genuinely Australian as any Anglo-Saxon writing, yet different in content, approach and form. In the United States, Canada and France, for example, immigrant writers like Czeslaw Milosz, Josef Skvorecky and Milan Kundera have been recognised as valued contributors to the literatures of those countries. It would be against the laws of probability to think that in Australia there are no writers of the same stature writing in their native tongues. The future Australian literature will be the poorer if they are not recognised and encouraged.

The political recognition of Australia as a multicultural society has coincided with the natural arrival of the Australian Anglo-Saxon culture at the previously mentioned fourth and independent stage of development. We have also arrived at an unprecedentedly opportune time to make the next stage a phenomenon never encountered before in the development of a civilisation: to make possible the emergence of a truly multifaceted and therefore truly egalitarian culture bound together by its common roots in the continent called Australia.

As for the statement I was trying to make, I'd rather continue the story about the intruder. Will the plot develop into high tragedy? A low comedy? Shall I write a realistic, polite account of the poor intruder and the benevolent host? What mode and manner will be most suitable? Satirical? Farcical? Shall I employ a turn of phrase à la Phillip Adams? Try to dazzle the reader with learned witticisms à la Max Harris? Or stick to the wry humour of the Eastern European peasant? There are many possibilities. I have a lot of thinking to do. If one wants to shout from rooftops, one should be as truthful as possible.

20 'In Australia, we read it differently …': Interculturality and the theory of literary criticism

Walter Veit

I.

One of the most promising advances in literary theory in German studies inside and outside Germany today is the development of intercultural studies within the cognitive theory of modern philosophical hermeneutics and the institutional framework of German as a foreign language. The process of teaching students from many countries linguistic and cultural competence in a German setting taught German academics a lesson in the cognitive potency of the 'other', of alterity, which is also an unacknowledged central premise for Australian scholars of German studies. I wish to use this example as a paradigm applicable to the studies of other cultures as well. The investigation of this most unsettling and challenging experience leads to my first argument: what is familiar to us in our own individual, social or national life forms the largely unexamined cognitive basis for our understanding of the foreign.

An earlier investigation into the theoretical and practical aspects of intercultural studies in Germany (Veit 1985;1987;1987a), a country which has finally accepted her cultural diversity, allowed me to point out deficiencies in the current widely accepted theoretical position in Germany: interculturality is still perceived there as a problem, a hindrance to the 'correct' understanding of a foreign culture. Neither in German nor in Australian literary studies is interculturality properly understood and accepted as a permutation of the hermeneutic category of pre-judgment. It is therefore a theoretical error—with far-reaching practical consequences—to try to eliminate intercultural perspectives in literary studies in order to achieve an 'objective' explanation of literary and other cultural or anthropological phenomena. Adapting to my own purposes a famous line by Martin Heidegger on the problem of the hermeneutical circle, I would like to advance my second argument: it is not enough to become conscious of the intercultural basis of all studies

129

of foreign literatures in order to neutralise it, but rather it is necessary to acknowledge interculturality as highly productive of meaning.

Such a position has wide implications for literary and cultural studies. It has particularly interesting results for German studies: it allows German studies in Australia to win a clearly identifiable position vis-a-vis German studies in Germany and worldwide and to contribute to and widen the potential for understanding aspects of German culture unexplored in Germany itself. The situation of an 'Auslandsgermanistik' (German studies outside Germany) obediently following the theoretical precepts of the dominant German paradigm which focus on the object per se is no longer tenable. In other words, and advancing my third argument: the study of a foreign culture is not necessarily, and certainly not in the first instance, guided by the interests of that culture but rather by the interests of the observer.

However, it is not only the productive and liberating effects of intercultural studies which ought to be stressed. There is an emancipatory implication of a different kind which reverses the order of the familiar and foreign in the cognitive process and produces my fourth argument: the study of German language and literature—or of any other foreign culture—is constitutive of, and therefore necessary for, the understanding of one's own culture. This fact has been acknowledged for a long time by linguists with regard to the study of languages, but scholars and teachers of literature have been slow to take up the parallel challenge of comparative literary studies. The recent report of the *Committee to Review Australian Studies in Tertiary Education* (Daniels 1987) has rightly deplored the striking lack of, or rather the systematic suppression of, an Australian perspective in all fields of study, but it has neither understood the cognitive foundation of the project nor taken the opportunity of enlisting the help of foreign language and literature studies in the establishment and development of an Australian 'identity'. In practice, however, many Australian students have chosen to study a foreign culture precisely for that purpose. It is time to acknowledge this fact more clearly in our curricula.

In the following analyses I would like to demonstrate the critical aspects of my theoretical propositions and the position of the cognitive subject with reference to three encounters with the foreign.

The first encounter records an experience with Australian students of German of interpreting a poem by the Austrian poet Ingeborg Bachmann. This experience highlighted some important aspects of the hermeneutics of German studies outside German-speaking countries, in particular in relation to the position of the teaching subject. The encounter demonstrated most forcefully that we read differently in Australia.

The second part analyses some of Georg Forster's encounters with foreign people in the Pacific during Captain James Cook's second voyage from 1772 to 1775. Here I am particularly interested in the way in which a European scientist adapts new impressions and experiences to scientific knowledge and, further, which cultural *topoi* and political interests serve as guiding cognitive conditions in his research.

Finally, I propose to look at a special case of writing in exile provided in the short but very complex novel *An Imaginary Life*, in which David Malouf has applied Georg Forster's insights to a particular Australian phenomenon: in order to understand ourselves and the antipodean world, Australian writers have to return to the *topoi* of an older world of European literature.

In all three encounters I wish to demonstrate that the understanding of the foreign is mediated through the mental luggage, the pre-judgment and pre-understanding of the cognitive subject. However, in all three encounters it becomes plain, too, that the confrontation with the foreign opens the door to a new understanding of the familiar. Whether or not this process could be described adequately as cognitive dialectics, I do not propose to discuss at this stage.

II. 'EXPLAIN TO ME LOVE . . .'

My first example reports on one of my own everyday experiences when interpreting German and Austrian writings with Australian students. As empirical evidence, the experience supports my claim as to the difference between the hermeneutic conditions of all teaching of and research in German studies conducted inside and that conducted outside German-speaking countries. I refer to the first stanza of a longer poem 'Explain to me Love' in the collection *Anrufung des Grossen Bären* (Invocation of the Great Bear) by the modern Austrian poet Ingeborg Bachmann (1961). In spite of some semantic intricacies, this poem does not seem to create particular difficulties for the native reader:

> Explain to me Love
> Your hat lifts gently in greeting and floats in the wind,
> your bare head is caressed by clouds
> your heart is otherwise engaged,
> your mouth incorporates new languages.
> The shivery grass takes over the land,
> star-flowers are set alight and blown out by summer,
> you lift your face blinded by flakes,
> you laugh and weep and go to ruin yourself,
> what could happen to you now—
> Explain to me, Love!

In an Australian context, every image has to be explained in a constant comparison between Australian and German linguistic and cultural idio-syncrasies in order to produce an adequate understanding.

To take just one example: the line 'the shivery grass takes over the

land' will most probably evoke the antipodean association of an introduced weed, since native grasses are less likely to be thought of as
'taking over'. In Australia I have not come across any equivalent associations to those suggested by the German popular names for grasses:
'ladies-hair' (*Frauenhaar*) or 'love- or amorette-grass' (*Liebes-* or
Amorettengras) or 'hare's bread' (*Hasenbrot*). Therefore there is no possibility for an immediate understanding of the symbolism. No Australian
student can be expected to take the hint, just as in the case of 'star-
flowers' or 'flakes', that particular references imply a range of specific
events or metaphoric structures which are conventionally evoked. The
chain of associations which one would expect a German student to find
is simply not available to Australian students. That means that they do
not see and understand the temporal structure of the poem, with its
oblique presentation of a seasonal sequence from summer to winter.
This sequence, in turn, evokes a time of waiting and the increasing
emotional numbness of the speaker in the observation of the loved one.

The discussion of these findings in class led to some remarkable
observations: that there is a great deal of symbolism attached to flowers
and plants which is well-known in the Australian community. But it
refers only to European flora introduced by European settlers. Hardly
any Australian native plants seem to have any symbolic significance, and
very little is known about the symbolic or mythological values attached
to them by Aborigines. Thus a symbolic chasm between Aboriginal and
European Australia becomes visible. The fact that the early settlers frequently gave popular names of European species to native plants may
serve as an empirical example for the process of recognising the foreign
through the familiar. (Smith 1960; Flower 1975; Veit 1983; Steven 1988)

At this early stage of the analysis, we can already say that the
interpretation of poetic imagery has pointed to some important
hermeneutic conditions guiding students and teachers. It has to be
recognised that the 'native' meaning of cultural phenomena may remain
hidden if viewed with 'foreign eyes'—which goes to show how much the
cognitive perspective determines the production of meaning. It points
also to the complexity of the hermeneutics of the foreign—not only for
the student but also for the teacher, who in many cases may be a
foreigner among foreigners with regard to the object of analysis.

III.1.

'. . . two travellers seldom saw the same object in the same manner . . .'
(Forster 1986:13)
I wish to turn now to the second part of my considerations of the
cognitive and epistemological conditions of scientific research. I have
chosen Georg Forster's *A Voyage Round the World* (written in 1777),
which is of crucial importance for the German perception of the Antip-

odes in the late eighteenth and nineteenth centuries.

In his preface, Forster moves straight into the questions of interest here. He specifies what was expected of his father, who had been chosen in lieu of Joseph Banks to accompany Cook on the second voyage (1772–75) as 'natural philosopher':

> He was only therefore directed to exercise all his talents, and to extend his observations to every remarkable object. From him they expected a philosophical history of the voyage, free from prejudices and vulgar error, where human nature should be represented without the adherence to fallacious systems, and upon the principles of general philanthropy; in short, an account written upon a plan which the learned world had not hitherto seen executed. (Forster 1986: 9–10)

Five years before the publication of Kant's *Critique of Pure Reason* and completely conscious of the fundamental differences between the French and German philosophical tradition of the Enlightenment on the one hand and the British on the other, Forster embarks on a critique of the rationalists' insistence on an *a priori* system and the empiricists' hunt for facts, and comes to the following observation on their own approach:

> Besides this, two travellers seldom saw the same object in the same manner, and each reported the fact differently, according to his sensations, and his peculiar mode of thinking. It was therefore necessary to be acquainted with the observer, before any use could be made of his observations. The traveller was no longer to trust to chance for a variety of occurrences, but to make use of his first discovery, as the thread of Ariadne, by the help of which he might guide his steps through the labyrinth of human knowledge. It was therefore requisite that he should have penetration sufficient to combine different facts, and to form general views from thence, which might in some measure guide him to new discoveries, and point out the proper objects of further investigation. (Forster 1986:13–14)

We recognise that Forster juxtaposes his own critical method of observation with the assertion of blatant prejudices in earlier travel reports: quite in keeping with the directives issued by the Royal Society, there first must be a number of empirical observations which have to be connected later into a rational sequence. But it seems that Forster did not see all possibilities of misunderstanding eliminated. He therefore continues with obvious reference to the heated contemporary epistemological debate:

> I have sometimes obeyed the powerful dictates of my heart, and given voice to my feelings, for, as I do not pretend to be free from the weaknesses common to my fellow creatures, it was necessary for every reader to know the colour of the glass through which I looked. Of this at least I am certain, that a gloomy livid tinge hath never clouded my sight.

> Accustomed to look on all the various tribes of men, as entitled to an equal share of my good will, and conscious, at the same time, of the rights which I possess in common with every individual among them, I have endeavoured to make my remarks with a retrospect to our general improvement and welfare; and neither attachment nor aversion to particular notions have influenced my praise or censure. (Forster 1986:14)

It is interesting enough that as a foreigner in England Forster has to reject any suspicion of national prejudices and, by the same token, can hint implicitly at their virulence in England at the time, but it is also important to consider why it is easy for him to do so: in contrast to England, Germany was not yet a nation in the political sense, nor a power with vested economic and political interests in sea power and colonisation. But as far as I can see, Forster does not take the foreign to be a cognitive problem. The hermeneutics of the Enlightenment follow the authority of the *topos*: '*Homo sum, humani nil a me alienum puto*' (Terence): 'I am a man, nothing human is alien to me'. We therefore have to turn to the empirical data themselves as they are described in Forster's text. It is here that we come face to face with the culturally specific, that is Eurocentric pre-judgments as conditions of understanding a foreign culture.

I have pointed out how deeply and thoroughly the description of the first landfall on Tahiti is predicated on the *topoi* of the Golden Age syndrome, and how the 'observed facts' give rise to a theory of history which not only anticipates in many ways that of Marx one hundred years later, but in its severe critique of instrumental reason as the essence of European society looks forward to Theodor W. Adorno's and Max Horkheimer's *Dialectics of Enlightenment* (1971). But on this first visit, the experience of which eclipsed all later visits, the pleasure of perceiving an almost ideal society in an ideal landscape is painfully disturbed by the encounter with a 'very fat man' who 'was . . . lolling on his wooden pillow' and had himself fed by his servants: 'His countenance was the picture of phlegmatic insensibility, and seemed to witness that all his thoughts centred in the care of his paunch.' The English text (and even more the German rendering) betrays Forster's indignant reaction to this encounter. But it is precisely the description of this experience which provides the analyst with an array of *topoi* of European ethnology of the eighteenth century and is worth a closer look. But first the decisive text from Saturday, 21 August 1773:

> The great degree of satisfaction which we had enjoyed on our different walks in this island, and particularly the pleasure of this day's excursion, was diminished by the appearance and behaviour of the chief, and the reflections which naturally arose from thence. We had flattered ourselves with the pleasing fancy of having found at least one little spot of the world, where a whole nation, without being lawless barbarians, aimed at a certain frugal equality in their way of living, and whose hours of

enjoyment were justly proportioned to those of labour and rest. Our disappointment was therefore very great, when we saw a luxurious individual spending his life in the most sluggish inactivity, and without one benefit to society, like the privileged parasites of more civilised climates, fattening on the superfluous produce of the soil, of which he robbed the labouring multitude. His indolence, in some degree, resembled that which is frequent in India and the adjacent kingdoms of the East. (Forster 1986:178)

Forster goes on to quote a passage from the 'original manuscript' of the *Voyage and Travayle of Sir John Maundeville, Knight, which Treateth of the Way to Hierusalem & of Marvayles of Inde, with other Ilaunds and Countryes*, describing graphically the abomination of Asiatic luxury.

The whole description feeds on the confrontation of an economic, social and political utopia in the tradition and spirit of the European Enlightenment with an alien, disillusioning reality. But the disillusionment does not lead to a change of perspective, nor even to a reflection on possible alternatives of interpretation. Significantly, the method of participatory observation did not yet exist (Moravia 1970; Lepenies 1976; Krauss 1979). Although Forster recognises the image of a civilisation of 'frugal equality' of all classes, with an equal share in enjoyment, rest and work, as a 'pleasing fancy', he continues to analyse it in terms of the European Enlightenment critique: for him there exists a division of classes between the 'labouring multitude' and 'the privileged parasites' who rob them of the fruit of their work and live 'without one benefit to society'. The foreign is easily subsumed under the analytic categories and the value system of the European 'philosophy'.

We can look at the procedure from a different point of view again to make abundantly clear what cognitive pre-judgments inform the observer: what Forster wants to describe was hitherto known only of a depraved Orient wallowing in its luxury and voluptuousness. Mysterious India and the Far East are the preconstrued examples to which Forster can refer as paradigms without the need for any further explanation. In his argument he successfully uses the classical rhetorical strategy of proving and authorising through examples. It does not matter at all that we know today that the travel log of a certain Jean de Mandeville (1322–72), *Les Voyages d'Outre-mer* of 1357, printed first in 1480, is most probably a popular but clever compilation from various sources. In my context it is decisive that this text has become one of the sources of hermeneutic pre-judgments for early ethnology, still providing the *topoi* for Forster's recognition and evaluation of the foreign. Forster's many open and hidden quotations—the German rendering of this passage harbours at least two Biblical images which cannot be identified in the English text—serve the same purpose. They are the nuclei of his *topoi* which in images and concepts draw a Eurocentric conclusion from his observations: just as Gibbon uses the *topoi* of the decline and fall of the

Roman Empire, Forster uses the Orient as the symbol of the alien which can then serve as the spearhead of his critique of contemporary European civilisation (Said 1978).

But the cultural critique presented in the passage under scrutiny is only coincidentally directed at the islanders and even less at the Indians or Chinese. It is directed against the 'privileged parasites of more civilised climates' in Europe.. Not only this half sentence but also the *topoi* of work which characterise the text support this interpretation. Indolence is recognised and criticised through the European work ethic which developed not from the classical myth of the Golden Age in Arcadia, but from the Christian tradition of the Lost Paradise and the extreme dictum of St Paul that someone who does not work may not eat (2 Thess. 3,10). The dream of freedom from work has today turned into the nightmare of unemployment.

For Forster, the dream of human equality in work and rest had not yet ended. The Enlightenment searched for utopia and hoped to find it 'at least [in] one little spot on this earth': Tahiti seemed to be that spot. But when utopia was found on one of those Pacific islands, it immediately became the strongest indictment of European prerevolutionary and early industrialised civilisation, as well as, paradoxically, of 'Asian', i.e. alien, elements in Europe's own culture. Furthermore, it can be shown, as Forster does, that the peaceful culture in the Pacific is already infected with the virus which will cause inevitable destruction, apparent in the image of the indolent and gluttonous man whose sloth is the beginning of depravity and the sign of the rise of a class society. If that is so, it has to be asked whether the cultures in the Pacific were, in 1773, at the beginning of a development which at that time had come to an end in European civilisation. Forster puts this question himself and sees the answer in 'the natural circle of human affairs' (Forster 1986:217) which has its origin in the necessity to work.

Thus the perspective of the 'foreign eyes' (Wierlacher 1980) has been rigorously re-established to the extent that the observed foreign culture has slipped from the centre of discussion. The *topoi* of European civilisation enforce the structure of Forster's understanding and literary presentation. The departure for an understanding of the foreign has led to an acknowledgment and severe critique of the familiar.

And why would we read Forster's account differently in Australia and in Europe? The rationale for my reading of Forster's description lies precisely in the fact of a changed perspective which has given me, and all those who are working on similar problems, a chance to change and add to a purely Eurocentric meaning of Forster's text. The next step would be to reverse the process and analyse in detail the *topoi*, themes and interests inherent in the Australian perspective in order to come to an acknowledgment and understanding of what is deeply familiar to the antipodean reader.

III.2.

The Eurocentric perspectivism is even more conspicuous in a second example from the same text. During the Antarctic winter of 1774, Cook and his companions sailed further into the northern Pacific in order to restore their health for a second advance into the southern polar region during the antipodean summer. During their foray into the Melanesian archipelago, they discovered New Caledonia and Tanna in the group of the New Hebrides. From the abundance of observations on Tanna I shall select only a few which demonstrate particularly well the effect of an unavoidable perspectivism, and I shall show that the analysis of the foreign proceeds from the understanding of the familiar and is recognisable as a cognitive structure.

The relationship of the sexes on Tanna aroused Forster's particular interest, but his description is completely guided by the pre-judgment of an idealised position of womanhood in European society. When he describes women and girls, he assumes that their garments and adornments are indicators of their age, and he further assumes that they are exploited by the men who, according to Forster, regard them as little better than beasts of burden. Their heavy labour is presumed to be the cause of their smaller stature. These phenomena and others observed elsewhere are then linked together in a causal nexus into a 'natural' law of economic character. And again the *topos* of work is used, this time to describe its civilisatory function.

On Saturday, 13 August 1774 Forster writes:

> It appeared to me that the women were not held in any esteem by the men, but obeyed upon the smallest sign; and according to the accounts of our waterers many were seen in the humiliating guise of drudges and beasts of burden. Perhaps the laborious tasks which they are forced to perform, contribute to lessen their stature, especially if they are in disproportion to their strength. It is the practice of all uncivilised nations to deny their women the common privileges of human beings, and treat them as creatures inferior to themselves. The ideas of finding happiness and comfort in the bosom of a companion only arise with a higher degree of culture. Where the mind is continually occupied with the means of self-preservation, there can be but little refined sentiment in the commerce of the sexes, and nothing but brutal enjoyment (*thierischer Genuss*) is known. Infirmity and meekness, instead of finding a protector in the savage, are commonly insulted and oppressed: the love of power is so natural to mankind, that they eagerly seize every opportunity to exercise their superiority over those who are unable to resist. The increase of population necessarily brings on a greater degree of polish; the cares of self-preservation are in great measure removed from the individual to the community; affluence takes the place of want and indigence, and the mind more unemployed, takes pleasure in the more refined enjoyment of life . . . The savage is not wholly incapable of tenderness and affection; we trace

them in the boy whilst he remains thoughtless and free from care; but as soon as he feels the urgent wants of his existence, every other sentiment or instinct is forced to lie dormant. We observed an instance of affection among the natives of Tanna this evening, which strongly proves that the passions and innate qualities of human nature are much the same in every climate. (Forster 1986:520)

It is obvious that Forster here takes the position of the Enlightenment philosopher whose basic principle is the common rights of humanity which, however, can be realised only in economically advanced societies. He clearly constructs a nexus between the satisfaction of needs, the overcoming of destitution, and 'a greater degree of polish' (*dem Maas der Sittlichkeit*). The high moral ground of the Enlightenment determines the tone of the text; it also provides categories for the evaluation of the foreign which, at the same time, by their very generality—'that the passions and innate qualities of human nature are much the same in every climate'—reveals its intention to be a critique of the familiar, specifically the condition of women and the working classes in industrialised Europe. From his description of Tahitian society, in which Forster uses the same contrastive *topoi* of civilisation versus nature and of the economy as the driving force and motivation behind any cultural progress, we know that these European ideals are not realised even in Europe to any larger degree. Within the framework of Forster's hypothesis about the causal nexus between material needs and morality, European civilisation itself has therefore not reached the acme of perfection. Again the view has turned from the foreign to the familiar, with an intention of self-criticism which was a characteristic feature of European anthropology and ethnology of the eighteenth century and which allowed the reader of 1780 to review together the progress and the deficiencies ofEuropeancivilisationwhilebeingconfrontedwith'savages'.

A little later, Forster notices some civilisatory 'progress' in the everyday activities of the Tannanese which reveals more cognitive *topoi* in his observations—this time arising from a comparison with the practices of the Tahitians. Although neither the clothing of the Tannanese nor their bodily cleanliness betrays any 'refinement' as yet, Forster detects certain harbingers of future refinement in their cookery and music.

On Saturday, 20 August 1774 he writes:

The people of Tanna do not appear, according to this standard, to be far advanced; their houses are mere sheds, which barely cover them from the inclemency of the weather. Dress, another distinguishing character of civilisation, is as yet entirely unknown to them; and in the place of cleanliness, which everywhere renders mankind agreeable to each other, we observed diverse sorts of paint and grease. They seem however to be in great forwardness towards receiving a greater polish. Their food is much varied by the arts of cookery which the women put in practice ... The domestic life of the people of Tanna is not wholly destitute of amusements

... but, on the other hand, their music is in greater perfection than any in the South Sea; and it cannot be disputed that a predilection for harmonious sounds implies great sensibility, and must prepare the way for civilisation. (Forster 1986: 540)

There is no need to stress any further than the text already does, the European conventions of dress, cleanliness, enjoyment of food and music. We only need to note that they remain the standard for adjudicating and describing *all* civilisation. The standard arises from the *topos* of the necessity of historic progress, so much so that Forster feels obliged to correct observations which he has not made himself and which became more widely accepted in Europe only after Charles Darwin. His reasoning is that because these phenomena are present in Europe on a very high level, they have to be present on Tanna on a lower level, for the law of progress from savage to civilised reigns without qualification. Forster can therefore write:

We know nothing of their religion. ... Civilisation enlarges and unravels the idea of a Deity, which is not unknown to the savage, though his more immediate wants prevent his giving attention to it. When the exigencies of nature are supplied with less trouble, and in a shorter time, the intellectual part expands and mounts to heaven to find some occupation.' (Forster 1986:541).

The German text closes even more strikingly with the sentence: '*So hängt selbst das Wachsthum der Gottes-Erkenntniss von dem Fortgang der Civilisation ab*' (II,281. 'Even the growth of the knowledge of the divine depends on the progress of civilisation').

In this comparative confrontation of the savage and the civilised, the foreign and the familiar, Forster permits us to recognise once again the fundamental cognitive parameters of his observations: in his perception and in that of the Enlightenment, the familiar is seen to be, in principle if not in reality, at a higher stage of civilisatory development than the foreign which European travellers and researchers are so eagerly investigating in the Pacific and elsewhere. It means that the researcher is able, before any critique, to grasp the prehistory of the familiar in the study of the foreign. In the language of hermeneutics, the foreign is the forgotten or suppressed familiar which the Enlightenment needs for the substantiation and confirmation of the self and therefore seeks out in restless research activities. The focus of all exploration of the foreign is the exploration of the self.

Forster is very conscious of this nexus. But it still comes as a surprise when, in the context of his appraisal of Tahitian alterity, he embarks on a critique not only of European culture and civilisation but of the European enlightenment project itself. It includes a critique of European science and scholarship which seems to anticipate analyses given by Adorno and Horkheimer (1971). The following passage from his account of the sojourn of HMS *Resolution* on Tahiti in September 1773 demonstrates this:

> This is the natural circle of human affairs; at present there is fortunately no room to suppose, that such a change will take place for a long series of years to come; but how much the introduction of foreign luxuries may hasten that fatal period, cannot be too frequently repeated to Europeans. If the knowledge of a few individuals can only be acquired at such a price as the happiness of nations, it were better for the discoverers, and the discovered, that the South Sea had still remained unknown to Europe and its restless inhabitants. (Forster 1986:217)

Further scrutiny of the text will reveal how the *topos* of the historical nexus between economy and civilisation set up earlier as a cognitive strategy has turned into a dialectics into which Forster is now firmly wedged: on the one hand he finds in the desire for 'superfluities' the motor for progress and a necessary step in the direction of cultural development; on the other hand, luxury remains the fundamental evil in all societies since antiquity and constitutes the fatal threat to the antipodean paradise. Precisely science and scholarship, as the finest flowers of the European need for an understanding of the self, are also the beginning of the destruction of 'the happiness of nations' and the European dream of utopia itself.

We can describe the cognitive mechanism in the following way: all earlier analyses have indicated that in the European project of understanding the *other* there lies the fundamental but mostly unreflected quest for an understanding of the self. The self-interest of the cognitive subject overpowers the alien and exotic and reduces it to the importance of an object, of the non-identical. Its 'true' identity remains undiscovered.

Bernard Smith (1979) has drawn attention to this cognitive process in rationalist science and its theory formation. While the Enlightenment still searched for the original state of human equality among the nations of Africa, Asia, the Americas and in the Pacific and created the image of the 'noble savage', after Charles Darwin the new discipline of social anthropology recognised in the 'savage' only a primitive form of humanity. This could become an advanced form only by means of a superior technology which could only be found in Europe.

If I am not mistaken, the cognitive conditions for the understanding of alien phenomena in the eighteenth century inherent in Forster's description correspond to the general conditions of understanding as described by modern hermeneutics, especially by Hans-Georg Gadamer. And it does not come as a surprise that the cognitive categories of the foreign and the familiar still show some of the vestiges of their Enlightenment origin in modern hermeneutics when in *Truth and Method* (1975) Gadamer discusses Schleiermacher's contribution to its development:

There is a polarity of familiarity and strangeness on which hermeneutic work is based: only that this polarity is not to be seen, psychologically, with Schleiermacher, as the tension that conceals the mystery of individuality, but truly hermeneutically, i.e. in regard to what has been said: the language in which the text addresses us, the story that it tells us. Here too there is a tension. The place between strangeness and familiarity that a transmitted text has for us is that intermediate place between being an historically intended separate object and being part of a tradition. The true home of hermeneutics is in this intermediate area. (Gadamer 1975:262)

The analysis of the whole syndrome can be taken one step further. It suggests an interesting reason for differences between antipodean readings of Forster's text and Forster's readings of the antipodean 'text'. The difference arises from the postcolonial situation in Australia. Australia is still not free from the vestiges of her colonial past. For this reason we have at least two possible readings of Forster's text: the first reading is that of the European colonist who is imbued with a feeling of superiority; the other reading is that of a colonial who is conscious of his or her economic, political, and cultural dependence on the European mother country. This situation gives rise to a painful dialectic: because neither the transported inherited cultural and intellectual identity nor the forbidding new land permits a simple dissolution of the old in the new, the 'wild colonial boy' of the Antipodes is forced to submit his European heritage to a rigorous critique in order to create his new spiritual and national identity. Australian cultural life and Australian literature in particular show that this process has not yet come to an end.

IV.

The analysis of the epistemology inherent in Forster's descriptions of the discoveries in the Pacific has demonstrated the existence of a Eurocentric perspective and a set of powerful interests in the form of pervasive cognitive *topoi*. The conflict in the modern Australian reader's mind arises from a changed perspective, that of a consciously non-Eurocentric reading of the Antipodes. This has had a marked impact on Australian writing. A notable example of this shift can be found in David Malouf's short lyrical novel *An Imaginary Life* (1978), which is generally acknowledged as one of the most important pieces of Australian fictional writing in the last decade. Not only does Malouf use a number of well-known new-world *topoi* in his story, he also uses the theme of the exiled poet in a way that foregrounds the polarity of familiarity and strangeness. His work provides an incisive and complex poetic articulation of the theoretical and practical concerns I am exploring here.

In five chapters the narrator, Ovid, tells of his childhood experiences, his banishment to Tomis and his daily life at the very edge of the civilised world, his hardening to the misery of a barbaric village life, the learning and appreciation of a new language, the capture and gradual civilisation of the wolf-child and, finally, the reversal of the relationship between poet and child when the child becomes the teacher and leads Ovid to the ultimate recognition of his identity and his merger with the land. The following brief explanatory remarks will provide a starting point.

The novel has an obvious chiastic structure; the intersection is occupied by the encounter with the wolf-child. As long as Ovid the poet–narrator finds himself a stranger among aliens, the only civilised one among barbarians, everything is seen from a Roman perspective, from the past. He therefore has no chance to comprehend his present environment. First signs of a change become visible in his efforts to learn the language of the barbarians, which is described as a primal language. This process is accompanied by the first vague news about a wild child. But the real turn starts only when the wolf-child, the child of nature, is captured and is civilised step by step. Only then does the past finally fall away and so allow him to settle into the present. Together with the painfully slow education of the boy towards a consciousness of his own self by means of learning human speech, the process of Ovid's appropriation of the foreign begins: he tells the reader of his increasing knowledge of the country, his acclimatisation and the loss of his old Roman self:

> I have come to a decision. The language, I shall teach the child is the language of these people I have come among, and not after all my own. And in making that decision I know I have made another. I shall never go back to Rome . . . . More and more in these last weeks I have come to realize that this place is the final destination I have been seeking, and that my life here, however painful, is my true fate, the one I have spent my whole existence trying to escape . . . . So I admit openly to myself what I have long known in my heart. I belong to this place now. I have made it mine. I am entering the dimension of my self. (Malouf 1978:94)

Tomis, the place of exile, becomes the temporary home until the identification with the land is achieved. But who then is the exiled and the foreigner? Ovid or the wolf-child, or the natives of Tomis? In the beginning, it is Ovid, the narrator, exiled and alien among the barbarians. But from the point of view of Rome, the acme of civilisation, the Tomisians are barbarians, aliens beyond whose fields roam the Scythian savages. But later Ovid becomes a local who teaches the captured child the local language. From Ovid's earlier point of view, the child is brought back from exile among the wolves into its own predestined heritage and to its true self.

However, this projection proves to be erroneous: for all are exiles here, all are aliens in an alien place at the fringe of the civilised world. Only the child is at home. Behind the story of the wolf-child rises the foundation myth of the Roman she-wolf and her two wolf-children, the two eponymous heroes Romulus and Remus.

In his treatment of the Ovid story, Malouf turns to a theme of European literature in order to plumb the depth of the problematic of the European in a foreign land and of his own existence in Australia. In doing so he draws attention to and makes imaginative and cognitive use of very familiar *topoi* of Australian existence, namely exile, emigration, punishment and flight. His reading of the old-European story turns Tomis into Australia. Therefore, the next steps in the interpretation are no longer difficult: we recognise the patterns of alienation which impede and enforce the recognition of the self. Some festering wounds in our mentality are touched: it is argued that we know the country only from without; only very few of us speak its languages, the many old-Australian Aboriginal languages. Australian literature has frequently identified Tomis with Australia: a land with no heart, a land with a dead or stone heart, or a land with a dead centre. It is argued that the rejection of understanding is caused by our origins in old Europe which, however, after 200 years of Australian history has itself become alien.

In a wider sense, Malouf implicitly contrasts the two great European myths of Odysseus and Aeneas, of the 'sacker of many cities' and of the exile who founded a new homeland and city. He draws attention to the fact that there are many Odyssean characters in Australian writings but that few are in the image of Aeneas. In the context of his *Imaginary Life* the reader is given to understand that the 'homeseeking Ulysses' wants to return to his native Ithaka, the metaphor for the European home, and that only Aeneas is to stay, albeit unwillingly. It seems to me that Malouf argues for a change in Australia's mythical paradigm in order to achieve a new, more positive, identity in this country. It is a matter of contention whether this argument ought to be rejected as belonging to outdated romantic thought or whether it is potentially constructive for the future. It is, however, ironic, precisely in the understanding of the German romantics like the brothers Schlegel, that it is two European myths which offer the cognitive potential necessary for Malouf's argument. It might be added here that his proposition is supported by a number of Australian authors, in particular by Patrick White in his novel *Voss*.

As it stands, the rejection of an identification with the new land indicates an effort on Ovid's, Malouf's or our part to reduce it to a 'creature of our own will', to an object of domination and exploitation. Ovid has to learn that the rejection of the indigenous language is not only a denial of any discourse with the land but also a refusal of its symbols, its myth and its heart. His overcoming of the old identity opens the way for his literal incorporation into the new which has become his 'true' self.

On the level of the analysis of the cognitive conditions for the understanding of the foreign and the familiar, of the self and the other, I have

interpreted Malouf's novel as an explication of the theoretical foundations which were laid earlier, e.g. of Alfred Schütz's proposition (1974)
*that the deepest understanding of the foreign is based on acts of an
understanding of the self and vice versa.* In Malouf's *An Imaginary Life*,
the understanding of the self is based on the acknowledgment of some
basic conditions of human existence: its dwelling in a landscape, in myth
and in language. At the same time, Malouf elaborates the problematic of
the other, the alien and marginal, which the dominant culture does not
trust. For Ovid, the Roman poet, Tomis, the outpost of the Empire, is
the other in terms of uncivilised human behaviour, full of shamanistic
ritual and superstition; in Tomis, however, he himself is the marginal
other who is suspected to be in touch with evil forces. The same is true
for the child, the incarnation of the uncanny and therefore persecuted,
first by the narrator and then by the village community, for quite different reasons in each case.

We have also become aware that Malouf's vision of the foreign is
informed and guided by paradigms and images from European literature,
not only from Ovid but also from writers of German romanticism and
even Martin Heidegger, as is evident in his thinking about language and
death. With regard to his own origin and upbringing, he hardly has a
choice if he wants to communicate with an Australian reader. But like
Moses in the desert, he must necessarily remain in the centre of the
contradiction: by using European imagery and *topoi*, and the theme of
the exiled Ovid, he can communicate his message and, at the same time,
is prevented from entering the new and desired land. This may also
provide an explanation for Malouf's decision to live in Italy for part of
the year, following in the footsteps of so many Australian writers and
artists who have created in foreign countries many of their works that
deal with Australia.

V. CONCLUSION

The conditions for an understanding of the foreign which emerged in
the discussion of our chosen texts in terms of a complex relationship
between the foreign and the familiar are at the same time the foundation
for an intercultural literary criticism. This, I would like to argue, has a
considerable advantage over the theory and practice of a traditional
comparative literary criticism. Phrased differently: comparative literature, as practised in Australia and Europe, needs to take note of and
absorb the epistemological insights of interculturality in order to retain
its central role in literary criticism in uncovering the wider but mostly
hidden potential of meaning in national literatures.

The same will be valid for any foreign-language philology. Whether
we know it or not, any teaching of foreign languages and literatures is
necessarily subject to the cognitive precepts of interculturality.

Hermeneutics teaches that in Australia, before any attempt to understand the meaning of German writing as understood in German-speaking countries, readers will have to start from the Australian perspective. Not only is it necessary to give up the notion of an 'objective' reading, it has also become clear that an understanding of the meaning *per se* is meaningless. Meaning is always bound to a particular perspective and specific human interests. Furthermore, we have seen that when studied in Australia, the great works of German literature acquire an additional meaning not realised in their native lands. Their meaning 'for us' realises something of the potential that the foreign keeps hidden from the superficial reader. The meaning for us, finally, contained in apparently foreign German and European culture in general, is necessary in the development of an Australian intellectual and cultural identity.

German literature has a special importance for Australia. There are a wealth of shared historical, political, intellectual, and moral problems for which the German-speaking countries have or have not yet found paradigmatic solutions. These solutions may or may not be acceptable to us: but discussion of them in German writing will help us to find our own. The question of a national and cultural identity is a case in point. On a more personal level: someone plagued by the questions of the national and cultural, and even multicultural, identity of his or her native land stands a better chance of understanding what Australians are talking about. The obverse is also true: nowhere have I found more interest in German affairs than in Australia.

21 Promitheas and his offerings

Vasso Kalamaras

It was midsummer. A few of us remained at the school of Nikolits. Our ages ranged from seven to twelve years, both girls and boys. We played, argued, yelled, jumped and waved our hands about excitedly. It was just past nine at night. There was a full moon, pure silver, and it shone on our flushed faces and made long shadows near us. Shadows embracing, playful like us. I was eight years old and at boarding school for the first time. It was one of the best and most expensive schools in Athens. My mother died when I was two years old. Each child had a special reason for being there, and all were from well-to-do, stylish families.

On this particular evening I remember, while carefully studying their faces, a powerful force was churning inside me, pushing and forcing me to tell my tales. Words released the pressure. I was surprised by all the strange things I was saying. There was a sudden silence and then, here and there, the others burst into spontaneous laughter, rumbling like mini thunder. They listened, enchanted, and I was enchanted with them. A new world of happiness opened up to me even though the stories, at times, also released pain. These impromptu tales took form and substance and thus began my career as a creative writer.

When I was thirteen years of age my father became a resident of the suburb of Thission, number 20 Iraklithon Street. We lived on the second floor of a three-storey apartment block and out of my window I would gaze at the Acropolis.

Every morning the Acropolis waited for me to wake up to greet it. Each evening our neighbourhood filled with boys my own age. I was the tomboy, the leader of a group with a greed for learning. We played hide-and-seek around the columns of the Parthenon, Erekthion and Othion Irothou Attikou. We used to run up and down the sacred road or play amongst the ruins of the ancient market. We used the broken columns of the Temple of Efestos as riding saddles down to Thission.

Most of the time we would cart our hill-trolley to the top of the

Acropolis and would then ride down the winding road straight into the front door of my house. Automobiles at that time were rare. Only the old, slow-moving trams made a loud thundering noise.

When I decided to come to Australia my mind was bursting with big ideas of what I was going to do. I would become overwhelmed with joy thinking about my new land and there was the pleasure of anticipation of sharing my stories with new people and hearing theirs.

From the moment of anchorage in this foreign land all my hopes and dreams disappeared in the wind. The place felt alien and unwelcoming. I did, however, bring with me my roots and the culture of my forefathers and memories of all the days and nights that I lived surrounded by the little hills of Musses and Pnika, the memorial of Philopapou, the rock of Vima, the church bells of St Marina and St Athanassios, the landscape that gave birth to Western civilisations.

The land of my forefathers was not lost. Remembering the Aegean Sea and the snow-capped mountains of Olympos, I have never stopped worshipping the gods. Migration cannot alter the fact that I have been moulded with the same material, same faults and joys as the gods Era, Apollo, Efestos, Athena and others, and these influences will never lose their power. It is the same with a whole range of forces—mythological, geographical, spiritual. The fairies of the forest, the golden-scaled mermaids of the Aegean, all are part of my daily life even now. I also brought with me the whole Byzantine era—vespers, icons with gold ornaments, red and dark purple colours, and endless gentle madonnas.

Looking back now, I can see that I was burdened by all these offerings I was bringing to the new land. I treasured my language and wanted others to love it as I loved it. I yearned to hear these new people say in Greek: mother, god, sunset, my love (*erota mou*) and to say Omiro, and not Homer, to say Othisseas and not Ulysses. Steeped in the language, the stories and the things that I knew and loved, I found it difficult to be open to the new world around me.

In the early years I felt cheated and I was caught like a bird in a cage. Australia became an inhospitable land of exile and I became enslaved in work. The desire to return to my homeland became demanding. But when I returned for a visit it was painful and an unbearably bitter experience. The issue of migration stems from ancient times. It is central to the long years of vulnerable history, the rich civilisation, culture and tradition of the Greeks. Later, after a struggle, I succeeded in making myself heard and accepted and it was only then that Australia became my new country—without betraying either my old or new country.

Zeus, the god of Olympos, and Hellines (Greeks) protect all those who know how to give hospitality to strangers, who love and respect the land that gives them their livelihood and, on top of everything, who honour friendship.

The god Promitheas came to earth to offer fire. He did not come to allow the eagle to eat his liver, nor to be chained nor baked under the Australian desert sun. If we are able to recognise the virtue and good of all things, every country has such gods; only their names change.

22 The journeys within: Migration and identity in Greek-Australian literature

Nikos Papastergiadis

Greek-Australian literature—but what is it? This was the question that was repeatedly asked at the first conference on Greek-Australian literature. There was an obsession with *who* and *what* qualifies. For three days literary and national boundaries were negotiated. An aesthetic hierarchy and a sense of place were very much in demand. There was a strong call for clear and definitive categories. It was presumed that the term Greek-Australian literature obviously announced a new species, and the audience demanded that the speakers identify its characteristics. Expectations were divided. There were those who were looking for confirmation that it was time to celebrate, albeit belatedly, a sense of arrival in Australia, and those who interpreted the conference as another nail in the coffin of Greekness. Between the appeasements and the applause, the criteria for Greek-Australian literature that were agreed upon revolved around the author's language, origin and identification with Greeks in Australia. In other words, Greek-Australian literature was not only any literature *by* Greeks or *in* Greek, but also anything *about* Greeks in Australia.

The answer that I offered was quite simple, but for an audience insistent on resolute and comprehensive definitions it was difficult to accept. As suggested by the hyphen in the term Greek-Australian literature, there is a space that is in need of bridging. The hyphen draws attention to the time of transition, to a space that is neither Greek nor Australian, and to the emergence of a hybrid that is both Greek and Australian in experience. The hyphen reminds us that the transition between these positions involves a cut. Consequently, I argued, the term Greek-Australian literature signifies a rupture within identity and includes a displacement of the conventional sense of belonging. The logic of this argument was premised on the belief that neither the place of departure nor the place of arrival should enter as the privileged basis upon which to define this literature (Castan 1987).

The hyphen draws attention not just to the author's experience and creativity, but also to the ethnocentric presuppositions and divisive strategies of literary institutions.

Literature written by 'migrants' has often been described as literature *between* cultures, as if it unproblematically occupied the liminal spaces outside, the transitional space from one and towards another, or was the keystone that marked the boundary between two separate spaces. Either way, these hyphenated definitions proceeded by constructing a definite passage with fixed points of orientation whereby the literature was packed and transferred across distinct and policed borders. It was either in the process of *becoming*, that is immature, or registered as that small and slightly odd item at the edge of sight. Hence the virtue of literature by migrants was limited to the 'natural' or unmediated expressions of exotic or childish authenticity. Being between cultures is, for the modernist author, a place of objectivity and transcendence whereas, for the migrant, it was considered a place of traumatic subjectivism. Migrant literature was always positioned in the margins of 'Australian' literature. This unrigorous opposition between canonical and peripheral writers, however, questions the very principle of critical distance.

Such conceptions sought to incorporate migrant literature selectively and domesticate it within a more stable and greater unity. In the last decade the monolith of Australian identity has prospered by pointing to new entrants in the formation of its *being*. Contradictory origins have not posed a contradiction to this evolution in identity—possibly because the contradictions have been wittingly or unwittingly erased in order to secure entry as a symbolic or real contribution to the national identity. In this manner, diversity in people's backgrounds has been used to legitimise the increasing uniformity of their foregrounds. The dubious development of national identity from assimilation and integration through to multiculturalism has been expressed in fundamentally linear terms. Progress has been claimed on the basis that knowledge has been accumulated, and the collective 'we' has learnt from the errors of its past.

In a sense, Greek-Australian literature can only be located *in* Australia, but it is a literature with an ambivalent sense of location. Memory and dreams are the first reference points in its landscapes. It is a literature that is placeless, but by that I do not mean that it travels or that it hovers in mid-air. It is not a literature which constantly departs and returns; it is a literature of dislocation which questions the very possibility of arrival; it has been catapulted by the opposing gravitational forces of migration and yet it also demands an ambivalent anchoring.

While Greek-Australian literature is nomadic,[1] it is also not without its cultural geographers, who are trying to reterritorialise it either in the 'tradition' of the diaspora or in the canon of Australian literature (Kanarakis 1985; Castan 1986; Spilias & Messinis 1988). This approach implies a symbolic rehousing of identity, a resurrection of archetypes and myths that depoliticise the journey in order to secure entry into the master's house. The writer, of course, will go in the opposite direction, looking not for glorious structures but, as Deleuze and Guattari noted:

> Writing like a dog digging a hole, ... finding his own point of underdevelopment ... To bring language slowly and progressively to the desert. To use syntax in order to cry, to give a syntax to the cry ... To be a sort of stranger *within* his own language. (Deleuze and Guattari 1985: 18–25)

Antigone Kefala has had four shifts in place and as many shifts in language. In response to the often-asked question, are you a migrant or an Australian writer, she answered:

> I can only say that I am both, and that the positions are not mutually exclusive.
>
> The paradoxes under which a writer like myself works are twofold—on the one hand, to express a difference in either tone, assumption or approach, leads to constant rejections and isolates one from a community of writers and readers, that place where people who are interested labour all the time to redefine their cultural reality. On the other hand, the impossibility to absorb so rapidly, or take in wholesale the local colouring, because at the level at which a writer is working, one is dealing with forces that absorb very slowly, take years to change that transformation into an evaluation, a language, a style. (Kefala 1988: 81)

To call Greek-Australian literature diasporic is to use an optimistically bucolic metaphor. Diaspora connotes a mother tree and the scattering of seeds capable of growth on distant soils. Migrants, however, are born from the explosion of the tree (if there ever was one to begin with). The bits of culture that survived did so in the shape of a fragment rather than a seed. And the potential of a fragment is very different from that of a seed. Most of all it must not be presumed dead simply because its history is revealed to be discontinuous with that of its putative roots and sources.

To place Greek-Australian literature within the 'tradition' of the diaspora is a mistake. It is not an innocent error but a mistake of convenience. To talk of the diaspora is to talk of redemption and survival through a temporal continuity which disregards spatial disjunctures. Diaspora connotes an organic sense of resilience, whereas the traumas of migration, as expressed in the texts that I focus on, are of an opposite order. They talk of the inorganic condition of identity and history in the time and space of migration. They confront the very need to reinvent the self, rather than passively allow the seed of the old self to re-emerge under foreign skies and on foreign soil. I am sceptical of terms like diaspora because they tend to gloss over the fissures in identity and the ruptures of time-space frameworks. The semantics of the word 'exile' carry a different set of meanings; the Latin word *salire* (to leap) is the appropriate term to describe the trajectory of migrants. *Salire*, however, also produces the word 'exult'. Thus this desire to find grandeur from the very depths of sorrow is etymologically based. However, the celebration of arrival should not be used as an excuse to erase the tensions of the journey. We must never forget the violence of migration. And we must find a language that can speak into this violence, rather than pass over it with silence. For, rather than presuming that the journey is over, we must consider the possibility that we are still 'leaping'. This is evident in every social function in which Greek Australians try to rehouse themselves in the traditions from which they came, and also find some accommodation within the traditions to which they aspire. In this act there is always something that doesn't quite fit. This discordance must not be deprecated but renegotiated in theory, as it is in practice.

Migration involves a displacement from one social location to another. This transportation, which usually implies a radical change, has the effect of questioning the social values which sustained both individuals and the community from which they came. This questioning is what consciously concerns the writer discussed here: Antigone Kefala.[2]

For Kefala, vision is in part constituted by a dismantling process. This involves the taking apart and the putting back together again of the tools with which one makes meaning. But then meaning is not restored to some pristine whole; it is reproduced with all its scars—precarious and mutable. These fractures suggest that the transitions in modernity require a language that is neither bound by the despair of nihilism nor sustained by the hopes of romanticism.

The tension between absence and presence is not just a principle for the imaginative re-creation of personal identity but is also the constitutive force of our epoch. Modernity is made up of migrations. Even those who have not left their homes have been displaced. The literature of modernity oscillates between the unsustainable polarities of exile and home.

In John Berger's recent ruminations on identity and migration, he argues that the physical departure from one's original home also involves an ontological and psychological severance which is irredeemable. After migration, identities, habits, personal memories and social history can no longer be embraced within the four walls of a home (Berger 1984: 67).

Antigone Kefala has also noted that migration undermines the identity of the individual not just by exposing the particular flaws in the family structure but also by undermining the assumption that *inside* the home the outside world could be analysed, understood, and that the external could be placed into a form:

Suddenly everything in our lives reduced to the most simple elements, unplaced in a country that belonged to other people, a lack of knowledge or intimacy with the landscape, a disconnection in ourselves in what we had been or experienced before, a cut.

The change had a profound effect on the family, on its structure, it broke the unity as we had known it in Romania, each one was thrown out of the group, made to rely much more on their own resources. The struggle underlined both one's intrinsic vulnerability, as well as the family's inability to offer much support, and re-arrange the world for us. Not that it had been able to do this in Romania, but there it had not been asked by circumstances to prove it. (Kefala 1988: 77)

In Kefala's novella, *The First Journey*, the narrator returns home as a stranger, lacking the assured intimacy and reciprocity which anchors others to their place of belonging.

Time had cut us from each other and we had lost the familiar. Then we spoke to each other carefully, as if strangers, attentive. I was trying to fit again into the silence of the house and of the rooms that did not contain me any longer. (Kefala 1975: 30)

Even his feeling of estrangement is expressed through a metaphor of 'unhousing': 'as if all the walls were falling away and an indescribable emptiness would start encroaching, silent and sly' (p. 38).

In Kefala's poetry the stranger never arrives with a surplus of choices, freely juxtaposing the past against the present. The stranger is the person who has lost the past and for whom meaning is the present and is problematical. Meaning in culture involves 'migration as well as rootedness' (Clifford 1989). Yet the relationship is not an open-ended one.

The process of transformation, the trajectory of a personal and social history, illustrates how the impact of the external is mediated by a 'system of dispositions' that are engendered by internal practices. A past that is isomorphically reproduced in the present tends to perpetuate itself into the future by a principle that Bourdieu describes as 'an internal law relaying the continuous exercise of the law of external necessities' (Bourdieu 1987: 82). The foreign is pursued but then assimilated within familiar principles.

If strangers are those whose names do not affirm commensuality, and if in their memory there is no recollection of the history of the group to which they are attached, then in such a system what identity can be conferred on the stranger? In Kefala's poem 'The Death Cycle', the fire that burns the house, blinding the narrator's friend, is also the threat of oblivion. The desolation caused by the fire reveals that the house served as the outer skin of the self, providing the 'measure' for both the minute and the infinite. While the proportions of the house are shaped by reveries and stories, without it the narrator's friend is approaching death.

According to Bourdieu, the house 'is the place *par excellence* of cohabitation and the marriage of contraries' (Bourdieu 1987: 125). The apprehension of the house as tomb returns to challenge the protective borderline between wet and dry, in and out, by tracing over them with the more pervasive fear of death against life. These oppositions are also played out with a contest between darkness and light. The stanza ends with the negative dominating, as the nocturnal 'terrors of darkness' assail any counteracting signs of protection. In the fourth section of the poem the narrator retells a dream in which the death cycle is re-enacted through a ritualistic passage. The estranged friend is seen 'swimming in ditches full of mud', in 'an unknown country', and finally the familiar face reappears, but held 'above the misty blue flame of a charcoal fire' (Kefala 1988: 75).

The value of fire lends itself to contrary direction because its properties, as Bachelard so lucidly remarked, 'appear to be charged with numerous contradictions' (Bachelard 1964: 102). But in this poem the fire principle symbolises an irredeemable separation. Left alone, the narrator must contemplate a darkness which is framed by monstrous inversions and condemnations.

> The darkness alive with faceless breaths.
> A curse that moved in heavy, unheard chains. (Kefala 1988: 75)

The dialectic between life and death, the possibility for affirmation to emerge from negation, is disrupted by the stranger, whose death offers no hope of regeneration and for whom there is no ritual which can bear out any symbolic resurrection. Bourdieu argues that the definition and status of an outsider are most deeply applied at the point of death; here 'the descendant' is most truly alone (Bourdieu 1987: 138). It is not a coincidence that the erasure of the stranger's identity from the collective memory is referred to as a linguistic problem of 'citability'—for this repeats the dilemma of naming the unnameable.

The concluding section of a 'The Death Cycle' conveys the 'unnaturalness' of such a death through the imbalance between lightness and darkness, memory and forgetting, speech and silence. Rain, which may symbolise the primal marriage of sky and earth, does not offer the stranger any hope for reunion. Kefala depicts the grave of the stranger as a place of utter oblivion. Disconnected form his ancestors and denied the possibility of being 'cited' by his descendants, the death of the stranger 'is the only absolute form of death' (Bourdieu 1987: 154).

> Pity the dead who cannot rise again
> to see the light
> but move in darkness heavy chained
> and sigh when the rain falls
>
> Pity the dead for the earth has no memory

and no tongue, but of trees and of rock
and they can tell their truth only
but not ours. (Kefala 1988: 76)

Life histories have been fragmented, traditions undermined or reinscribed, the centre of the world has been permanently dismantled. A return is now precluded; perhaps more than ever before, the mythical escapes are considered deluded. Identity can no longer be conferred by cross-reference to timeless and fixed central points. Shelter is found partially and only through the haphazard process of putting together the bits and pieces; the significant and the arbitrary are stitched together by repetition and translation. For when a name is not a home but just another transient thing, then the only creative process that redeems is a form of ingenuity and improvisation that Berger calls the 'bricolage of the soul'.

In Kefala's writing very little happens. Events and desire are revealed through dreams and memories rather than expressed in dialogue and action. In *The First Journey*, dreams not only anticipate outcomes but reveal estranging fantasies that are doubly unsettling. For example, in one passage not only does the narrator's dream predict the death of his beloved but his anguish is tinged with a mixed sense of relief and revenge (Kefala 1975: 52). Her death ushers forth a guilt which bears no direct connection with his conscious wishes. The compulsive crisscrossing of impressions and memories, dreams and fantasies reflects not just an instance of moral transgression but a pervasive anxiety over the stability of values. The benchmarks with which to measure the solidity of experience seem to shift constantly, and this obsessive introspection has the effect of permanently wedging not just a sense of dissatisfaction but an ontological doubt between desires and reality.

By revealing the interiors within the interior, dreams open up not just the relationship between the personal and the social but also the relationship of the other and the self. The language of dreams belongs both to the individual's and to the collective's unconscious. Gunew argues that 'Kefala inserts what often appear to be very personal and idiosyncratic dream sequences but this may be, more precisely, a strategy for constituting a new body of myth'; furthermore, 'myths are predicated upon journeys . . .' (Gunew 1988: 65). To understand the myth, we must therefore follow a journey. And we must ask, Is *The First Journey* a repetition of the Romantic journey where foreignness and familiarity were the two counters of objectification, or an expression of a critical journey where objectivity pulses in the rhythm of transgression and renewal?

Dreams and mirrors dominate the narrator's fascination as they stage the self in a threatening double act. Is the obsession with the internal double a symptom of a neurosis or an expression of a reassuring romanticism? Alexis, the narrator, is associated with figures for whom this is the case. His uncle went mad whilst staring at the mirror:

> And he remained there, in the library, refusing to move, in front of the mirror, watching his reflection, waiting for the second one. The one that had plotted everything, that undermined his movements, waiting for him to come out . . .
> . . . But however much patience he displayed, the other one had more. (Kefala 1975: 4)

His friend, Mr Caragea, is the 'Romantic' artist who liberates his self from the strictures of time and space through 'heroic' abandonment in work.

> Concentrated, totally absorbed. This I admired in him above all other things, this ability to become lost, unaware of time and place, suspended in an undercurrent in which nothing outside mattered. (p.53)

Alexis, both saturated in self-consciousness and haunted by the inner other, is, however, set apart from these figures: 'I had to invent ways to appear natural' (p.53).

Alexis's estrangement is not tinged with a 'luxurious, voluptuous sadness'. His ambivalence does not revolve around the pathos of unrequitedness, but erupts from the unhousing of identity.

For Alexis the nocturnal view of the city is like an upturned vision of the sky, 'An unknown potential in the air whose subtle position gave me a feeling of intoxication' (p.55). Flickering lights suggest the alluring sense of being elsewhere within the here and now; the ever-changing horizon both promises and threatens to split him from the solidity of his own form.

> In the dream, that night, I was going up a spiral staircase in an empty white house. I was with someone else. I and another I. Sometimes I was I, and sometimes the other person. (p.15)

The two I's are opposed, but it is not a moral opposition whereby the conscience marks out the exterior boundaries to contain the excesses of passion. Rather, it is a parasitic opposition, a 'subtle enemy' that feeds internally yet demands authority. This internalised stranger persecutes the self, not by connoting moral transgression but by splitting the vision of the self's exterior performance. The I becomes a seeing I and a seen I.

> So that the moment became split, between a doer and a watcher, and the watched being the stronger, the doer tried to maintain such a level of concentration and involvement leaving no room, no crack, for the second one to insinuate itself. (p.39)

In contradistinction to Judy Brett (1985), I believe that despite the differences in the narrators' genders and social positions, *The First Journey* and *The Island* are not discontinuous with each other; like

Kefala's poetry, both deal with the philosophical and cultural questions of homelessness and ambivalence in modernity.

There is clearly a shift in the attention to sexuality between the two novels, but this shift should not simply be read as evidence for the emergence of a new form of agency that presupposes the negation of others. The women in *The First Journey* are far from being the caricatures of domesticity and sentimentality that Brett reads them as being. For instance, Aunt Sophia's resilience is not attributed to her 'nurturing faculties', but to the fact that she is 'full of stories':

> One imagined that she would have started a household in the middle of
> an empty field with the bombs dropping from everywhere, and would have
> produced a tradition of cooking, of living, made a myth of it in no time.
> She had warm brown eyes, with copper tinges, and neat plump hands, very
> well kept, and her table manners were elegant. (Kefala 1975: 12)

Throughout Kefala's poetry there are repeated references to the home as the place of stories. And in Greek there is no semantic difference between story-telling and history-making. For Kefala stories and the domestication of fire are what transforms a space into a home. The proximate relationship between the domestic and the historical is what provides the shelter and the reference point from which the individual can interpret the exterior. As noted earlier, Kefala's writing is about the loss of faith in such a structured relationship between the physical and the metaphysical. Perhaps because Brett has bracketed out the effects of cultural dislocation, she has confused the representation of loss with a nostalgia for previous ethical certitudes and cosmological orders.

In *The First Journey*, the narrator's introspectiveness is not the consequence of an immature disavowal of social dislocations. While the novella is set in the aftermath of the war, the external devastation is only rarely directly represented, for Kefala's strategy is to examine how changes have been internalised. Metaphors of the body and the house interweave with each other:

> The destruction of the war [*was*] visible everywhere, in the dignified
> skeletons of houses following each other empty-socketed, watching with
> invisible eyes abandoned streets, charred trees, craters where the bombs
> had fallen. (Kefala 1975: 7)

Throughout Kefala's poetry and stories, the eye serves as a metaphor for both the unarticulated gaps in communication and the silent estrangement of solitude. The eyes are the home of the soul. In her story 'The Boarding House', people are constantly 'watching the unpopulated country of each other's eyes . . . Ravaged eyes . . . eyes of the deep . . . eroded eyes' (p. 95). In her poetry, Kefala speaks of eyes that have seen better times but belong to a mother who is absent (Kefala 1988: 17); eyes that contain a deep and elemental wisdom, yet are those of an octopus at the feet of a subterranean goddess (p. 18); and the eyes of a silence which is welling within nostalgia (p. 19).

Brett suggests that Kefala's novel, *The Island*, moves on from where *The First Journey* flounders. But before we can dismiss *The First Journey* as a repetition of the conventional decadence and masculinist narcissism inherent in the *Bildungsroman* genre, we need to evaluate the ambivalent cultural attachments in this novel. Brett celebrates *The Island* because it draws attention to the maturation of the narrator's psychological states. *The Island* succeeds, she argues, because Kefala demonstrates an 'ironic stance' towards the preoccupations of the narrator. That is, in comparison to a singular series of obsessions there is a plurality of perspectives, and in this multiplicity the author gains a critical distance from the emotions that are represented.

Brett's argument makes uncritical use of the opposition between domesticity and independence to suggest a further distinction between inward and outward vision.[3] Melina, the narrator in *The Island*, does question her friends' and relatives' vision of the past; she rejects Erik's engulfing sense of the past because it forbids the present any specificity. She is resentful of the bureaucrat who preserves the past and thereby cauterises it from any relationship with the present. Similarly, she is dissatisfied with her Aunt Niki's internalisation of her 'exotic charms'. Thus, while Melina is sensitive to the rhythms of continuity, she questions her own power to transform society and, in general, the possibilities of cultural differences are veiled by ambiguity:

> And I felt in their eyes an immense pity, a pity for myself, as if there on top of the waves I was burning out in a last effervescence of sound, burnt by a gift that I possessed that could not save me now, a gift that was my doom, that divided me from them, but which was useless. (Kefala 1984: 78)

Thus we must distinguish not just between insular attachment and self-assured detachments, for Kefala's novels reveal that the process of becoming is not resolved by defining a place of arrival, but rather that identity oscillates in an ambivalent zone of horror and hope.

I began with a story about the problematic location of Greek-Australian literature, and I want to return to the idea of history as storytelling.

In *Imagined Communities*, Benedict Anderson (1983) suggests that the pervasiveness of nationalism is not limited to the rise of specific political powers but is coeval with a particular way of seeing history and emergent cultural patterns. This has far-reaching implications for the complicity of modernity with the so-called pathology of nationalism. Modernity, which was born with the emergence of the nation state, is still haunted by nationalism as if it were a spectre from its premodern past. Anderson, realising that there is a radical potential within history to alter the conventional perceptions of nationalism, soundly advises us to 'do our slow best to learn the real, and imagined experience of the past'.

Anderson's concluding quotation is from Benjamin's celebrated description of Klee's painting 'Angelus Novus'. The angel—with contemplation fixed towards the past, and wings caught by a storm that propel him backwards into the future—symbolises both the chiasmatic paths of history and the contradictory burdens of the visionary.

Benjamin's philosophy is not directed towards the celebration of the transmission, or a lament for the loss of putative wholes, but is a method for understanding the relative autonomy and irreconcilability of the parts which migrate across and within various histories. There are no ready-made solutions lurking in the past which prefigure the problems of the present. The past does not arrive intact or in a passive form. Through the structure of crisscrossing patterns, the past is constructed as it constructs an interminable agenda of catchment and deferral. Benjamin (1985) suggests that the past is woven into the realisations and choices that a historical role of the present is called upon to resolve.

Kefala also perceives that the significance of events can be catapulted across history, that meanings transpose themselves incongruously with and against linear chronology. Similarly, in Kefala's poetry, the pervasive past exists not by virtue of some adoration of dusty or sterile museum pieces but in its ability to infiltrate the dreams and obligations of the living. The significance of dream sequences in her poetry (and her prose) is not just to confront the nebulous border between consciousness and unconsciousness, i.e. between self and non-self, but also to gauge the 'measure' of atavism through the visceral projection of the past.

> To find our measure, exactly,
> not the echo of other voices.
> The present growing out of our lungs
> like a flower, with a smell
> that we have re-traced through our veins
> some dark, secret smell
> that will bloom when the hour has struck
> an animal smell
> reminiscent of blood
> the world's scent.[4]

The earliest poem in *European Notebook*, and perhaps the most resonant, is 'Memory'. It is metaphorically embedded in one of the archetypal dramas of conflicting obligations and exile in ancient Greek drama, Sophocles' *Antigone*. Its second section (which acts as the pivot between the desolate plains of banishment in the opening section and the austere world of madness in the conclusion) begins by recalling images of a foreign land. Yet is this the distant past, or the distance passed?

The wind would stop abruptly and the silence
would fill the moonlight, falling unceasingly
like a blue still rain over the sleeping hills,
and in the deep of night the silk tearing
sound of waves would break over the dead sand (Kefala 1988: 54)

Such images of the external landscape cannot be sustained
unproblematically. Vision is punctured by the 'echo of that foreign
laugh' which surfaces like a traitor from within the self. Betrayal is
doubled by the conflation of past and present. The self is alienated by
unforgettable memories and uncontrollable meanings. Time and vision
fold in upon each other and the conflicting pressures hollow out the
substance of both. This section ends by suggesting that a reconciliation
is, at best, a detached and idealised one:

and sometimes in a stray sunray, some meaning
of the past would come to you, in strange blue shapes,
and then before our blind eyes,
the crystal vision of the world would rest untouched. (p.54)

The third and final section moves out of this reverie and into a stark
asylum. The narrator is no longer embracing the victim within, but
prevaricating over the confrontation with an outcast—an in-patient
whose approach cannot be faced and whose final passing will not be
witnessed. It is from this by now distanced 'you' that 'we' hear the truth
about the inalienable link between the passage of history and the passage
of a life:

They steal my time, you said in a low voice.
Then watched the floor as if my presence were too much.
And in the silence, the white men moved,
their pockets full of time, their steps so sure
cushioned by what they stole.
'They steal my time, I shall not last much longer,'
And I protested, unconvinced, for you had aged so much.
And who could say what they forced out of you
behind those walls. The essence maybe of our time,
dripping so slowly in our blood.
Maybe they stole the measure. (p.55)

By stripping away the certitudes which divided fantasy from reality,
Kefala echoes the broader project of feminism and cultural difference:
the construction of new 'measures'. Gayatri Spivak has argued that 'the
deconstruction of the opposition between the private and the public is
implicit in all, and explicit in some, feminist activity . . . Displacing the
opposition that it initially apparently questions, it is always different
from itself, always defers itself' (Spivak 1987: 103).

The questions of past and present, self and other, tradition and
modernity must be posed through the axioms of migration and

rootedness. To do this would involve a rethinking of history, identity and culture and a displacement of the 'nationalist' narratives of being and belonging. it would herald the productive tension of what Bhabha calls the 'Third Space': a dual process of enunciation and negation that leads us to a conceptualisation of alien territories, 'based not on the exoticism, or multiculturalism of the *diversity* of cultures, but on the inscription and articulation of culture's *hybridity*' (Bhabha 1988: 22).

So far the discourse of politics has considered migrants only in terms of *their* success or failure at integration; history has shown a marginal interest in the migrant's oral testament as an expression of 'new beginnings'; in literature the fascination with the migrant's innovative use and abuse of language has not managed to break free of patronising categorisations—hence migrant literature is now referred to as 'emergent' literature. Yet, in all this attention, the journey of the migrant has never been seen as a metaphor for the ontological homelessness of the metropolis, and the dynamism of modernity.

Part IV: Subversive re-readings

23 Exoticism is just a boutique form of xenophobia: Writing in a multicultural society

George Papaellinas

I don't see Australian history as successive waves of easily definable cultural homogeneities crashing into each other. Things are messier than that. And since one's identity, after all, is defined by one's race, gender, class, language or languages, regional association, age, and not simply and immutably by a generic culture set romantically in an original homeland, arguments that speak solely and mystically of 'ethnicity' appear rather impoverished and simplistic.

We talk here of 'multicultural writing' as though we were speaking of some temporary oral phase. Reportage. Literature is what others do. Multicultural writing is said to be performed by people here in Australia who aren't of British stock. These people are often referred to as migrants. As opposed to the British.

I could simplify things entirely by assuming the usual congratulatory tone whenever the term 'multicultural' or even 'multicultural writing' comes up (and I don't want anybody to confuse congratulatory with patronising) . . . and say something like: we are here to discuss migrant writing . . . or ethnic writing . . . or multicultural writing . . . or non-Anglo writing . . . or writing by writers of a Non-English-Speaking Background. I could say all of the above in one long and windy breath. They're all synonyms of each other, aren't they? Or are they? I could add that my personal favourite, my chosen form of description because it is just so tortured, is the last, the Non-English-Speaking Background one. Or NESB, as it's even more simply said; and then I'd pause a moment and have to clarify my meaning by reminding you that that I am talking about Australian writers, of course. Oh, and Aboriginal as well. They're Australian too. And Non-English-Speaking Background. Though not migrants. Though there is some dispute about this. Not that Aborigines are migrants, they're not—well, long ago, sure—nor that they aren't Australian, there's no dispute about that, not since the 1967 referendum . . . well, I suppose there is . . . amongst racist Australians, which nobody reading this is. No, the dispute is whether Aborigines are ethnic. Or NESBs. No, sorry. They are NESB but they're not multicultural, if you see what I mean. Well, they are. Everyone is. Anglos too, necessarily, if Australia is a multicultural society. But I mean bureaucratically . . . they're not multicultural, surely, that's for migrants . . . oh, and their children . . . who may not be migrants but are, if you know what I mean. And I'm sure you do. I mean, as writers, they're not migrants. Are they? Well, I suppose they are. They're not Anglo. We are talking about politically and aesthetically meaningful ways of dealing with writers, don't forget.

I hope you haven't misunderstood me or anything. It is not my wish to insult anybody.

I could then reel off a list of NESBians (that's a term I recently heard a very important advocate of state funding for multicultural art and artists use to describe the objects of his concern . . . I mean, his passionate interest, recently. His tone was warm and congratulatory. Not patronising.) Amongst others: Loukakis, Kefala, Houbein, Cappiello, Tsaloumas, Don'o Kim, Tzoumakas, Skrzynecki, Walwicz, Papaellinas, Malouf . . . no, sorry, not Malouf, he's not one, a multicultural writer, neither is Elizabeth Jolley, remember, Anglos aren't, though she is an immigrant, and though Malouf is of NESB, he isn't one. He is well known overseas and says he is Australian, so it's official.

I could instead just suggest that all of the above comprises offensive cultural politics, even worse a theory of aesthetics which is marginalising and discriminatory. And that it is a response that excludes all notions of class, gender, stylistic or political intention, not to mention ethnic differentiation. Or, as Dimitris Tsaloumas suggests, that it 'reflects only the official sanctioning of a cultural ghetto for non-Anglo writers which is to be patronised but only as a margin of Australian literature'.

This is what happens in Australia. Writers who are writing of as central an Australian experience as, say, Rushdie is of a British one are bureaucratised into margins. Or sometimes exoticised, in spurious praise without any reference to a text's critical value but with much reference to the writer's 'ethnic' origins by a muddle of marketers, critics, reviewers and bureaucrats, as if ethnicity in itself is grounds for congratulation in superficially guilt-ridden, middle-class, literary Australia. Exoticism is just a boutique form of xenophobia.

And what of the question of language? What about writings other than in English? This in itself needs a very full discussion. Is English the only Australian literary language or is it simply one of them, at best the lingua franca?

And don't many non-Anglos speak in the terms that I have just outlined? They do! Trivialisation is not an Anglo province alone, and I reject non-Anglos' practice of it as deeply as I do any Anglo treating my own or anyone else's writing in that fashion. My feeling is that when many non-Anglos use this separatist and apologetic terminology, they do so having dubiously decided that the margin you create for yourself is a prettier one. This has all the moral force of an argument that cultural suicide is so much more preferable to suffering homicide.

The Rushdie experience indicates many cultural inadequacies and chauvinisms, from all sides. It speaks of many tottering hegemonies—a tense and uncomfortable process but inevitably, a rich and worthwhile one. Such a process could be called 'Australia'.

This is the text of a speech delivered at the Canberra Wordfest, March 1989.

24 Speak as you eat: Reading migrant writing, naturally

Efi Hatzimanolis

Recent critical analyses of literature have been largely devoted to the novel rather than to poetry. Whilst these efforts have in many ways attempted to redress the New Critical emphasis on poetry (and on ideas of high culture), poetry continues to be conceptualised as a self-enclosed totality according to self-fulfilling critical approaches that locate and define poetry's value through ideas of its inherently unifying and underlying structures rather than through the differences and the contextual conflict and contradiction which inform its material production. Yet increasingly, poetry has become one of the genres used most by migrant women writers in Australia. Although it would be interesting to speculate on how contemporary critical interest in narrative has perhaps unintentionally contributed to the marginalisation of migrant women's poetry, and hence to a large amount of migrant writing, the central questions I wish to address are how migrant women writers use the genre poetry, and how this is related generally to ideas of migrant writing. Two poems written in English by Silvana Gardner are exemplary. Since these poems are difficult to find they are reproduced below.

Little Words (naturally)

If you can't get your meaning across
without using little words, you can forget
the art of communication, *parla come magni*
you said in your native tongue
and who would like to appear a gluttonous
pachyderm with no concern for etiquette?
But if I am to speak with the simplicity
of I like you or I don't, I will or I won't
and there's truth in your slogan,
what will my diet consist of? I am only

asking because the mince of a 'nice day'
or 'I am sorry' has no sauce
in the dry recipes of some situations,
the meaty parts dessicate with lack
of turning over this meaning and that
till the juices of improvisation
lose their tang. Still, I must be modest
and speak in small amounts
so as not to be considered a big eater.

Big Words

Helminthology
is only the science of worms,
don't be overcome by the *helms*
and the *minths* preceding in formal
procession the *logos*. The taxonomy
need not alarm you nor make you feel
I am showing off. I just love big words,
that's all, but I can see by your avuncular
disapproval that you are not convinced.
Can't you see that the word is only
the chondroid cover of tiny phalanges
articulating in the joints of the alphabet?
Little letters,
inflorescing all kinds of gestures
in the schizogenesis of meaning,
flagellate each other to reproduce
a chain in the palaeontology of our race
now well and truly cut
from the Sumerian umbilical cord.
Big words fatten on the tongue
and sometimes they are difficult
to swallow in the education of a dictionary,
but you are the one who sees them as plums,
I suck the preposterous bulls' eyes
down to the rich red vein.

Silvana Gardner arrived in Australia with her parents in 1952 as a
migrant refugee from Zara, Dalmatia. She is a bilingual artist and poet
(Italian), and a graduate of the University of Queensland in Fine Arts,
History and English Literature. She has had five books of poetry published, the most recent being *The Devil in Nature*. The two poems 'Little
Words (naturally)' and 'Big Words' were first published in the collection
With Open Eyes (1983; now out of print). Since then they have been
anthologised by Π.O. in *Off the Record* (1985). This important anthology of works not part of Australian mainstream literature, presents
experimental and performance poetry written by migrants as well as

Anglo-Celtic Australians. Many of the texts confront issues of race, class and gender. They challenge the discursive formations which describe the use, value and achievement of poetry as apolitical, that is, as some sort of transcendental and essential unity expressive of a universal human condition. This type of 'practical criticism' informs the dominant literary and critical discourses in our society—what Spivak (1987:115) calls the 'neutralising permissiveness' of the humanities—and functions to marginalise works by migrants and women.

The strategies used by the poems 'Big Words' and 'Little Words (naturally)' foreground the textual production of meaning, and construct reading positions in the texts which implicitly relate the discourses of multiculturalism and sexism to restrictive representations of migrant writing. So these poems engage in and are part of the social relations of power which inform representations of both migrant women and their writing. Like all discursive formations, poetry is a site of conflict and contradiction, the material realisation of competing discourses (Kress 1985:18). Any discussion of poetry, then, must pose the question: 'How is it that one particular statement appeared rather than another?' (Foucault 1986:27) To answer this, poetry must be analysed in terms of the discourses that inform its conventions, and 'Discourse has to be seen as ideological not simply because it is an historical product but because it is one which continues to "produce" the reader who produces it through a reading in the present' (Easthope 1983:24).

Both poems position the reader as critic of the 'ideal' language user, that is, the bourgeois patriarchal subject, by simultaneously defamiliarising expectations of both the form and function of writing by migrant women. The uses of polysyllabic verbosity and punning in 'Little Words (naturally)', and of bourgeois mystification in 'Big Words', satirise and subvert the idea of a 'natural' language that should perfectly match the occasion of social interaction. Excessive displays of metaphorical language construct an oppositional voice in the poetry. These textual strategies suggest struggle within poetry as a meaning-making system and interrogate the privileged positions of enunciation implicitly defined by the texts as patriarchal. In the opening lines of 'Little Words (naturally)' the speaker's resistance to patriarchal ideas of representation also signifies resistance to assimilationist views of language which naturalise repressive conventions:

> If you can't get your meaning across
> without using little words, you can forget
> the art of communication, *parla come magni*
> you said in your native tongue

The informal and colloquial words in the first line introduce the commonsense view of language as transparently referential only to subvert this in the third line by the use of Italian words. The slogan *parla come magni*, which in the dialect of Trieste means literally 'speak as you eat', suggests ideas of what Bakhtin (1987) describes as authoritative discourse[1] and what Barthes calls 'fragments of ideology' (Silverman 1983:274). To put it another way, it addresses or constructs the ideal reader/writer as passive consumer of the idea that meaning should naturally be self-evident and self-unified, thereby concealing its material production in terms of the conservative aesthetic and political investments in ideas of plain speech. What, after all, could be more natural than eating—except perhaps, speaking in your native tongue? But how is language to be viewed as 'natural' or even used 'naturally' when a subject occupies a bilingual position? Or when a subject is both an immigrant and a woman? The poem addresses these questions in two crucial, ironic ways which suggest that poetry '. . . can also be the site where language is at its most radical in its refusal to take itself for granted' (Parmar 1990).[2] For example, while obscuring its complicity in any 'unnatural' or artful use of language, the slogan is also, ironically, a figurative construct, a simile. Moreover, the 'native' Italian words operate as an estranging device in a way that produces a displaced critique of the discourses which define one language as natural, unmediated and accessible to all regardless of race, class and gender differences. That is, the 'native' words are 'foreign' words whose self-evident meaning, ironically, is meaningless to most readers of poetry in monolingual Australia. However, the poem's critique of the opposition natural–unnatural is implicitly related to bourgeois ideas of poetry both as an artifice and as an elevated form through which to create meanings and, as such, is implicated in contradictory ways in ideas of aesthetic neutrality, that is, in ideas of art for art's sake.

Moreover, the text's critique of the idea that meaning should be self-evident is given satirical edge in the rhetorical question posed in lines 5 and 6. These lines reconstruct a bourgeois subject position which is then deconstructed by the use of an exaggerated formality and by the excessively clipped sounds of the polysyllabic words. This is precisely the sort of language that would position the speaker as an insensitive pig, but it is used here to parody the conventional constructs and arbiters of good taste. And because the text transgresses these bounds of good taste it implicitly signifies the ways in which patriarchal ideas of poetry function to exclude and devalue women's writing as a displaced domestic activity and as excess. In the following lines the simile 'speak as you eat' is extended and 'feminised' into a hyperbolic conceit satirising the idea of 'good taste' and self-evident meanings:

> . . . the mince of a 'nice day'
> or 'I am sorry' has no sauce
> in the dry recipes of some situations,
> the meaty parts dessicate with lack
> of turning over this meaning and that

The use of metaphor here recalls 'the unnatural yoking' so disliked by Samuel Johnson in the eighteenth century, when propriety and decorum were the moral foundations of good sense and good writing.

Commonly seen by dominant cultural practices as aberrant and unnatural, excessive or extravagant writing constitutes a textual strategy which contests culturally defined norms. It is, after all, in the prevailing ideology's favour to appear as commonsense—as natural, obvious and inevitable as eating. In this way the social practices which determine discourses and subjects, and which are in turn determined by them, are internalised and naturalised. The poem's use of exaggerated images of the preparation and consumption of food signals this idea of cultural assimilation whilst transgressing the bounds of a polite 'art of communication'. In these terms, the poetic subject's non-assimilation of patriarchal ideology articulates the struggle to free poetry from a repressive authority. So the playful and punning metaphors construct the idea of language as tasty food, that is, as a 'thing' sensual rather than transparent. Without figurative speech, then, language is not only tasteless but also meaningless. According to these ideas the text inverts conventional ideas of good taste and bad taste, and subverts assimilationist views of one language as natural. Significantly, the term, 'assimilation', used in Australia before the introduction of 'multiculturalism' in the 1970s to describe euphemistically the repression of migrants, is a metaphor of digestion and excretion (Carsaniga 1986). The 'aberrant' cultural practices of migrants were not so much 'naturalised' as marginalised. The popular representations of their contributions to Australian cultural life have been mostly restricted to a celebration of new foods. Culture becomes pasta and brie. Displacing such cultures into the private, feminine and domestic sphere effectively silences and disempowers them. How much more so when you must 'speak as you eat'. Moreover, multiculturalism engenders these 'alien' cultural practices as feminine in terms of a liberal pluralism that reifies ideas of multiculturalism itself for bourgeois consumption. In this sense, the poem's 'feminisation' of language through images of food engages in and interrogates the racist and sexist discourses which conceal the ideological assumptions implicit in the textual production of feminine subjects and which inform the reception of migrant women's writing.

Like Anglo-Celtic Australian women, migrant women must negotiate dominant discourses, systems of representation which marginalise them by constructing positions of passivity for them. The poem's final lines, for example, produce the speaker as a feminine representation:

> ... Still I must be modest
> and speak in small amounts
> so as not to be considered a big eater.

Modesty becomes a woman, women must be seen and not heard, men

are bigger eaters than women; these sociocultural constructs of femininity are also informed by the poem's earlier use of the epithet 'gluttonous'. Gluttony is one of the seven deadly sins in Christian discourse, and
its use here together with the lines above suggests the moral and social
investments of patriarchal ideology. While the poem attempts to
neutralise this reading by displacing the violation represented by patriarchal restraints into a textual display of an individual's lack of self-
restraint, it nevertheless is open to a plurality of meanings. The text
suggests that poetry itself is an aberration, a perversion of everyday
speech incorporating foreign tongues, a type of sinful indulgence in
forbidden and sensual forms of meaning or an uncontainable excess, an
artifice, a perversion of sincere and authentic communication, of good
and proper behaviour. Its subversive revelling uses the repressive 'speak
as you eat' as a departure point for the construction of new possibilities
of representation. In the process the idea of the poet as masculine is
interrogated. Again, the last lines of the poem inflect this strategy. The
measured rhythm and restrained use of imagery, the seemingly straightforward and plain meaning, meekly conform to the Italian maxim.
Gardner gets her meaning across, but she does not really mean what she
says. The use of irony here undercuts the representation of feminine
passivity and continues the poem's subversive strategy. This tactful, and
tactical, 'retreat' into 'silence', particularly since it is constructed after
the excessive sibilance and ideas of orality suggested by the images of
food in the previous lines, produces a further irony. That is, the final
lines ironically imply the safe containment and framing of unnatural and
potentially eruptive material to prevent it from corrupting the bland but
'natural' language of ordinary man.

What is important here is the attention focused on the issue of
language and writing and, as a consequence, on the idea of assimilation
to the dominant culture through conformity to aesthetic norms. By
engaging with the problem of meaning as self-evident, Gardner's poem
also suggests a variety of questions concerning the literary status of
English as a second language. Too often multicultural writers are
essentialised, defined by their ethnicity where their writing is relegated
to the realm of sociology, to a content-based criticism which seeks
confirmation of its commonsense view of the 'migrant problem', and
therefore of the migrant as problem. Brian Castro succinctly writes:

> These definitions are ways of closing off. They are ways of saying: 'You
> cannot write in any other way but that of the Greek Australian because
> you are Greek Australian; you cannot write in other way [sic] because you
> are Italian Australian,' and so on and so forth. In my case I have been
> described as Chinese Australian. The assumption would be that there is no
> other way I can write besides that of dealing with racism and the Chinese
> question. If I launched into something else I would be described as
> inauthentic (Castro 1984:48).

Similarly, Sneja Gunew writes:

> If we accept the suggestion that migrant writing signifies only within the formations of sociology and history then, paradoxically, its value lies here with speech rather than writing. In other words, the migrant's speech (rather than writing) is solicited and the more disordered it is the more authentic it supposedly sounds. In those terms, migrant writing is valued precisely insofar as it is inscribed with the marks of linguistic naivety and (even) incompetence: broken language being symptomatic of subjects not yet assimilated (rendered the same) or 'naturalised' (Gunew 1986:65).

Gardner's texts, however, invert this idea of the production and reception of migrant writing. Clearly the poem does not uncritically re-present dominant views of migrants; instead it actively engages in the textual production of meaning. Because poetry is characterised by the ways it foregrounds it generic conventions, theoretically at least, it would be an ideal form by and in which to interrogate the 'transparency' of language. In practice, of course, this is not always the case, since poetry is informed by discourses which naturalise its conventions in constructing reading positions in ideologically orthodox ways. This is perhaps most evident in both poems' use of metaphors through which Romantic and New Critical approaches to poetry are fetishised. That is, Romantic ideas of poetry's heightened (and masculine) self-presence and self-generative nature are opposed to ideas of the pedestrian, straightforward nature of prose. Similarly, the Practical Criticism of the New Critics emphasised the coherence and unity of poetry achieved through poetry's use of metaphor (Murray 1989:10). While implicated in these ideas of the production and reception of poetry, Gardner's texts, nevertheless, produce reading positions critical of the ways ideas of unity ('speak as you eat') function oppressively for migrant women writers. Moreover, it is important to note again that the majority of writing by multicultural women writers seems at present to be in the form of poetry. As Sneja Gunew writes: 'To write poetry means that one is staking a claim to the literary and hence to public cultural participation' (Gunew 1986:65). This is not, however, an assimilationist view of aesthetic and social norms. In Gardner's poem, for example, the play on 'bad taste' can be seen not only as the textual transgression of aesthetic ideals, but also as an interrogation of what constitutes multicultural women's writing.

Although the poem's textual strategies resist patriarchal ideas of language, they do not imply a radical epistemology and aesthetic because finally the speaking subject is constructed in ironic distance from her transgressions of propriety. Indeed, the discourses which inform the representations of natural attitudes and of excess, position migrant subjects in relation to the latter. In one sense (according to such oppressive oppositions), the only strategies left to the migrant subject who desires to be heard are constructed by the text through ironic representations of the socially constructed self not only as the quiescent, feminine and assimilated subject, but also as the excessively 'oral' migrant, that is, as a 'proper', naturalised migrant subject. But because of this the text foregrounds those who are excluded from the privileged positions of enunciation, namely women and migrants.

Thus the poem is not just the site of prevailing ideology; rather, it is the intersection of numerous discourses: those of the conventions of poetry as a literary genre; those of wider social proprieties; and those of the cultural distinctions of race, class and gender. This is not to define the text as a 'tension-filled unity' but to see it as dialogic (Bakhtin 1987:298)[3] and as a negotiation of culturally defined subject positions, of possible and impossible meanings.

Resistance to social and literary conventions and to the authoritative discourses which inform them requires articulation. The poem 'Big Words', for example, uses a strategy similar to that of 'Little Words' by parodying the privileged voices produced by phallic discourses. Paradoxically, knowledge of the conventions that exclude or restrict the voices of marginalised subjects provides the very means of subversion. The final lines of 'Big Words' suggest that in the process of internalising 'the education of a dictionary', that is, of becoming a subject in and of dominant institutional discourses, the marginalised subject may also redefine the rules which regulate the use and value of English and generic conventions:

> but you are the one who sees them as plums,
> I suck the preposterous bulls' eyes
> down to the rich red vein.

Although the text's strategy is described as child's play, the metaphor 'bulls' eyes' also suggests that this is not an aimless verbal play. Rather, it is a strategy that breaks conventional rules, exposing the ways in which those whose voices are excluded from privileged subject positions are marginalised by racist and sexist discourses. In this sense, the representation of pretentious language and of the poem as child's play signals the usurpation of an exclusive and patriarchal subject position. However, the implied equation of poet with child is problematic. It signals the Romantic idea of a child's immunity from gendered and culturally defined subject positions and suggests the ideology of the aesthetic text as unconstrained by political and social realities. And it does this whilst also suggesting that marginalised voices can articulate new meanings and defamiliarise conventional social representations. By not employing correct usage, the 'child' (i.e. the marginalised subject) de-bases and de-constructs patriarchal language. But this type of resisting representation is potentially conservative, not only because of its Romantic implications, but because it implicitly reproduces the equations woman = child and migrant = child. This recalls stereotyped ideas of the authentic migrant voice as disordered and broken.

In a general way, Deborah Cameron describes how the proper use of English represents the investments of dominant discourses:

> Although English is not subject to a centralised authority, it has the trappings of an institution (e.g. dictionaries etc). Those who subscribe to the institutional view of language are quite clear that English is a cultural artifact which needs to be regulated and protected from abuse (for instance, debasement by foreigners and the lower orders). 'Language' is just a kind of shorthand for 'correct usage' or the 'language of the most educated/privileged speakers.' Communication is taken for granted: it is assumed that people know how to communicate and only need to be taught the most elegant way of doing it. (Cameron 1985:137)

It is this view of language as informed by the repressive distinctions of high and low that the poem debunks in a highly articulate textual play. Aesthetic ideals of clarity, elegance and accuracy, and also of obscurity and mystification, are parodied in a type of literary Darwinism which satirises the view of a 'fit' and decorous language:

> . . . but I can see by your avuncular
> disapproval that you are not convinced.
> Can't you see that the word is only
> the chondroid cover of tiny phalanges
> articulating in the joints of the alphabet?

The parody of obscure language as self-evident meanings, like the parody of good taste in 'Little Words (naturally)', also constructs a patriarchal subject position in the poem which the speaker addresses, and threatens, with coy reassurances. The protestations of innocence and neutrality, like the false modesty in 'Little Words', foreground an evasive textual strategy and signal a feminine representation of the speaker's voice. It is here that the conflict between contradictory subject positions is most evident. The speaker is positioned both in conflict with patriarchal norms and as a feminine construct of those same values. The problem is, to what extent does the coy tone subvert the text's subversive strategies?

Constructing a new language seems the only way out; a language, furthermore, that highlights its contradictory origins, and challenges definitions of poetry as unified:

> Little letters,
> inflorescing all kinds of gestures
> in the schizogenesis of meaning,
> flagellate each other to reproduce

The metaphor of 'the schizogenesis of meaning' not only undercuts the idea of Genesis, 'In the beginning was the word . . .', but also suggests the construction of a hybrid, anti-hierarchical language.[4] Words are both constituted and constitutive of other words; language is both product and process. New ways of articulating are made possible by combining disparate meanings, and by splitting and dividing language. The word 'schizogenesis' itself is a construction of two combining forms which suggests both its own split origins and the idea of writing as a synthetic, self-generative process. The text here implicitly pits an evolutionist view of language against a creationist view. The word is not made flesh, rather, it is satirised as a 'chondroid cover', a type of impenetrable exoskeleton represented by hard consonantal sounds and a dense overlay of obscure scientific language. Meaning is not incorporated or fixed, but represented as being renewed and regenerated in a type of primeval alphabet soup where little letters engage in a savage, protozoan-like mitosis. Similarly, the formalistic and reductionist approach in the opening lines, where the impressive-sounding 'helminthology' is decomposed into its component structures and exposed as being merely the study of worms, exemplifies the subversive textual strategy to defamiliarise and mystify whilst purporting to familiarise and demystify pretentious language. Using big words which mean 'little', the text constructs a parody of what Fowler condemns as abstractitis, a type of chain reaction of abstract words which conceal meaning. In doing this, the text exposes the patriarchal bourgeois authority invested in ideas of plain talk. In other words, ideas of plain talk are shown to be displaced ways of repositioning marginalised subjects in essentialist subject positions, so that when they use language according to bourgeois conventions, their linguistic competence is considered at worst, inauthentic or unnatural; at best, merely pretentious.

Whilst the textual punning and satirical exaggerations act as estranging devices, in both poems the textual strategies used to defamiliarise conservative expectations of migrant writing are implicated in the conventions they subvert. The deviant and subversive representations of ways of speaking are constrained by the positions of femininity constructed by the coy tone. However, to speak in aberrant and mocking ways, ways that are difficult to understand directly, is also to resist the repressive discourses that naturalise social representations of the migrant's 'aberrant' speech. According to these discourses it is almost impossible for the marginalised subject to use the privileged speech of institutional and aesthetic discourses without distorting and de-basing the privilege. Furthermore, the texts' constructs of migrant speech as a type of childish orality[5] where words are treated as things, and where sensual pleasure in the sounds of poetry estranges and subverts the patriarchal idea of a 'high', lexical determination of language use, foregrounds and interrogates the opposition speech–writing. In these poems, then, parody not only is a strategy of resistance, but also functions as the displaced speech of marginalised voices.

25 The migrant and the comedy of excess in recent Australian writing

Ivor Indyk

One of the benefits bestowed by migrant humour on the host culture is the way it allows adherents of that host culture to step outside and look at themselves—though whether they will be amused by what they see is another matter. The possibility of misunderstanding—wilful or otherwise—is all the greater when the host culture places great value on restraint, on strict but unspoken rules of propriety, as has been the case in Australia. What right has the migrant to poke fun at his hosts when it is the migrant, with his excesses of speech, his outrageous tastes, his extravagant gestures, who is the ridiculous one, the object of fun?

In such cases, humour may well function as an instrument of revenge, turning the accusation of excess against the accusers themselves. This is the way it works in Antigone Kefala's novella *The Island* (1984), where the migrant narrator, a student at university, constantly feels herself exceeding the limits of decorum observed by her fellows. In one scene, she portrays herself sitting in the cafeteria, surrounded by young men with heavy jaws made of iron. Her friend Ashton, a man who 'felt at ease only in a world of small, distant approvals', is only marginally more animated than the others, 'clenching and unclenching his teeth, staring vacantly before him':

> There was no need to get excited, his hands said, his coat, his face. He looked around at the other tables, overwhelmed by my vehemence. He had never asked for this, he told them, he was not responsible. He opened a packet of cigarettes laboriously, offered me one, and waited for the thing to pass.
>
> It was obvious that the effort was not worth it. I was suddenly silent, the air getting rustier and rustier and so heavy that a movement became impossible to imagine—my jaws became of iron and left a bitter taste in my mouth. I wondered for a moment how I could ever find the energy to break those insurmountable mountains of resistance.

It was only at sports that the animal in them leaped out across the
well-trimmed lawns, jumped and ran letting out hoarse cries, and when
the game had finished they all collapsed again, trailing their iron chains
across the wet corridors in the semi-darkness of the stained glass windows
and into the cafeteria where they stayed at the tables mute as statues.
(Kefala 1984: 23–4)

The trick here is to have made restraint itself seem a form of excess,
something grotesque and monstrous. The stiff upper lip becomes
through magnification the iron jaw, while the constraining bonds of
decorum become the dragging chains of full-blown Gothic. English
Protestantism has always had a penchant for the Gothic, especially when
it could be made a Catholic affair—but here the bird of prey comes
home to roost.

Excess seems to be one of the basic qualities of migrant humour in
Australia. According to conventional wisdom, truly Australian humour
depends on quite different qualities—it is understated, laconic, sardonic,
ironic. But this is to ignore the element of farce, an essential ingredient
in Australian humour, though admittedly one which is not primarily
verbal in nature. The humorous excess of our migrant writers seems, on
the other hand, to be primarily a matter of language—certainly, it is the
style of the writing which is most likely to offend, as exceeding the
bounds of good taste and judgment.

Perhaps the best example of this in recent Australian writing is Rosa
Cappiello's *Oh Lucky Country* (1984), a novel-length monologue which
ranges from insult to fantasy, and from the depths of self-pity to the
heights of exuberance, in its manic urge to expression. One might easily
think of this apparently uncontrolled torrent of words as ineptitude on
the part of the author, but this would be to ignore the perspective from
which the book is written. The novel is about the effects of migration,
particularly on unmarried women who, by virtue of their displacement,
come to have value merely as sweated labour, or as sexual commodities
to be possessed or employed in the business of child-bearing. The prose
is, in a way, a rebellion against this degradation, a relentless assertion of
value haunted by the possibility of denial, so that it swings between
extremes, at times becoming intoxicated with the illusion of power, at
other times tormenting itself with loathing and disgust. Hence the
description of Beniamina, desperately saving so as to be able to return
home with a little money:

Her aim is to beat the bank book deposit record in as short a time as
possible and then to buy herself a prefabricated cottage back home with
pots of geraniums on the balconies, terracotta tiles, a fire place, a little bit
of garden where she can grow lettuce, cucumbers, beans, tomatoes, where
she can keep a pig, some chickens and maybe raise mink. In the meantime
she complains of migraines, rheumatism, pain in the joints, swollen feet,
dry losses because of the strain under which she works. The tepid piss

which comes out she drinks for tea. In the morning she squeezes her tits to obtain a drink of milk. She wrings vitamins out of mice. Reads by the light of the street lamp on the corner. Catches the bus two steps further on so as to save five cents. Searches for cress and edible herbs in the park ... (Cappiello 1976:121)

And so on. The humour springs here from two traditional sources, obsession and incongruity—you know the task is an impossible one even as she hurls herself into it. There is a sense, too, in which the language aims to compensate for the sense of reality lost by the migrant—the incessant cataloguing seems like an attempt to conjure the world into existence, or at least to give it substance. This applies also to the novel's narrator, for as the novel is her utterance, so its language gives her substance and identity. The inflationary rhetoric works therefore to magnify the speaker herself—it proclaims her value, and in the largest possible terms. The social order which places the migrant in inferior positions is inverted: once the migrant discovers power in speech, the slave becomes the master and the master race sinks, buried beneath the weight of the speaker's scatological invective. Thus Rosa's response to the TV scriptwriter who fails to recognise her talents:

I'll give you something sensational you fucking, big-nosed, tropical-climate bitch. Kneel down and kiss me there. Together with the migrant masses I am contributing to the process of your civilisation, to widening your horizon which doesn't extend any further than the point of your great ugly nose. I tear the weeds out of your ears. I give you a certain style. I teach you to eat, to dress, to behave and above all not to belch in restaurants, trains, buses, cinemas, schools. You probably don't know, but I'll tell you in confidence, for your information, that your country, which is now mine too, is based on a gigantic belch. Its flag flutters in the wind created by the toxic gases produced by your stomachs which are choked up like sewers. The myth about being happy and lucky is based on your drunken bouts. Go on, then, drink. You offend us. You don't like wine? You prefer beer? Waiter, a huge bottle of beer for the lady. (Cappiello 1976:192-3)

I don't mean to suggest that the habit of magnification is peculiar only to migrant writers. It can be found in women writers like Miles Franklin and Eve Langley, whose novels are regarded as expressions of the Australian tradition, and also in such essentially 'Australian' male writers as Joseph Furphy, Patrick White or Les Murray. The sense of vulnerability, the discrepancy between the value one might want to claim for oneself and that offered by the culture in which one finds oneself— these experiences are not confined to migrants in Australia, though they may be suffered by them with particular intensity. Π.O's self-lauding poem 'MAYAKOVSKY a la KOCH (sortov)' suggests a migrant perspective in the sense it offers of the poet creating himself in a vacuum; but it also captures in comic terms the social isolation and egocentricity of a whole generation of Australian poets.

i'm brilliant.

      i'm fantastic.

            i'm great.

         i'm brilliant.

             i'm fantastic.

                i'm great.

arn't i,

    brilliant.

        fantastic.

            O, me, O, i!

      o-me-o-i

      o, i! o, Π!

you're great.

    (i'm great)

        you're brilliant.

              (i'm

brilliant).

        you're fantastic.

             (i'm fantastic).

    i'm brilliant

    fantastic

    great

(Π.O. 1978: 41)

The humour here springs in part from the distribution of words on the page—those empty spaces suggest responses, objections to the poet's extravagant claims which are not forthcoming, simply because the poet is not speaking to anyone but himself. And so the claims are repeated, expanded, as if to fill the surrounding silence.

There is a similar kind of excess in Π.O's demotic poems, those written in the patois of migrant English, where the speaker struggles not against silence but against the restrictions of an unfamiliar tongue. In some cases the urge to expression overflows the close bounds of language and manifests itself in gesture, threat and violence, as in the beginning of 'Tekish Men'.

Tekish men sten lake dis (   )

      lit'l boi, d-air ( )

        a men kik bawl ( )go'l!

        hit the boi in het (poom!   )

Tekish men: "weye? yoo hit bawl hUT!?"

(Π.O. 1978: 69)

Elsewhere, the energy is felt within the language itself, molesting, deforming, transforming it, producing an utterance which seems (by normal standards) to be grossly laboured and overwrought.

Pita! yoo rayt leta!

the akchell rock hit me was the size of
evrij pilow (apox 40/50lb).
the walls whor saif. w-hay? it hepen, I do not know.
thet was up to the pepol abav me.

I was drilling whit my machin.
the rock hit my halmat and give me conchshn,
and I hev 2 to 3 tayms a wek sever hadaks.

I went to fissioterapiss, 7 munts
bicoss I was paralaiss
and my lef ensait is very wek.

they mus giv me compensation, Pita.

rayt letta, big lettas, a?

law institoon.
dear sir, I steven petdro wod lake to know
of my case wat happen bicoss is

sach long time. I have to cut of my penticion
to pay the bils for the doctor and
all addar expenses.

(Π.O. 1978: 76)

The comedy here may seem obvious enough—it is the 'funny' language of the migrant, so much effort for such a simple end. But the joke is more complex, and certainly more subversive, than it appears to be. On the one hand, as the bizarre spelling suggests, there is a sense in which the utterance 'takes the piss' out of standard English; on the other hand, by focusing on the dangers which prey on unskilled migrant labour, the poem manages to evoke sympathy for what would otherwise be a stock comic figure, 'the migrant bludging on worker's comp'. The joke, that is to say, is on the Australian reader, who may have thought he was laughing at the migrant, when in fact it is his own superior standpoint which has been subverted.

The examples I have given are all essentially monologues. The form is well suited to capture the migrant's experience of isolation and loneliness, and also something else—within the boundaries of the monologue, which may be extended at will, the migrant imagination creates a country of its own, finds there the voice, the presence, the power, which it is otherwise denied. The monologic utterance is therefore capable of extraordinary intensity, since it is not just a medium of expression, it is the speaker's world, the speaker's reality, outside of which there is no existence.

Despite the fact that they have this remarkable intensity, Ania Walwicz's prose-poetic monologues have gone largely unrecognised by the Australian literary establishment. Again, one suspects that it is the quality of excess which has stood in the way. The poems are composed of a barrage of sentence fragments, with frequent repetition, as if the urgency of the emotion constantly overwhelmed the limited means of expression available to it. In addition, the poems often build up to an ecstatic pitch, to an overflowing of excitement or joy, as the speaker beguiles herself with fantasies of her own unsurpassed beauty, wealth, fame or brilliance. In this deliberate *débordement* there is a yearning for release, both from a deep sense of fragmentation—for the fantasies draw their disparate elements from dreams, fairy tales, popular romance, pathological confession, and memories of a European past marked by violence, fear and desolation—and from a terrible isolation in which the speaker feels herself unloved, dispossessed, displaced, without identity or reality. In 'Glowing World' there is the line 'I come from nothing. I make myself', which exactly describes both the inventiveness of Walwicz's monologues and the *horror vacui* from which they spring.

It is not easy to separate the humour from the horror, but a discourse as extravagant as this, with its bizarre conjunctions and obsessive energy, necessarily has a comic side. In 'landlord', a burst water pipe produces in the speaker an unstoppable torrent of anxiety:

> landlord he the mister next door talk to me talk to me he greek forgets that me that i don't that i can't greek speak no understand see but he he he landlord greek talks greek to me just a slip a mistake error funny sorry embarrassed he greek to me sounds are words to look at me look at me landlord greek talks to me greek in i can't see tell me what happens what the plumber said what did happen little sounds out of his mouth bubble says come to me tell me very thing what plumber pipe burst told landlord pipe burst told me landlord what about the pipe what about the washer what about my plumbing the connecting all joining what about everything don't want to live with my parents . . . . (Walwicz 1989:81)

The poem plays ironically on the cliche 'it's all Greek to me' as a dismissal of foreignness, for here there is no escape from foreignness into familiarity. Landlord and tenant may both be foreign, but there is no bond in this since each is also foreign to the other. In such a world even the simplest matters become intolerably complicated. The power of excess is most likely to be felt here in the way the burst pipe builds in intensity until, under the pressure of the speaker's anxiety, it suddenly overwhelms us with the fear of total disintegration. This overinvestment of the object is crucial to the humour of excess, and to migrant writing in general. It stems, I think, from the drastic reduction or thinning of the cultural milieu which the migrant suffers as a consequence of dis-placement. The culture of the past now comes to reside in only a few surviving objects—it may be a photograph merely, the contents of a suitcase, an old clock. On the other hand, the culture of the present, from the migrant's point of view, may seem not to exist at all, other than in those sites popularly mythologised as Australian, or specifically reserved for the use of migrants in Australian culture. In the following example Walwicz's heroine creates herself, inflates herself, by way of the objects in a delicatessen, a site where the migrant is conventionally applauded for making a contribution to Australian culture.

> I'm healthy pink in an apron. I fat sausage. Sit in the cheese. I'm the shiny sweets. You don't run out here. Never hungry. Or stuck for. Something to say. I'm the whirly colour in a bouncy cake. I grow small and fat and happy for no reason. I sparkle in the polished steel counter. I get so well. I'm sweaty pink ham. In thin slices. I dance in the red iron coffee grinder. I'm pastel sugar almond. I let my belt out. I'm pretty sweet. Two years old. I'm all flavour gelati. I don't talk to anybody. I get big on me. I get full of myself. I eat me gently and slowly. Delicate me. Dainty and dainty. My sweetest sweetie ... (Walwicz 1982:29)

There is a similar kind of inflation in Morris Lurie's work, and a similar kind of comedy. Lurie's most compelling narrator is one haunted by the demons of the past, confused by the absurdity of the present, alternately filled with elation and feelings of release, or else utterly devalued in his own eyes, rendered impotent and insignificant. In *Flying Home* (1978), again essentially a monologue, the narrator's Jewish–Polish heritage is embodied in a severely reduced form in its three ghostly guardians—his father, mother and grandfather—who return as gro-tesque caricatures to haunt him. As soon as his egotism falters, they are there, larger than life certainly, monstrous, oppressive, accusing—and he so small in comparison, so weak and insubstantial. In addition, there is the samovar:

> Do you know what a samovar is? An urn. An urn for making tea. We had one at home, in Australia. My grandmother brought it with her, all the way from Poland, from Bialystock, and she gave it to my mother, a memento of the good old days. My mother used to polish it every week. She made it shine. It was like gold. But she never used it. It wasn't even in the house. She kept it in the garage, on a shelf. In the house she used her new electric kettle. And do you know what happened to it, in the end? When she died, and my father died, I sold it to an antique dealer. Rappaport. Rappaport Antiques. And do you know what he did with it? I'll tell you. He drilled a hole in the bottom, pushed in a bit of flex, stuck

on a globe and a shade, and made it into a coffee table lamp. That's my Bialystock. It's become an electrical appliance. (Lurie 1978: 116)

Significantly, Lurie seizes on the object, and pumps value into it, with a staccato prose style similar to that employed by Cappiello for her elaborations, and by Walwicz. The humour in all three writers comes from the sense of arbitrariness which accompanies the process of inflation, or which is revealed when the process is abruptly punctured, as it is here, by some wildly inappropriate or bathetic attribution. Walwicz often foregrounds this sense of abitrariness by deliberately seizing on very common or stereotyped elements as a means to express the most intense kind of emotion, or alternatively, by focusing insistently on objects which seem to have no particular value at all, like hats, or boats, or buttons:

> what am i doing push my button up my nose push it and push it and push push button up nose i i don't know why i don't know why i am pushing this button up my nose i didn't know i just have to do it i don't know why i do it but i do i have to push a button up my nose i just had to do it i had to push a button up my nose i had to i have to i have to do it . . . . (Walwicz 1985:58)

It is worth mentioning, finally, that the comedy of magnification and debasement has in some of these writers a marked scatological tendency. The ruling object in *Oh Lucky Country* is the vagina, with all the ills it is heir to—'genital prolapse, bacterial flora, Doderlein's bacilli, fungus and parafungus, trichoma, lactic acid, dry mucus, over-heated vulvae, bacteria, parasites, gonococco, streptococco, pneumococco, straphylococco'—and Cappiello often counters the social debasement of the migrant through scatological invective which either drags down the pretensions of the host culture, or elevates the least regarded and valued of objects, as in the case of piss:

> For years now all social strata have been pissing on me from a great height . . . . I have stored up so much of that piss over these wretched years that I could piss down from the top of the wall for centuries on end and unleash a second flood of biblical proportions. The truth of the matter is that my piss is priceless, piss streaked with blood and cancer, piss that asks no quarter, not to run to waste because in its flight it curves like a colour-changing rainbow and paints cities, plains, mountains, rivers, lakes and seas. Gather the sparkling fluid in buckets, bins, baths, troughs. A woman who has suffered too much and has learnt to piss for want of any better consolation offers it to you as a gift. (Cappiello 1976: 234–5)

In *Flying Home*, Lurie's narrator joins a group of American Jewish widows and divorcees in Israel on a bus tour to Eilat. As it crosses the Negev, the party is stricken with diarrhoea. As so often in Lurie the comedy dwells on the absurd effects produced by cultural displacement:

> From my seat I saw them squatting all around the bus, roosting chickens in the sand, middle-aged ladies with their skirts fluffed out, their slacks dropped down, with their tinted hair, their flashing sunglasses, most clutching their handbags, some even with cigarettes. (Lurie 1978: 170)

Unexpectedly, though, the subject of defecation fosters a sense of community as everyone warms to the topic of bowel movements:

> Everyone was tired, exhausted, depleted, but look how friendly. The bus rocked with talk. Everyone took part. Private confidences buzzed around the bus. We had boarded as strangers and now we were a solid group. Bowels had broken the ice. We had common ground. (Lurie 1978: 171)

The episode neatly captures both the complexity and the comedy of the consequences of migration, for here is a group of people with a common cultural heritage, travelling in a country which is in some sense their spiritual homeland, yet the only common ground they share is this, the lowest of all common denominators.

26 Irritations

Dewi Anggraeni

I used to feel sick reading stories that depicted non-white races as inferior, underdeveloped in ethics yet overdeveloped in deviousness, therefore prone to crime and corruption. This kind of literature is self-perpetuating. If you feed readers this kind of concept, they will look for more. When these readers become writers, they will in turn produce the same kinds of stories, because the concept of white supremacy has become second nature to them. They have become unconscious racists.

A dear friend of mine told me that when he was sent to India as a British soldier, he felt infinitely superior to the local people. There he was, a working-class lad from southern London, now part of a ruling class. And the whole population, even their kings, were his subordinates. He was never consciously cruel to the Indians, but his feelings of benevolence was in the same vein as that toward animals. He treated them with caution. Their humanity only sank into his consciousness much, much later. This friend, in his youth, was not ignorant. In fact, amongst his peers, he was regarded as an intellectual, widely read.

The realisation that the majority of racists are unconscious ones pacified me somewhat. Now I can read such books with detachment and, depending on the degree of credibility and feasibility of the plots, I can smile with condescension or collapse in hysterics. I also realised, however, that unconscious racists are often hard to identify and target. They are not a homogeneous group who can be identified by their professions or vocations, residential areas, or income brackets. And in many cases, because they are unaware of their racism, they feel self-righteous. A conscious effort to 'educate' them, therefore, would not be well received.

Literature has often been regarded as the mirror of a society. It depicts its values, its various classes and its ways of life. It reflects the richness of the society's culture. Literature also plays an important role in informing the members of a society about what they think of each other. Except for students of literary studies, the process of learning through literature does not occur in an esoteric way. It is an unconscious process. One learns while being entertained. The power of literature cannot be underestimated.

Through literature, unconscious racists see themselves depicted but they can also see the 'others' presenting themselves in their own stories told from *their* points of view. Because of its non-threatening manner of 'educating', literature is likely to be more effective than direct criticism. I am not suggesting that writers should be didactic and purposeful when writing fiction. As a writer of fiction I would feel very constrained in my creativity if I were asked to write with a particular purpose. I do not even have the slightest purpose in mind when writing, beyond telling a story the way I see it, the way I feel it. Writing is a liberating experience. When I finish the first draft of a story and give it to my readers, the first question I ask when I see them again is, 'Did you enjoy it?' This is probably because I have enjoyed writing it, so I think my readers should enjoy reading it. I only realise its 'side effects' afterwards, when these readers tell me how it made them cringe when they saw themselves in it, or how they didn't realise that was how I felt about such-and-such people. Letters I received from general readers about *The Root of All Evil* were incredibly varied, yet one common thread runs through them: the book gives them tremendous insights into the contemporary culture of the Indonesian middle class. By doing this it also helps them understand the Indonesian community in Australia, which, especially in Victoria, mainly comes from this social class.

Australian literature, however, is still far from comprehensive. If it is a mirror, it is a slanting one. Large parts of Australian society are not represented. Many in the publishing fraternity would still like to believe that Australian society is Anglo-Celtic. Sifting through Australian fiction, one would have to look hard for stories which use non-Anglo-Celtic names for main characters. Many of the stories start in England or move to the United States. When a story moves to Asia, southern Europe, the Middle East, or even to Aboriginal communities, the tone changes. The main character (an Anglo-Celtic Australian, of course) feels constantly threatened by the dangerous and untrustworthy locals. The main character becomes a hero larger than life, no matter what s/he does. If his untiring vigilance conquers the deviousness of the locals, he is clever and sharp; if he shows empathy toward the locals and joins them, he is utterly compassionate. The fact that he is probably having a good time is often overlooked.

I have very little objection to this side of Australian fiction, considering that an author can only depict a situation within the scope of his or her own perception. However, what I would welcome is exposure of the society from other angles. I would like to read more about non-Anglo-Celtic communities in Australia, not just about their leaders or heroes, but about the ordinary people, just as we read of the ordinary people of the Anglo-Celtic community. Stories told from their varying points of view would help to disperse common prejudices, such as those relating to the inscrutability or the exoticism of these communities. Such stories would go a long way towards creating an understanding of their specific behaviours or customs or mannerisms considered weird by the uninitiated.

Who in the publishing community should take the first step to fill this gap in Australian literature? Very few of these works appear in our bookshops. Publishers are reluctant to bring them out because of the perceived financial risk. They are convinced that Australians are conservative readers. In reality, they only count the majority of readers those of Anglo-Celtic background. Non-Anglo-Celtic Australians don't read Australian literature because they don't find themselves in it. Unless we rectify this under-representation, we are going to reinforce the situation and increasingly alienate these people from the reading community. It seems that the first barrier to break through is that of publishers' resistance. One reviewer candidly told me once, 'You mustn't use so many foreign names and so many foreign words. Readers find them irritating, for they interrupt their enjoyment of the story.' When I pointed out that there were only three such 'foreign' names and the same number of 'foreign' words, this reviewer replied, 'People put it down at the second foreign word. I do anyway. There are so many books to read, why plough through one which gives you so much trouble?' I wanted to point out that there were some books which I found uninspiring, but I never had the arrogance to think that other people would necessarily find them boring too.

I don't know how widespread this attitude is among editors and reviewers. At that time, I did try to comply. But when my fellow writers came across such a ridiculous passage as:

Jemima [anglicised from Juminah] looked in the mirror and slowly undid the lowest safety pin of her blouse. Her waistband failed to disguise her bulging stomach.

they either laughed their heads off or screamed in exasperation.

'Well,' I defended myself, 'I couldn't very well write, "Juminah looked in the mirror and slowly undid the lowest safety pin of her *kebaya*. Her *stagen* failed to disguise her bulging stomach," because it would mean that in one paragraph I'd have three foreign words!'

My readers could well reply: 'Okay, but here it sounds as if this Jemima had a weird sense of dress. She put her blouse together with safety pins. Why? Had she lost all the buttons? And what waistband would disguise a bulging stomach? One wears a waistband around one's waist, not around the belly!'

Should I abandon the 'ethnic' description of an Indonesian woman's dress? Should I paint Jemima as completely Anglo-Celtic and so create a story in an Indonesian setting where the main character is a transplanted Anglo-Celtic woman? The how will she fit in with the plot? The problems multiply with each step that is taken to 'simplify' the text by reducing cultural difference. How long will Australian readers remain unaware of these other angles in our society?

If your book or story passes the screening of the editor and arrives safely in the 'to be published' basket of a publishing house, you still cannot celebrate. The bookshops might find it too 'up-market' for their readers.

I had heard about *Inside Black Australia* (Gilbert 1988) some time before it was even reviewed. When I cheerfully went to my local bookseller (a branch of a major chain), I was confronted with blank faces and the comment, 'Never heard of it.' A few weeks later, I saw a review and took it to the same bookshop. The manageress gave it a cursory look, then said, 'We can order a copy for you. It will probably take about a fortnight.' Surprised, I asked, 'You mean you aren't going to stock any, even after seeing the review?' She gave me a look as if I were too naive to have any opinion about the reading world. 'No,' she said, 'It's a specialist book. We have no readership for it in this area.' I was too disgusted for words. A few days later, I happened to mention it to a friend, who said, 'Yes, when I tried to promote your book *The Root of All Evil* in Geelong, the bookshop managers told me that it was an up-market book with no readership in that town.' How true a reflection is this attitude of the real readership of Australian society? One thing is certain, if a book is not on the shelves of bookshops, readers will not find it, considering that not everybody scours review pages of publications or listens to book programs on radio. Many of the letters I received from readers of *The Root of All Evil* and *Parallel Forces* found the books while browsing in bookshops and liked the few lines that they read before buying them.

A heartening factor I have noticed lately is the increasing number of writers of Anglo-Celtic background who write empathetically about other cultures. There are also growing numbers of reviewers and producers of radio and television book programs who adopt an enlightened attitude towards the diversity of Australian literature. There is a need, however, for this attitude to be more widespread. The tendency nowadays is still to label non-Anglo-Celtic writers as 'ethnic' and their writing as 'fringe' literature.

Multicultural Australia will remain a myth for a long time if Australian literature does not give more recognition to multiculturalism by beginning to reflect it not only in published writing but also in the distribution and promotion of that writing. Non-Anglo-Celtic writing can no longer be pushed to the side and labelled with names which mean anything but 'real literature'.

27 This eternal curiosity: The search for a voice in the wilderness

Cornelis Vleeskens

I walk along the street I lived on 30 years ago, stop outside the house from which my family migrated to Australia. It is pouring, and icy rain mingles with teardrops rolling down my cheeks. This is the first time that I have returned to the land of my childhood and I feel that I am a stranger here. I do not know how to fit into the society. The basic knowledge one gains through living in a place is missing. I stand here, frightened like the ten-year-old child that was forced to leave. No! More frightened, because I suddenly become aware that I am a stranger in Australia, as well as in my native Holland, that I am no longer able to wholly fit in anywhere.

Did I ever fit in? When we arrived in Australia in the late 1950s it was impressed upon us that we had to become integrated, become indistinguishable from the Anglo-Australian majority. The Dutch were considered model migrants! We threw off our own culture and became invisible. By the end of my first year here I topped the class in English, a language I had not heard before my arrival. I forgot, or rather unlearned my mother tongue and took on the squawking of the cuckoo.

When the first Anglo convicts, guards and settlers arrived on these shores they dislodged the Aborigines in the manner of the cuckoo chick hatched in the unsuspecting donor's nest. They demanded more and more of the frazzled mother until they left her exhausted. Their squawk was louder, their gullet wider. The only way to get a share of the food was to adopt their ways, to squawk so much louder.

Only the English language was permitted. The Aborigines were herded into camps and punished if they attempted to maintain their languages, their cultures, their identity. With the postwar flood of migrants the old tried and proven methods were continued. From the airport we were taken to camps where we were sneered at for our inability to communicate with the authorities, where we were forced to learn their language and eat their unappetising food.

But let me put it straight. I am not saying that we were like the Aborigines, for they belonged here and we didn't. What I am saying is that the methods used by the Anglo-Australian authorities were similar in both cases.

And what is the English language after all? It is a tongue removed from its Germanic roots by excessive and often irrational borrowings. Wave after wave of invading cultures overran the British Isles and left their mark on the language, tainting it until it became the language of the invader. Research into old English and the northern European languages shows the degree of corruption. The indigenous tongues lacked words for commands and orders that had the same shades of meaning as those conveyed by the words of the Roman conquerors. The northern 'barbarians' of Europe resisted the Empire and retained more of their original words, although these often were adapted to the new concepts.

Language is a reflection of the people and the land. For centuries the northern languages maintained their relation to the complex society where everything had its place, where the roots of speech were tied inextricably to the social patterns and shades of meaning were conveyed by variations on a root word rather than by the adoption of foreign expressions.

These continual incorporations into the English vocabulary have resulted in an overburdened language. The splits have been evident for quite some time and sociolinguists have written volumes on the various speech codes, the various sub-languages now contained beneath the umbrella we commonly refer to as the English language. Because English became a language of invasion and command, minority groups in those countries overrun by the invaders developed their own speech patterns, selecting from the vocabulary those words they could adapt to their own cultural and social systems.

The invader, however, looks down on the other speech codes within the umbrella group, just as he looked down on the indigenous languages of the countries he invaded and the languages spoken by the migrants who entered English-speaking regions. The laws are written in the most removed form of English and no longer relate to any living form of culture or society. They are formulated in a language that is incomprehensible to the majority of native-born English speakers, and even more so to the many minority groups. They are the ultimate example of oppression through language.

The greater part of my formal education was received in Australia, and ultimately led to an honours degree in English. In the late 1970s my writing became overly influenced by the easy rhetoric available in the English language. I could write endless poems where the music of the language took over, because English through the adoption of Latin and French words has a musical quality that belies its more guttural roots. I became dissatisfied. In 1979, the year after I completed my degree, I started to write a series of poems which were later published in the volume *Orange Blizzard* (1981), in which I explored the extent and effect of the influences exerted over my writing by the English language and the easy rhetoric of the American poets.

A number of reviewers failed to perceive the intent of that volume. One said it was '63 pages in search of a subject', which it was. And what it was intended to be, though he failed to see that! Another saw it as one of the most humorous examples of modernism in Australia. He'd missed the boat, too.

But how to break out of the rut? Having dismantled the language in which I wrote my poetry, I was left with a vacuum. I had become increasingly aware that language had become the subject of my poetry, instead of a vehicle to lay bare the subject. The modernist belief that there was no subject but language was somehow unsatisfactory in English. What was needed for a true modernism was a language in which the words used approximated the social structure in which we live: a language less corrupt than that which was available to me.

I turned more and more back to my roots and the Dutch language, a language I hadn't used for twenty years at that time, and I was childlike in my rediscovery of it. I managed to get hold of a handful of Dutch literary works and a battered dictionary. I started my first attempts at writing in my native tongue.

It was extremely difficult. Each word had to be wrestled loose from somewhere in the back of my memory. I had been so successful in becoming Australianised that I had almost completely blocked out the first ten years of my life. And, of course, when the words did come I found my vocabulary limited to that of the child I had been.

I became obsessed with trying to regain my abandoned mother tongue, devoured every word of Dutch I could find: labels on imported goods, newspapers, magazines, trashy detective fiction . . . anything. The few works of literary worth I had in my possession started to show signs of wear as they were read and re-read. I scoured the second-hand bookshops, found a few offerings to supplement my diet. I became aware of the level of language oppression exercised in this country.

Those first attempts at writing poems in Dutch were, as I said, an attempt to break out of the language patterns I had evolved. I had not thought through the process fully because I felt that my knowledge of the Dutch language was too limited.

But I soon found that the poems I wrote in Dutch, when I translated them, had a power in the mere use of words that had been lacking in much of my English-language poetry. These poems were more thought-out, more complete, and yet appeared extremely simple. I became more and more aware of the actual words I used, of the precision that is possible within language. And then I realised that some of the things I wrote in Dutch were very difficult to translate. The English language was too loose, the connections between words that were obvious in Dutch and that added to the impact of the poems were often lost in translation.

It was to be years before I fully realised the importance of this, and the implications.

Preoccupations shifted sideways. I laid aside the Dutch attempts to be worked on later. I had gained what I had aimed for, a fuller awareness of the language I wrote, and I tried to carry this through into English-language poems.

I realised that I had to come to terms with living in Australia, and my writing began to explore the place where I found myself: the hinterland of Queensland's Sunshine Coast. I threw myself into my next book, *The Day the River* (1984), in which I tried to tie the strands together. The migrations: first from Holland to Australia, then from the city to the country, and finally the migration into language itself. The first two I had to come to terms with before the third could progress.

For the middle section of the book I realised that much research was needed in order to create the valley that provided its setting. To feel at home in a place, you must become a part of that place, a part of its geography and its history. You must know the place as well as the Aborigines know their place, every tree, every watercourse, and how they came to be where they are, and why. An impossible task for an outsider. I researched the valley, with the help of a librarian friend who was able to direct me to the written source material. I gained an understanding of the valley. But I could not become the valley.

I am of another place, and it is that place that must provide me with that sense of belonging. I could come close to a feeling of belonging, but without knowing my own roots I would never be fully able to feel at home anywhere.

It was at that time that my father's older sister, Marie, came to visit the family in Australia. She brought me some Dutch books as a gift, but brought a greater gift: for many years she had been studying and researching the family history. She was a little surprised, but very pleased, that I expressed an interest in the photocopies of documents dating from 1700. They were handwritten—calligraphy would be a better description—records of the testimony of witnesses to an incident involving my earliest known (patrilineal) ancestor.

Deciphering them was almost impossible for me. They were written in an old language, using words and speech patterns no longer current, but the biggest problem lay in making out the words. My aunt, who had studied old languages and calligraphy, was able to provide me with a typescript. I worked with the typescript for several months, bringing it up first into modern Dutch, then English prose, and finally working it into a sequence of poems. This was the start of my new book, *Sittings for a Family Portrait* (1988).

Over the next four years my aunt provided more and more documents and long letters explaining how the family history had been traced and how parts of it had been handed down orally. Here was an oral history with documentation. Here were my roots. I started to do additional research into the periods I was working with. I was catching up on the history I would have been taught if it hadn't been for the dislocation.

By this time I had moved to Melbourne, where I discovered a bookshop that sold Dutch books and was willing to obtain others I ordered. Armed with a list of names of writers culled from the books I had already managed to get hold of, I spent long hours going through catalogues. For years I read very little other than Dutch literature, trying desperately to catch up on the 30 years since my departure. Until I finally felt that a return could no longer be put off.

Exactly 30 years after arriving here I boarded a plane, flew again over the red deserts of Aboriginal tribal lands (Aboriginaland) and the oceans and continents that had separated me from my own land.

I felt an incredible sense of relief as we descended over Schiphol. The feeling became even stronger when I caught the train back to the Hague and walked through the streets of Scheveningen, my birthplace. I felt a load slip from my shoulders and walked and walked. Took in.

Took in my country. Took in my being. Took in my culture. Never to be lost. Never to be stolen from me again. I stood in the Hague, in Amsterdam, in Enschede. I stood alongside Koories who were there to ask the Dutch Queen not to come to Australia for the Bicentenary, I stood alongside Robbie Thorpe of the Kurnai of south-eastern Victoria, and for the first time could really understand why the sense of belonging to a place is paramount, why dislocation from one's culture and land is like murder. I stood there and was proud that the first book of mine to have been published in Amsterdam (*Het gedrang van de leegte*, 1987) was about the Aborigines and Australia, about what has been done in this land. I was proud, and finally felt that I had something to offer. I knew who I was.

28 Artists and islands in the Pacific

Satendra Nandan

It is almost exactly twenty years since the first students graduated from the University of the South Pacific, an institution that has become the symbol of higher education and a new hope for the peoples of more than a dozen countries in the region. The South Pacific, with some of the smallest countries in the world in the largest ocean of the world, has its peculiar strengths and problems. The written word came into the seascape via the translation of the Bible. The coming of the Biblical mythology and its overwhelming impact on the life of the people have been profound and protean. Added to this theological exploration and adaptation has been the experience of colonialism in both its benign and brutal impositions.

But colonialism is part of our heritage, like the Taj Mahal, St Paul's Cathedral and our own Parliament House. It cannot be denied, for although British colonialism was brief compared to the lives of more ancient empires, its impact has been vast, and it permanently changed the contours of a varied world; through language and education, the configurations of the interior landscape of our mind and imagination were radically transformed. That is why the decolonisation of the mind is almost impossible, for the mind is shaped by multiple layers of experience. Colonialism is a vital stratum embedded in it.

Colonialism implies migration in many aspects: of explorers, settlers, migrants, mythology, ideology, language, literature, ideas, awareness, institutions. And wherever there's migration, a multicultural world is in the making, which means, at the turn of the twenty-first century, the whole earth. Space shall be no exception.

'Migration', as Salman Rushdie, that creatively controversial Indo-British writer, puts it, 'also offers us one of the richest metaphors for our age. The very word metaphor, with its roots in Greek words for *bearing across*, describes a sort of migration, the migration of ideas into images. Migrants—borne-across humans—are metaphorical beings in their very essence; and migration, seen as a metaphor, is everywhere around us. We all cross frontiers, in that sense, we are all migrant peoples' (Rushdie 1987). The crossing of frontiers of education is perhaps the most exciting. The South Pacific, like most of the world we know, has been peopled by migration. The world's most powerful and inventive nation is a migrant nation. In our own region our largest and perhaps most generous neighbours have been created as nations by immigration. So migration is a non-negotiable and an integral reality of our landscape.

Islands though the South Pacific was, it acquired a monolithic view of the world that came to it through the religious construct most prominent in colonial times. Indeed, Christianity has been a colonising religion: the Europeans carried it with the zeal of the converts which they really were. Gavan Daws puts it thus in his eminently readable book, *A Dream of Islands*:

> The nineteenth century turned into the century of imperialism, in which the white man stood above all others. Increasingly it was thought that the best that could be done with the savage was to control him. This was part of a great exercise in control in the nineteenth century, control over self as much as control over the world. The civilisation that recoiled in horror from cannibalism was itself swallowing up place after place, the islands of the South Seas along with the rest. Polynesia was being incorporated in the body politic of the world.
>
> The white man deserved to rule: this was the truth that made the West strong in the nineteenth century, and it was a truth that the West set out to teach all the peoples of the world. That truth came to the South Seas by way of the Bible. The nineteenth century was the great missionary era in the Pacific, as elsewhere.
>
> In its way missionary work was a form of imperialism, and in Polynesia the empire of God in the making was British. The founders of this new empire had been seized by the grand vision revealed to them by the eighteenth-century explorers of the Pacific. The Englishman William Carey, a driving force in the setting up of overseas missions in his day, had read the published voyages of James Cook. Carey was a bootmaker, and over his workbench he kept a map of the world on which were shown the natural resources of the earth and the various religions of man, civilised and uncivilised. Carey's idea was that as the world was made to yield up all its treasures, so all its religions would become one, and that one would be evangelical Christianity.
>
> In this view there was no such thing as a noble savage; he had never existed. The South Sea Islander was in a state of sin, and the missionary would have to voyage to the South Seas to redeem him, to save him from himself. (Daws 1980: 20–1)

This is my first point about education: that the monolithic view of the world propounded by colonialism in terms of race, religion and culture needs critical scrutiny in all its forms and facets. Edward Said has made a significant beginning in the context of the Orient, demonstrating how education and educated men of the imperialist tradition—of philosophy, lexicography, history, biology, political and economic theory, novel writing, and lyric poetry—come to the service of Orientalism's broadly imperialistic view of the world. In the Pacific of our region there wasn't even the religious–cultural resistance that was part of the Orientalist world. In the South Pacific, certainly the feudal chiefs of these highly hierarchical societies, opened themselves to the colonisation of the soil and soul. And it is that decolonisation of the spiritual seascape that we find so difficult to attain in our lifetime in the islands of sun and sin.

The consequence of this monocultural view of the world has been inimical to other cultures within the South Pacific. With all their empty pride, the Pacific Islands' feudal leaders have tended to bully those who are least able to defend themselves, the indigenous and immigrant people. They have acknowledged the superiority of the Europeans and their tradition in many things and the psychology of the bullied is often reflected in their attitudes towards Asians, who are their neighbours. Fiji, of course, is a telling and tragic case in point.

II.

I do believe that artists often generate thinking that changes our perception of the world. Dostoyevsky's and Picasso's works make the point rather well; in our own region, Patrick White's writings do. The images of the artist as a mirror, reflecting our world, and a lamp, illuminating the darker regions of our interior landscape, are well known. But there is a third dimension to this concept. And that is the artist as a warning system or as a surgeon who plies the steel and foreshadows the nature of the malaise. It is not always acknowledged that many of today's most powerful ideas have been spawned by the artist–philosophers. In our own colonial world, think of novelists: Bankim Chandra Chatterjee, Joseph Conrad, E.M. Forster, Wole Soyinka, V.S. Naipaul and Salman Rushdie. In subtle ways they laid bare before us, layer by layer, the colonial experience and our shared condition in all its horror and occasional glory. They changed us more profoundly than politicians and affected not the quality of our life but the quality of our humanity. They educated us into a new consciousness.

The artist, therefore, has to look for new possibilities and suggest ways of healing the wounds of history. In the very wounds, he may find the healing blood. Isn't that the image of Christ, too, or the Buddha: perhaps two of our greatest artist–thinkers? And how often in one's own personal experience does a line of poetry, a song, a dance, a work of art give one that sense of wholeness and understanding and a feeling of permanence and life's creative continuities. The artist then begins to understand, with compassion, the dislocation of a people, the displacement of values, and the encroachment of new ones as part of the disjointed scene.

The second aspect of the artist's role is to give back the self-esteem that was trampled on during the juvenile delinquency of colonialism. It is relatively easy for a people to get their political and economic independence, if that's possible at all among colonial geriatrics, but what takes a long time to recover from is the pyschic abortion caused by the arrogance of being ignorant of the past. Let me give one example. In Fiji we have, broadly speaking, three traditions: the Pacific, the European, and the Indian. The European tradition, through its association with power and monopoly, reinforced by a monolithic and proselytising religion, did enormous damage to the multiplicity of the vision of life that the ancient faiths believed in. The 'I am the only way' syndrome chopped away the idols which were really works of art, humility, openness and accommodation. This sublimely egotistical view of life came into existence barely 2000 years ago. The world has surely been in existence for many more millennia. At the turn of the twenty-first century our children are paying a tragic price for that view of history and the world.

There are other faiths which survived the ravages of history and man's inhumanity to man and have long been ignored. I am, of course, talking not of religious experience—that is every person's mystery with his or her God. What I am stressing is the attitude of mind created by this evangelical fervour of faiths born in the deserts of the Middle East. As a result, we began to feed our imagination on borrowed fairy tales and lost faith in our own truths. And I think this is our fundamental challenge as educationalists: to bring back into our education the variety and subtlety of life as perceived by other earlier civilisations. It is not enough to continue to parrot Plato if we have no knowledge of Pānini, the first Sanskrit grammarian. We continue to quote from Homer's *Odyssey*, but Vayasa's *Mahabharata* is not even mentioned. The list could be endless.

Take Fiji, for instance. We had enormous possibilities, but rarely did we explore them for the benefit of our nation. We have been so dominated by the Anglocentric thinking that has come to us via New Zealand that education has been thought of as largely a European phenomenon. This at times has been dehumanising and alienating and the Eurocentric tradition is seen to be all-encompassing, mature, subtle and sophisticated, while the others are primitive. Over a century and a half ago, Lord Macaulay said that the wisdom of India and Arabia could be put on a single shelf of an English schoolboy. And this—in the case of India—about a civilisation that has at least 5000 years of *written* literature.

Only the other day I was reading a book published by a group of American scholars on *The Literatures of India*. This is what they had to say about the Hindu epic the *Mahabharata*, written almost 1000 years before the Christian era. This book, which became the founding library of a whole civilisation, includes history, legends, education, edification,

religion and art, drama and morality. What interested *me* most was this
paragraph:

> If an analogy were to be made to western culture, one would have to
> imagine something like the following: an *Iliad* rather less tightly structured
> than it now is, incorporating an abbreviated version of *The Odyssey*, quite
> a bit of Hesiod, some adapted sequences from Herodotus, assimilated and
> distorted pre-Socratic fragments, Socrates by way of Plato by way of
> Plotinus, a fair proportion of the Gospels by way of moralising stories,
> with a whole complex of 200 000 lines worked over, edited, polished, and
> versified in hexameters by successive waves of anonymous church fathers.
> In the Western tradition this seems incredible. In the Indian civilisation the
> *Mahabharata* is a fact. (Dimock et al 1974: 53)

Peter Brook has now, of course, given the epic a universal audience
and appeal. Like a great master educator he has given us new eyes with
which to read old books about our times and lives (Brook 1988).

But it is not simply this fact, or the lack of it, in our education that I
am concerned about; it is a more disturbing confession I wish to make.
My parents knew no English but were well-versed in the *Mahabharata*
and the *Ramayana*. Because of my education, whenever someone asked
me if they were literate my answer was always 'No', simply because they
did not know that an 'a' was for an 'apple' and a 'z' was for a 'zoo'. This
is how we were fed and trained in our little zoos. This is the great
blasphemy of our generation's education, controlled by people who
admittedly had their own limitations. We, however, do not have *their*
excuse.

There is another aspect of our life to which an artist in our society
must give definition and direction. That is to give an uprooted and
transplanted people a sense of place and belonging. It is, I think, a
question of the faith of the artist in his people and place. Colonial
people are brutalised in many ways. One of the lasting injuries done to
them is this lack of an established past or a continuous culture. At Fiji's
independence in 1970 some of us were beginning to feel the first sensa-
tions of rootlessness. After all, we were defined only as 'Indians' in the
Constitution, the supreme law of the land. This is the price we paid for
the awesome awareness that came with the coups. The more educated
we get, the deeper will become our recognition of this deracinating
reality. And a sense of alienation is setting in at many levels. It is,
therefore, necessary for the artist to give the people strength of mind
and resilience of spirit. He becomes involved in an act of self-becoming,
individually and collectively.

In the Pacific, if artists fail to move us towards a synthesis, integration
and new orientations, then while some communities will continue to
suffer from this lack of the country of the mind and consequently see
their achievements mainly in material terms, others will move deeper

into the well of the past. And the past can kill. It can trap us into thoughts which have no real bearing on our contemporary lives and we will tend to romanticise a version of the past because we're unable to confront the harsh realities of today. This fascination with an imagined past is not confined to the South Pacific. It is becoming a worldwide phenomenon, where the countries grappling with the bits from their colonial wreck have not been able to grasp the present and are falling back into the myth that the old was gold. As V.S. Naipaul said:

> The 'Third World' notion is itself a cliche. I feel there is a great universal civilization at the moment which people would say is Western. But this has been fed by innumerable sources. It's a very eclectic civilisation and it is conquering the world because it is so attractive, so liberating to people. What disheartens me is that there are certain cultures where people are saying 'Cut yourself off. Go back to what you were.' There is nothing to replace the universal civilisations they are rejecting. The Arabs, the Muslim, some Africans [some Pacific Islanders] are doing this. I think it's a disaster. The great Arab civilisation of the seventh to twelfth centuries was the world's most eclectic civilisation. It wasn't closed to outside influences. It was endlessly incorporating the art of Persia, the mathematics of India, what remained of the philosophy of Greece. The mistake of Western vanity is to think that the universal civilization that exists now is a purer racial one. It's not the preserve of one race, one country, but has been fed by many. (Naipaul 1980; 1991.) [My addition in parenthesis]

Finally, the artist may bring us to the realisation, particularly in the South Pacific, that though living on islands we are not islands. Alone we are yet not alone, uniting as we do the themes of so many other lives. Indeed the interest the artist's self has for others lies in the extent to which that self has embraced the lives of others. We are all stiffening in rented mansions or mortgaged houses: the house is no more a fortress and human relationships are more like the oceans—ever changing, restless and creative, with palpable love, but demanding the daring of the early explorers. Only such people will discover new horizons and see the oceans that connect us all. I believe there's an Indian–Pacific that runs through the heart of Australia. Once we begin to recognise the growing relationships with others then we begin to recognise ourselves, and often a work of art leads us into that kind of illumination. This imaginative exploration of our lives is often more true than the so-called facts of life. At this level, then, art *makes* life, and living becomes an endless, exalted faith in the ordinary world of all our being.

A longer version of this chapter was presented at a seminar on 'Higher Education in the South Pacific', September 24-28, 1990, at St Hilda's College, University of Melbourne.

29 The Goulash Archipelago

Rosa Safransky

I'm glad Captain Cook was eaten on the Sandwich Islands. I just wish someone had stuck him between a bagel *before* he discovered Australia and not after. Perhaps if Captain Cook had been blown off course by Hurricane Platypus, he might have discovered somewhere else and years later my family and I might have helped populate the Far North by opening a dress factory in Darwin. I don't think bagels and gefilte fish were easily obtainable in Arnhem Land, so we came to Melbourne. Melbourne might as well have been the lost city of Atlantis. I was hardly aware of myself as part of a 'tide of migration'. I thought it was only us. My mother arrived in Melbourne with a pair of nail scissors and my father with six shillings in his pocket. Later a complete set of dishes came in a cardboard box. I'm still not sure who sent them. The confusion and dilemmas are part of my stories.

I was born in Paris of a Polish-Jewish background and grew up in an inner Melbourne suburb, though which part of me is Polish, French, Australian, Jewish, I have never been able to figure out. A hand? Left or right? A foot? An arm? The high school I attended felt like it was in England, though I never had to get on a plane. I took trams across the Yarra into the third-largest Victorian city in the world. Before it was pulled down.

'Where did you learn to speak such good English?' a headmaster in my local state school once asked me. From the radio serials. I even took the mantel radio to bed and listened to Dr Floyd on the ABC. Food I ate at school. Salami, pickles, rye bread. What, no Vegemite or white-bread sandwiches without crusts? There was also a slight communication problem. How did people communicate with each other? They didn't seem to at all.

'You're a good sport!' I told my father. At school it was a great compliment. He hit the roof!

'No one would dare say such a thing to their father in Poland!' Of course not. No one played cricket in Poland.

When my parents arrived in Australia they were totally involved with survival and acquiring the language. They didn't have a clue where they were. I have spent years trying to find out. Was Captain Cook any more perplexed than I was? Food and customs at home were Polish-Jewish. I could have grown up in Poland. Polish bush, Polish gum trees, Polish kookaburras. I wasn't in Poland but where was I? I tried to read Ion Idriess but why do the things that happen to Idriess never happen to me? To this day I haven't met even *one* frilly-necked lizard on Acland Street. At school, the '*Queensland Drover's Song*' drove me to distraction, and '*I Love a Sunburnt Country*' by Dorothea Ma-ck-ell-ar bored me to tears. Melbourne (before the greenhouse effect) was wet and bitterly cold most of the year. My toes were covered in chilblains. We went to the museum, where I saw for the first time a stuffed horse called Phar Lap and an enormous glass case full of stuffed snakes. We sometimes went as far as Geelong or the Dandenongs in the Morris. My father always sent postcards from various country towns in the bush, where he sold the dresses he, my mother and uncle made in the factory. Australia to me meant 'a factory'.

The factory was a shopfront called 'Maurice of Paris' in a back street in Brunswick. The mantel radio talked and talked. Sometimes it sang. The factory was split in two. Downstairs was my father's territory, the non-smoking section; upstairs belonged to my uncle and was officially the smoking area. Australia was a Turkish steam bath. Clouds of smoke drifted through the entire house and the factory as well. At one point we had 22 cats. As always, my uncle and father were divided on this issue, my uncle being a fanatical cat fancier and my father unable to abide them. My most vivid memory around this time is of my mother clutching a basket containing saucepans of food wrapped in tea-towels, running for the train so we could get to the factory before dark and eat supper. The factory absolutely dominated our lives.

Apparently I hadn't been born in a factory. I made my first appearance in Paris, a city graphically captured for me in the tinted postcards of fountains, Eiffel towers, public monuments, parks and gardens my mother kept in a black leather handbag. I spontaneously combusted somewhere between the postcards, the train, the factory and the black handbag. I arrived in Melbourne in a vehicle which was a cross between a time machine and a ship and moved into a house that had always been there, with three ready-made uncles, one of whom turned out to be my father. The mystery took a while to unravel. My family ran as a collective. When my uncle and mother won £100 in Tattslotto, we threw the icebox out and bought a fridge.

A shoebox with some photographs was my map of the world. My

great-grandfather, a conscript in the Tsar's army, poses against an ice-berg. The photograph lives in the top right-hand corner of a chest of drawers on our back veranda. The photographs know why we are here and are part of the secret horde of stories that live in my family. No book I read approaches the stories my family tell as common everyday events. My 149-centimetre godmother, who always insists I help myself to another slice of her delicious honey cake, worked in Nazi headquar-ters as a spy for the French Resistance. In fact my family's odyssey through Europe seemed closer to fiction than fact. Australia, or more specifically Melbourne, was almost without context. I often walked around the streets trying to make sense of things. Maybe it wasn't only me that had combusted here, perhaps it was the entire city. Melbourne itself might have had a parallel existence on some other planet and then, through a cataclysmic event, found itself sucked through the universe and deposited off St Kilda beach. Its imitation Gothic buildings and ornate Victorian mansions seemed like palaces belonging to kings and princes. My own weatherboard was in a back street on the edge of the world.

A teacher sticks an Australian flag in my hand. What am I supposed to do? 'Wave it when the Queen comes.' The cheering grows louder, crowds of people line the streets. An open-topped limousine comes into view. A feather boa, diamond tiara, rows of medals. The crowd goes wild. Why? The Queen and Princess Margaret are the patron saints of the idle and the lazy at home. But home and me at school are mutually invisible. I ate food most Australians could not pronounce and had never heard of, spoke, read and wrote Yiddish, the language of the eastern European *shtetl* and brought notes from home asking to be excused on religious holidays most of my teachers had never heard of. No book on any English reading list explained me to me or why my friends were all Greek, Jewish, Italian or Chinese or what any of us were doing in Melbourne with our olive complexions, dark hair and unpronounceable names in WASP schools geared to perpetuating the English middle class.

Culture reflects society. By the year 2000 over half the population will come from non-English-speaking backgrounds. Australian writing is not multicultural, it's not English, it's not American. Its influences extend from the convicts through to Geoffrey Blainey. Arguments about what is and isn't Australian literature seem to me meaningless and to attempt to pursue a kind of literary white Australia policy would be antediluvian. Joseph Conrad, Primo Levi and Vladimir Nabokov, writing in Australia today, would be labelled 'multiculturals'.

Multicultural has become synonymous with Martian. The term denotes a literary kiss of death and sends academic critics scurrying for their bedside Virginia Woolfs. Ethnic or multicultural writers are little green men and women from Mars landing on Anglo-Celtic Australian soil with their foreign-sounding names and ray-gun typewriters.

A new energy is pouring into Australian writing, created by migrants and the children of migrants who are coming to grips with language in exciting and original ways. Their prose breaks through cultural stereotypes which relegate migrants to an intellectual and cultural backwater in Australia, labelled and defined by those who themselves have never experienced the traumatic, often long-ranging effects of uprootedness and displacement which have come increasingly to characterise the lives of so many people in the latter part of the twentieth century. After eluding political repression, torture or death in their countries of origin, many migrants found themselves confronted with a situation of economic exploitation on arrival here. The cultural dislocation, confusion, alienation and inter-generational warfare can take generations to work out.

The definition of what constitutes Australian writing and culture in the late 1980s has widened. There is not one voice, there is a multitude of voices. The writing indicates that it has not been a quick or easy path to assimilation, that Italian cuisine does not change to meat pies overnight, but why should it? Australian society itself has changed and is changing. The writing reflects this.

Part V: Re-writings

30 Move over Shahrazad

Zeny Giles

I like all kinds of stories—folktales, legends, fairy stories, parables. A special favourite of mine is 'The Onion', one of the fables from *The Brothers Karamazov*. During the holidays I was reading some Italian folk tales collected by Italo Calvino and was surprised to find the same story called 'St Peter's Mamma'. The one good deed of the Russian woman was to give away an onion, whereas St Peter's mother was so stingy she had given away in her lifetime only one leaf of a leek. There is more than a hint of spite and conceit in her words as she yells out to the other damned souls trying to grasp hold of her leek and be pulled into Paradise, 'You should have had a saint for a son.' Even St Peter can't save her. Like her Russian counterpart, she loses her grip as she tries to kick off her fellow sufferers, and falls back down to the everlasting flames.

Closer to home, there's a story my father told me about a Greek who came to Australia and managed to find a job cleaning toilets in Martin Place in Sydney. He did his work conscientiously and everything went well until he was asked to sign a form. The Greek admitted he couldn't write and he was told that, in that case, he couldn't be an employee of the City Council. The Greek had to do something for a living so he bought boxes of fruit at the markets and sold them at bargain prices to shopkeepers in the eastern suburbs. He worked long hours, steadily increasing his customers, and by the end of the year, he'd earned more than 60,000 dollars. When he went to see an accountant about completing his returns, he was asked to sign the tax form. Once again, he had to explain he couldn't write his name.

'You can't write your name and you've earned all that money!' said the accountant. 'Where would you be if you could write?'

'Cleaning toilets in Martin Place,' replied the Greek.

Of course you've heard it. Somerset Maugham used it so skillfully in 'The Verger' and I'm sure it occurs in many other places. Last year, I was delighted to have the story recounted to me by a neighbour. In his version, the Greek had become a Yugoslav and the cleaning job had moved from Martin Place to the offices of Newcastle's Hunter District Water Board.

Stories have a way of pushing through boundaries. In the light of the recent Salman Rushdie scandal, it's interesting to look at the popularity of the Islamic stories from *A Thousand and One Nights* with Christians in the early eighteenth century. And who would have predicted the European appetite for the novels of Walter Scott and the special empathy of the French for the stories of Edgar Allan Poe?

My grandfather came to Sydney from a little Greek island in the 1920s and, like most of his compatriots, was no lover of the Turks. Yet he would delight his family by telling them story after story of Astradihodja, the lovable Turkish *hodja* whose naive discoveries are such an amusing comment on human nature.

When I was telling my grandfather's story, I decided to include the fable of Astradihodja's donkey. You will have heard it in one form or another. Astradihodja decides that eating is only a habit and he's determined to prove this by training his donkey to eat a little less each day. On the first day, he cuts the beast's ration down to half, the next day a quarter, and so on. 'But talk about bad luck!' Astradihodja complains to his neighbour. 'Just as I trained him to do without food, the stupid animal had to die on me.'

I spend most of my time looking for stories. I listen for them at dinner parties and at the school where I teach. I pick the brains of parents and grandparents and ancient aunts. A few years ago, I went searching for them at the Moree Baths because when people meet they swap stories, whether they are Canterbury Pilgrims, or visitors to the Salzburg Festival, or people in Australia who go to take the waters. The characters I wrote about had come originally from Greece, Hungary, Yugoslavia, Ireland, England and Germany, and what intrigued me was their coming together in this small country town in northern New South Wales.

Once I used to say apologetically, 'Yes, I'm writing about my Greek background again,' as if that was something not worthy. And I would have liked to have proved myself by writing a *non-ethnic* story.

But what is a *non-ethnic* story? The *Macquarie Dictionary* defines an ethnic group as *'a group of people, racially or historically related, having a common and distinctive culture'*. Surely the term applies to all the different waves of migrants since 1788? The narrowing of its meaning to refer only to non-English-speaking groups serves to diminish the cultural strength of those who are described as *Anglo-Celts*.

Now I grab a story where I find it and celebrate the differences. I like having the option of retelling old tales or inventing new fables. And I don't want to hang labels on my characters. I like them too much.

One of my earliest memories is a class photo taken when I was six years old. I was perfectly happy with my image on the paper until golden-haired Patty Cooper blurted out to me, 'My mother says you look like a gypsy.' I was humiliated. I'd convinced myself I blended into that predominantly Anglo-Celtic classroom in the 1940s. I'd done my best to hide my relatives and to make sure Mum and Dad didn't speak Greek in front of my friends and yet I'd been discovered. I would have to try harder.

So I went on pretending through primary and high school and even after university. Now I'm too wise for such pointless games. And if I had a chance to go back to speak with Patty Cooper's mother, I would thank her for her compliment. How good to stand out. And how wonderful to be a gypsy. To have an older European language as well as English. To have skills in telling fortunes and camp-fire tales. To be swarthy and mysterious and wear golden earrings. Best of all, to live in a caravan on the edge of Australian suburbia, and be at the one time inside and outside the action; able to look from my special vantage point at the certainties of this society.

31 Concrete poetry and my work

Thalia

The rise of capitalism tended to devalue poetry as an unprofitable activity, except insofar as it became a commodity, for example in advertising. Books and reading reduced learning by heart and the attention and retention that are part of a tradition of oral literature. With writing came rules and grammars in which words and idioms are judged not by their expressive power but by their 'correctness', and language became almost a closed field.

We do not see words, we read them, which is to say we look through them at their significance, their contents. Concrete poetry is first of all a revolt against this transparency of the word:

> . . . a challenge to authority, including the authority of definitions. It undermines the power exercised when things are named and it draws attention to the limitations, and temporality, of such power. Naming, of course, is part and parcel of how we talk together. And so is the continual questioning of names and the process of re-naming'. (Reid 1989: 5)

The international movement of concrete poetry started in Brazil in 1955. But the poetry had been around long before the twentieth century, in fact one can trace it back as far as Egyptian hieroglyphics and Chinese and Japanese ideograms, all of which display an interfusion of visual beauty and literal meaning.

As Hugo Ball the Dadaist writer said: 'the word and the image are one' (Reid 1989: 6). Concrete poetry begins by being aware of graphic space as a structural agent. As Apollinaire pointed out, by exchanging the visual appearance of the words, by printing them in unusual shapes, larger, smaller, distorted etc., a visual dimension is added; one perceives the words with a combined sharpness of the eye and the ear.

The difference between visual poets and artists who use texts, letters, signs is:

In the work of the visual poets both the original and the transformed literal meaning of the words (or signs) is an important element in our response. Our response is a flash which occurs when we see literal meaning transformed by the space it occupies. In the work of the painters the literal meaning of the words, letters, signs, is either removed entirely or is vastly subordinate to their meaning as design and visual composition. (Reid 1989: 8)

Visual poetry is profoundly literary, for it deals with the effects of writing. It makes the sound and shape of the word/s its explicit field of investigation. It is a structure which explores elements of language itself, rather than one which uses language to explore something else. Here the poet uses unconventional methods, to shape and present the text to a point where even the inattentive reader is forced to pay attention to the word as word.

My introduction to shorthand and to concrete poetry was in 1971, the former at business college whilst doing a secretarial course. My first impression was amazement: all I could see was a visual context in which strokes and curves became symbols for words, symbols based on sounds. Marvellous, I thought, and my dyslexia almost disappeared.

Shorthand was invented by Isaac Pitman in 1837 and has been predominantly used by women. It is an international linguistic skill based on sound and was commonly known as sound-hand writing.

In Australia in the early 1970s, Π.O. had invited a group of poets to come together and exchange, share, circulate and pass on information to one another about concrete poetry on a national and international level with the intent of eventually bringing out a magazine. With access to a printing press, /* [Slash Asterisk] Press, run by Π.O., *Born to Concrete* was launched, a magazine to promote and circulate concrete poetry.

This group was as diverse in style as there are languages or dialects. Jas Duke concentrated on using Lettraset; Peter Murphy on the typewriter and the camera; Π.O. used Chinese ideograms as well as Lettraset; Rosemary Edwards focused on pictures, words, and cutouts of advertisements; A.C.R and Renee used Lettraset—just to mention a few. And I, to give the group as diverse a range as possible, looked to shorthand as the medium in which I was to execute almost all of my visual poems.

I have been attracted to the use of shorthand because of its visual beauty and the quick, free flow of the word as it rests and relaxes on the page. As we perused different overseas and local poets it soon became apparent to me that no one had ever considered or attempted to explore another dimension of visual poetry through the use of shorthand symbols. Shorthand is a language based on sounds and with its many visual permutations, cuts through international language differences. Isaac Pitman said that shorthand 'is the final stage in the history of writing'.

Within my poems I give (and pass on) a woman's visual understanding and meaning of a word in a symbolic manner which has traditionally existed for women within all their art work e.g., doilies, needlework, knitting, painting etc.

Suffering from RSI and out of the workforce (labelled unemployable), I have found in concrete poetry an outlet of continued communication via an international language.

Although there have been an overwhelming number of women writers throughout history, a women's language has been virtually nonexistent, and it is here that I feel I am to provide a language common yet refreshingly free from rigidly defined patriarchal concepts.

My poem 'Male Sexuality' deals with two words, 'religion' and 'worship'. The poem depicts the penis.

MALE   SEXUALITY

Worship

Religion

Within society, male sexuality is constantly assuring us of what and who holds the reins of power and the male penis has become a 'subliminal' religious sign worshipped and enforced by all within language, culture, sex, work, family and history. 'Male sexuality is not constructed as a mere reflection of the fact that men have power over women, but rather it is constructed and reproduced as an instrument of male control' (Coveney et al 1984: 14).

'Tides' is a poem with the one word, *'woman'*.

The word 'woman' has been turned into the ocean's splashing waves, an overpowering force of woman or women (the same shorthand outline). This is my statement of women's history, which is constant in struggle; a wave which one cannot hold back, it surges up in revolt and uprising.

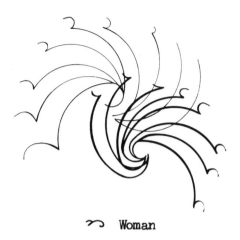

~ Woman

'Literature' is depicted as the earth with the four compass points (north, south, east, west) and with all points meeting in the centre—bullseye.

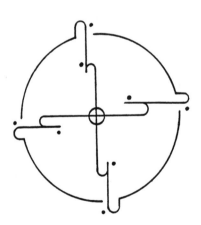

LITERATURE

It can also be seen as four dolphins rotating in harmony.

> Human beings are symbolising creatures, and we are constantly engaged in the process of producing symbols as a means of categorising and organising our world. It is our capacity to symbolise and the use (or misuse) we make of the symbols we construct that constitutes the area of language, thought and reality. (Langer in Spender 1980: 138.)

When executing a poem my first job is to research as much information as possible in order to understand and do justice to the theme, or text. The second stage is to single out key words that epitomise the essence of the subject matter. Once I've done that I execute the shorthand symbols for these key words.

In some poems, like 'Domestic Violence', I had to go outside the realm of written matter and work on words that do not talk on a generalised social scale but concentrate on a single or personal war, for example the words 'private' and 'silence'.

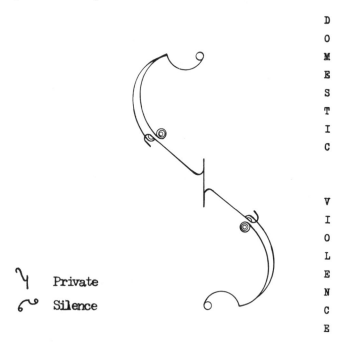

D
O
M
E
S
T
I
C

V
I
O
L
E
N
C
E

Private

Silence

Although domestic violence is a universal atrocity inflicted upon women (and children) it is always kept, or 'tolerated', within the home of the victim or victims. This poem shows two faces, one towering in a threatening way over the other. The other, of course, is being subdued by the known assailant who threatens or intimidates his victim.

Concrete poetry allows the reader to have a number of visual interpretations of a word, and generally calls for participation instead of passive appreciation.

With the use of concrete poetry I am able to create in writing a visual language that transcends all languages, dialects and cultures and which in turn allows me to dispense with the dominant written language.

32 Miklouho-Maclay and his dingo

Birimbir Wongar

I was eighteen years old when I first read the New Guinea diary by Miklouho-Maclay.[1] It was actually the first book I read, on a cold wintry night, sitting by a kerosene lamp. It took me almost the whole night to go over a chapter and I caught a cold. The following week I stayed in bed and finished the book.

Ever since those wintry days in Europe, I have kept looking for a rainforest with old hollowed trees known only to birds; trees older than man and his books—white man I mean.

In New Guinea, as in Australia, trees like that were still in the bush some decades ago, so that they were able to tell how the place looked when Maclay came to rest under them. He was the first white man to do so. That was in 1871, but in the life of a big tree a century or so is only a short space of time. Maclay was sent to the Pacific region by the Russian Imperial Academy of Science to study primitive life forms, but he soon found that plants and man belong to the same world and that without trees there would be no humans about.

It was a daring thing to be an ecologist and humanist in the last century, and very often lethal for a scientist.

Before Maclay's New Guinea expedition, which took him fifteen years (about one-third of his life), he was a promising star of a scientific community in Imperial Russia, a follower of Darwin and Haeckel and a pupil of the latter. Maclay was not particularly interested in the origin of the species, nevertheless he set out to prove that humans are equal whether their skin be black or white, a daring task at a time when slavery was the order of the day.

On 8 November 1870, the battleship *Vitiaz* sailed from the Baltic port of Kronstadt, calling at Copenhagen, Madeira, Christmas Island, Tahiti, Samoa and New Ireland before dropping anchor in Astrolabe Bay on the north-eastern coast of New Guinea on 19 September 1871. The ship had been at sea 346 days. This was no mission of gunboat diplomacy, as the *Vitiaz* was on its way to the Russian ports in the Pacific and Maclay was hardly more than an eccentric hitchhiker. I admired that scene he describes, after landing on New Guinea's shore, when he found himself surrounded by tribal warriors but still refused to use firearms. He took his shoes off instead and went to sleep, which astounded the Papuans. That incident led to a new concept of human behaviour: no native would harm a white man unless provoked to do so.

On his travels in Africa, Livingstone held similar views but Livingstone travelled with God while Maclay did it alone. He was more interested in knowing what the black man's God was like and he found him to be a very passionate and humane God. The Papuans, who had never seen a white man before, thought he had arrived from the moon; *tamo*, moon man, they called him. On the other hand Maclay thought that to welcome a white-skinned stranger could turn out to be lethal. He expected that after him, other Europeans would come in great numbers and with guns take slaves and conquer the land.

After a long stay in New Guinea's jungle, Maclay went on to Sydney, sailing perhaps on the same ship carrying *kanaka* slaves to Australia. He hoped to organise a worldwide campaign to protect the native man in New Guinea and his environment. Maclay wrote to Queen Victoria, Bismarck of Germany and any other ruler or politician he could think of, soliciting help, but the help never came. Sydney was the most appropriate place to campaign from, for Maclay's appeal was inspired by conflict between whites and blacks in Australia. At that time, extinction of the Australian tribes was proceeding at an alarming rate while the politicians debated whether it would be more humane to speed up the process of extermination, thereby not subjecting the Aborigines to lengthy suffering. This theory became practice in Tasmania when a single campaign by white settlers and colonial authorities wiped out almost the entire Aboriginal population of the island.

Maclay was allowed to stay in Australia and carry on his campaign from Sydney just so long as he spoke only about Papuans and their fate. He made his stay in Australia more comfortable by marrying the widowed daughter of Sir John Robertson, a society lady. I wonder how he must have felt sharing a dinner table with colonial pundits who refused to implement the British Abolition of Slavery Act and instead supervised a most savage extinction campaign against the native population. He would have been far happier marrying a Papuan girl or perhaps sharing his bed with dingoes, as he was especially fond of them. The dingo is the prehistoric dog of Australia and presumably the only living ancestor of all the mongrels and pedigreed dogs known to the world now. There could be no greater reward for an ecologist than to have one of these prehistoric creatures lying on his bed and listening to its heart—the heart of the wilderness, so old and still alive.

To this day to my knowledge Maclay remains the only scientist who has carried out positive research on dingoes. After the European conquest of Australia the dingo suffered a similar fate to that of the tribal people with whom Maclay used to share a camp fire and keep warm at night; the animal was often the tribal totem. To the whites the dingo was vermin to be poisoned, shot at and trapped for two centuries; even nowadays the dingo is generally regarded as a pest and is condemned to extinction. There is a tale dating back to the last century in Sydney which Maclay must have heard when he was there, that the dingo had earned a bad name for stealing the governor's chickens. However, the tribal Aborigines, who did not steal and were robbed of their land, had received the same treatment.

Maclay left his papers and scientific findings to the Mitchell Library in Sydney; much had disappeared, especially the material relating to dingoes and Aborigines. He returned to Russia in 1882 disappointed that he had failed in his campaign to stop the white man destroying the world. The Russians gave him a hero's welcome and the Tsar of Russia undertook to publish his work. Maclay thought of it as being too little too late, for by then the Germans were already on the move to colonise New Guinea and the Aborigines of Australia were vanishing at an even greater rate than before. In his will Maclay asked that all his papers should be burnt; they burnt them.

His ideas survived and for more than a century were used by most European philosophers when writing about tribal society and culture. One can trace Maclay's influence from Marx to Malinowski and Margaret Mead. The scholars often recycle his ideas without even acknowledging him. The International Treaty for Antarctica is actually his concept at work, except that he originally envisaged such a treaty for New Guinea. His finding that tribal man is far happier, more politically independent and more economically secure in his bush environment, where he lives in harmony with nature, than when he is dependent on Western culture has been ignored by the rest of the world. In Australia for the last 200 years the white man has cleared most of the bush and exterminated many species, including many tribes, creating an ecological disaster by turning land into desert. The Aborigines lived on that same land for about 50 000 years and could have gone on living there indefinitely had the Europeans stayed away from their shores.

Here at Dingoes Den, there is a patch of rainforest miraculously saved from developers. The place is in Australia and far south of New Guinea, but ancient tall trees do not mind where they grow so long as man does not cut them down. There is a huge tree hollowed out by time out in the bush; it has survived more storms and bushfires than history has recorded. I call it Maclay Tree, for it looks like the one where he pitched his camp in New Guinea's jungle. Nearby flows a stream. The tree's shade falls on a rock on which there are grooves left behind from the time when tribal people lived here, camped under the tree and sharpened their stone implements on the boulder. On the ground nearby I found a stone axe and the tool looked similar to those that the Papuans used when Maclay visited them.

When he was in Australia over a century ago, Maclay held that in ancient times there must have been a land bridge between Australia and New Guinea over which tribal man travelled, presumably with his dingo. This idea was at the time ridiculed by British and Australian scholars, who declared that no man or dingo could have crossed the Arafura Sea on foot, especially Aborigines, who were regarded as subhuman. The British bent over backwards trying to convince the world that tribal man in Australia was a relative newcomer, though they gave no evidence whence he might have arrived. Then the Europeans learned more about the Ice Age, which caused the level of the sea to rise so that it flowed over the plain between Australia and New Guinea and turned it into the Arafura Sea. Along came the theory of the drifting of the continents. At last the world learned the truth of what Maclay had said about a century ago, that tribal man is a part of the environment: he is as old as the land around him and should not be destroyed just because the rest of the world knows so little about him.

My dingoes often run into the bush and hang around the ancient camp site at Maclay Tree. They climb the boulder and howl, perhaps trying to call back the old tribal master, or perhaps they simply lament for him and for much of the bush which has gone. Some years back a botanist came to see the timeless tree and thought it could be thousands of years predating Christ. He suggested that the tree be cut down so that the age could be evaluated: 'We'll keep the trunk in a museum with the plaque and the name.' I told him to go and never come back. Before he left Dingoes Den I asked him if he had ever heard of Maclay. The botanist misunderstood my pronunciation and thought the name might be that of the British intelligence officer McLean, and he left, intrigued as to why one would name a tree after a spy.

Maclay did not invent humanism but he was probably the first ecologist, which is equally important. Ahead of the time he lived in, he recognised that life on earth would survive only if humans learned to respect it. He tried to warn a world driven by greed that man is breaking the covenant by which humans and other species have co-existed through eons of time. It was not accidental that he became attracted to the dingo—the Aborigines were the best custodians of the natural environment the world had ever known and the dingo, their common totemic symbol, is a living example of that.

33 all about ania

Ania Walwicz

she's my girl alright who are you you anyway what what is she then is she
foreign the foreign body of mrozek the little first frost writes about
emigrants in a cell cellar in paris the emigrants of mrozek then the
foreign body in a system the virus she is so foreign but not to me is she
foreign then she is avant garde they don't have any like her here sorry so
sorry haven't got any like that so she's different not the same to be far
different and not the same to be foreign then to stand out bit she likes it
like that she's so foreign here she's going to geneva that's why they don't
have any like her here that's why she's not local foreign means opposite
to local then she's foreign she's just danger with a stranger then she's
foreign she's going away she won't be local and at home she won't be
just here and put stay put she wants to go elsewhere she wants to get big
and bigger a big star then she doesn't want to be miss merimbula she's
going to become miss world and miss universe and miss everywhere all
over the world she's miss universe now she's international book year
she's everywhere but not all over the place yet she's centre earth she's in
contrechamps and chicago that's foreign to you she's miss world and
miss universe and miss intergalactic she's madame pompadour too she's
pompadour pink specially made she's my buttercup she's emigre conrad
and emigre nabokov writing around the clear lake now she's all books
now and in every country so she's not foreign then she's at home in any
book then she's at home around the world she's in radio television too
you can see here she does her picture in my words who is ania she's just
a singer of words she's bella and teller she's my big star in her worlds
she's my special letter she's all rosy now she was born in paris then she
always travels she's on photocopier of baudrillard she's post modern
post magazine she's pix she's just here she'll be everywhere soon just you
wait she's taking over she's elegant and far flung she's a book queen and
a word princess call her your highness she's too good for just here she's
the best writer that's what i say i am writing her reviews she strings

222

words in my pearl necklace she puts roses in my vase she's little red riding hood in every fairytale she can talk to everybody here she writes a pantomime for my child she puts on big theatres in my head and i bow she's so extreme where there's no extreme she's just wagner on a high mountain singing with her big clear big resounding voice she's a diva she so exotic they don't know how to take her she's just beckett in clacton on sea she has to leave and wave a hanky she's beckette a beckette in the provinces she has to go further away she has to be all over she has to send and send she's miss international and universal and intergalactic fame that's how far she goes to my head i admire i bow i stoop i make a flourish with my feather hat i throw my coat for her to walk on i'm sir walter she's my queen i'm in awe she's french and polish and italian she speaks russian she translates she's universal she's astounding i egg her on and on she sends me lovely letters and drawings she tells me good stories and i love her

Notes

INTRODUCTION

1. The use of the term 'Anglo-Celtic' under no circumstances attempts to homogenise either Britain itself or Britain in relation to Ireland. It is an unsatisfactory term and is used here merely to indicate the cultural links of roughly two-thirds of non-Aboriginal Australians, those who derive from England and Ireland.

2. Note here the work of Deleuze and Guattari (1986) on 'minority literature' in relation to Kafka.

3. That the use of terms such as 'migrant', 'multicultural' and 'ethnic' to designate certain bodies of writing is propelled by a particular politics is discussed in Gunew, 'Denaturalizing Cultural Nationalisms: Multicultural Readings of "Australia" in Bhabha 1990.

4. A Collection of Multicultural Literature has been established as part of the Australian Literature collection at Deakin University. See also Gunew, S., Houbein, L., Karakostas-Seda, A., & Mahyuddin, J. (forthcoming), A Bibliography of Australian Multicultural Writers, Centre for Studies in Literary Education, Deakin University.

LINES OF COMMUNICATION: MEANING IN THE MIGRANT ENVIRONMENT

1. The haptic experience of architecture forms a major theme in Bloomer and Moore 1977. The phenomenological argument their thesis rests on and its spatial applications are more fully articulated in Merleau-Ponty 1962; Bachelard 1969; Heidegger 1971; Norberg-Schulz 1980.

2. The relationship between voice and architecture is neglected by phenomenologists. A classic consideration of the spatial origins of rhetorical practice is Yates 1966. A recent essay of interest is Caws 1989.

3. Interestingly, the pidgin form was soon taken up by advertising copywriters—the connection between the pidginisation of language and

the ubiquity of advertising jingles, with their substitution of phonetic for grammatical logic, would make for a fascinating study.

PMT (POSTMODERNIST TENSIONS): READING FOR (MULTI)CULTURAL DIFFERENCE

1. The study of English as an historical institution complicit with British imperialism has produced an avalanche of analyses in the past two years. See Baldick 1983; Batsleer et al 1988; Spivak 1987; Widdowson 1982; Bhabha 1990.

BEFORE THE MIGRANT WRITER: JUDAH WATEN AND THE SHAPING OF A LITERARY CAREER

1. A new edition of *Alien Son* (1952) was published in 1990 in Angus & Robertson's Inprint Classics series. This chapter is based in part on my introduction to that edition.

2. I thank Ivor Indyk for the point about the Palmers' cosmopolitanism. Vance Palmer's review of *Alien Son* makes the point about the assimilation of Waten's writings into a national project: '*Alien Son* is bound to have an effect as an inside picture of a foreign group gradually beginning to merge into the life of this country' (Palmer 1952: 25). This essay could be read as an extended unravelling of all that is implied in Palmer's statement—and an analysis of the ways in which Palmer has proved to be right.

3. Little more has been said since Vance Palmer's early review cited above. See for example Hadgraft 1960: 267; Ewers 1966: 170; Bennett 1979: 124; Mitchell 1981: 130.

4. I'm thinking, for example, of their account of Kafka's relation to Yiddish 'beside' his relation to German (Deleuze & Guattari 1986: 25).

5. From an interview on the television program 'Spectrum': 'Judah Waten on Commitment' (ABC-TV, December 1966, interviewer Tony Morphett). The comment recalls that by Abdul R. JanMohamed and David Lloyd responding to the minority literature argument of Deleuze and Guattari: 'the collective nature of *all* minority discourse also derives from the fact that minority individuals are always treated and forced to experience themselves generically' (JanMohamed & Lloyd 1987: 10).

MENA ABDULLAH, AUSTRALIAN WRITER

1. All references are to the 1974 edition.

2. This quotation and other information about Mena Abdullah's life and career quoted here are extracted from autobiographical notes compiled by her in 1988 at the request of the author.

THE JOURNEYS WITHIN: MIGRATION AND IDENTITY IN GREEK-AUSTRALIAN LITERATURE

1. In the sense with which Deleuze and Guattari characterise a minority literature—'the deterritorialisation of language, the connection of the individual to a political immediacy, and the collective assemblage of enunciation'. See *Kafka, Toward a Minor Literature* (1986), trans. Dana Polan, University of Minnesota Press, Minneapolis (p. 18). This schema is particularly applicable to the poetry of Π.O. and his complex 'utilisation' of languages demands further examination. See Π.O. (1989).

2. For a comparison between Antigone Kefala and two other Greek-Australian authors, Dimitris Tsaloumas and Dimitris Tzoumakas, which relates the sardonic and satiric modes in their tragicomic view for representing identity to the fragmentary and palimpsest-like manner in which a migrant makes 'contrapuntal' connections across time and space, see Papastergiadis (1987).

3. Bachelard warns against the decisiveness of linear thought as he challenges both the symmetry and the exclusiveness of such oppositions with the alternative image of the spiral, whose 'invertible dynamism' collapses the boundaries of inside/outside. With the image of the spiral, 'One no longer knows *right away* whether one is running toward the centre or escaping.' (Bachelard 1969:214).

4. (Kefala 1988:58). For a critique of the mode of oppositional thinking that denies the emotional overlap between various subjective states and which fails to juxtapose the multiple historical reference points in every cross-cultural encounter, and for a more detailed account of the relationship between the experience of displacement and the renewal of a critical perspective in Kefala's poetry, see Papastergiadis (1989).

SPEAK AS YOU EAT: READING MIGRANT WRITING, NATURALLY

1. Bakhtin's definition of authoritative discourse describes how privileged language demarcates itself as monologic, and as a prior, given authority that permits no sense of itself as other than complete. It is, as it were, a 'dead quotation, something that falls out of the artistic context . . .' (Bakhtin 1987:344).

2. It is worth quoting more of Trinh T. Minh-ha's argument here, since she raises some interesting issues in relation to how ideas of poetry's use, value and achievement are produced and consumed differently according to race, class and gender differences. Trinh notes that:

> Theorists tend to react strongly against poetry today because, for them, poetry is nothing else but a place where a subjectivity is constituted and where language is aestheticised (such as building vocabulary and rhyming beautiful lines). Whereas poetry is also the place from which many people of colour voice their struggle. Consider Cuban and African poetry, for example. And if you look into Asian, Hispanic, African and

native American literatures here in the U.S., poetry is no doubt the major voice of the poor and of people of colour. So poetical language does become stale and self-indulgent when it serves an art-for-art's sake purpose, but it can also be the site where language is at its most radical in its refusal to take itself for granted (Parmar 1990:69).

3. Bakhtin writes that by 'stripping all aspects of language of the intentions and accents of other people, destroying all traces of social heteroglossia and diversity of language—a tension-filled unity of language is achieved in the poetic work' (Bakhtin 1987:298). I do not agree with this monologic notion of poetry. Indeed, the concept of a 'tension-filled unity' recalls New Critical ideas of how poetry resolves differences and contradictions through ambiguity.

4. For a non-hierarchical view of language not dissimilar to that suggested by the image 'schizogenesis', see the article 'Rhizome' (Deleuze & Guattari 1981).

5. I wish to thank Laleen Jayamanne for her helpful comments on this point.

MIKLOUHO-MACLAY AND HIS DINGO

1. According to the *Australian Encyclopedia*, Nicolaus Miklouho-Maclay (1846–88) was a scientist, traveller and explorer who was born in Russia, the son of an engineer. He travelled widely and married an Australian in 1884. He died shortly after his return to Russia. Some of his papers are held at the Mitchell Library, Sydney.

Selected bibliography of multicultural writing

BIBLIOGRAPHIES

L. Bodi, Stephen Jeffries & Susan Radvansky *Image of a Continent: A Bibliography of German Australiana from the Beginnings to 1975* Harrasowitz, Wiesbaden, Germany, 1990

S. Gunew, L. Houbein, A. Karakostas-Seda & J. Mahyuddin (compilers) *Bibliography of Multicultural Writers* Centre for Studies in Literary Education, Deakin University (forthcoming).

Lolo Houbein *Ethnic Writings in English from Australia*, Adelaide ALS working Papers, Department of English, University of Adelaide, 1984 (3rd rev. and extended ed.) *The pioneering compilation currently being revised by S. Gunew et al.; see below.*

Alexandra Karakostas-Seda *Creative Writing in Languages Other than English in Australia 1945–1987: A Bibliography* Unpublished M.A. thesis. Monash University, 1988

Serge Liberman *A Bibliography of Australian Judaica* Mandelbaum Trust, University of Sydney, 1987

Peter Lumb and Anne Hazel (eds) *Diversity and Diversion: An Annotated Bibliography of Australian Ethnic Minority Literature* Hodja Educational Resources Co-operative Ltd, Richmond, Victoria, 1983 *Annotated guide for teachers.*

ANTHOLOGIES (GENERAL)

The following cover a range of writing and will give authors whose work may be followed up.

S. Gunew (ed.) *Displacements: Migrant Storytellers* Deakin University Press, Melbourne, 3217, 1982

S. Gunew (ed.) *Displacements II: Multicultural Storytellers* Deakin University Press, Melbourne, 1987

S. Gunew & J. Mahyuddin (eds) *Beyond the Echo: Multicultural Women's Writing* University of Queensland Press, St Lucia, 1988

R.F. Holt (ed.) *The Strength of Tradition: Stories of the Immigrant Presence in*

Australia University of Queensland Press, St Lucia, 1983

R. F. Holt (ed.) *Neighbours: Multicultural Writing in the 1980s* University of Queensland Press, St Lucia, 1991

M. Jurgensen (ed.) *Ethnic Australia* Phoenix Publications, Brisbane, 1981

M. Jurgensen & R. Adamson (eds) *Australian Writing 1988* Outrider/Penguin, Melbourne, 1988

M. Jurgensen (ed.) *Earth Wings: The 'Outrider' 91 Almanach* Phoenix Publications, Brisbane, 1991

J. Kable (ed.) *An Arc of Australian voices* Oxford University Press, Melbourne, 1990

P. Skrzynecki (ed.) *Joseph's Coat: An Anthology of Multicultural Writing* Hale & Iremonger, Sydney, 1985

SPECIALIST ANTHOLOGIES/ORAL HISTORY

D. Chub (ed.) *On The Fence: An Anthology of Ukrainian Prose in Australia* Lastivka Press, Melbourne, 1985

B. Cugliari & D. Bradshaw (eds) *The Word is Round: An Anthology by the Migrant Women Writers' Group* Migrant Women Writers' Group, Collingwood, Victoria, 1985

A. Dezsery (ed.) *The First Multilingual Anthology in English and Other Than English* Dezsery Ethnic Publications, Adelaide, 1979

Gael Hammer (ed.) *Pomegranates: a Century of Jewish Australian Writing* Millennium Books, Newtown, NSW, 1988

George Kanarakis (ed.) *Greek Voices in Australia* ANU Press, Sydney, 1988

Nancy Keesing (ed.) *Shalom: Australian Jewish Stories* Penguin, Ringwood, Victoria, 1983 (1978)

Multilingual Authors Association of South Australia *The First Step* Dezsery Ethnic Publications, Adelaide, 1982

G. Rando (ed.) *Italo-Australian Prose in the 80s* University of Wollongong, 1988

I. Skof et al. (eds) *Our Paths: Multilingual Collection of Poems, Prose and Drama,* Association of Yugoslav Writers in Australia & New Zealand, Melbourne, 1986

Thanasis Spilias & Stavros Messinis (eds) *Reflections: Selected Works from Greek Australian Literature* Elikia Books, Melbourne, 1988

JOURNALS

Directions Multicultural Arts Victoria

Migrant 7 PO Box 2430V, GPO Melbourne 3001

Outrider: A Journal of Multicultural Writing in Australia PO Box 210, Indooroopilly, Queensland 4068

Rainbow Rising Multicultural Writers Association of Victoria

SECONDARY SOURCES (SELECTED)

L. Bodi & S. Jeffries (eds) *The German Connection: Sesquicentenary Essays on German-Victorian Crosscurrents 1835–1985* Monash University, 1985 Collection of essays which deal with German-Australian cultural interactions.

Con Castan *Conflicts of Love* Phoenix Publications, Indooroopilly, 1986 *On the work of Vasso Kalamaris, the Greek poet and writer now living in Western Australia; also offers a more general account of Greek writing in Australia.*

Dimitris Tsaloumas: Poet Elikia Books, Melbourne, 1990

Jacques Delaruelle & Alexandra Karakostas-Seda (eds) *Writing in Multicultural Australia 1984: An Overview* Australia Council, for the Literature Board, Sydney, 1985 *Proceedings of two conferences held in Sydney and Melbourne; contains numerous papers with a variety of ethnic affiliations.*

S. Gunew 'Discourses of otherness: Migrants in literature' in *Prejudice in Print: The Treatment of Ethnic Minorities in Published Works* eds R. & H. Rasmussen, proceedings of 'Prejudice in Print' conference, Melbourne Centre for Migrant Studies, Monash University, 1982, pp.48–58

————'Migrant women writers: who's on whose margins?' in *Gender, Politics and Fiction* ed. C.Ferrier, University of Queensland Press, St Lucia, 1985, pp.163–178

————'Why and how multiculturalism should be included in the English curriculum' *English in Australia* no.82 (1987), pp.28–35

M. Jurgensen & A. Corkhill (eds) *The German Presence in Queensland Over the Last 150 Years* Department of German, University of Queensland, St Lucia, 1988 *Proceedings of a symposium.*

J. Kable 'A multicultural perspective to Australian literature' *English Teachers' (NSW) Newsletter* May 1983, pp. 7–8

————'The immigrant experience: learning English and Australian literature' *Australian Studies Bulletin* no. 3 (April), Deakin University, Melbourne, 1985, pp.21–24 *The writer is an experienced teacher who has experimented with using ethnic writing in the classroom.*

Rudi Krausman (ed.) *Literature* MATIA, Multicultural Arts Today in Australia series, Australia Council, 1987

A.M. Nisbet & M.Blackman (eds) *The French-Australian Connection University of NSW*, Sydney, 1984 *Papers from a symposium held on this topic.*

G. Rando (ed.) *Italian Writers in Australia: Essays and Texts* University of Wollongong, 1983 *Fascinating collection of critical essays and writings by Italo-Australians.*

Meryl Thompson 'Migrant as meaning-maker' Australian Studies in Language & Education monograph series. Curriculum Development Centre, Canberra, 1978 *Explores how diverse cultural backgrounds and languages affect the process of creating meanings.*

Italians in Australia and Australia's Italian Heritage, Vaccari Italian Historical Trust, Melbourne, 1987 *Proceedings of two conferences held in 1985 and 1986.*

Selected bibliography of Greek-Australian literature

Compiled by Con Castan

This is the first part of a bibliography I have prepared of Greek-Australian literature. I hope to publish the whole of it in the near future. The second part is a listing of those authors who have either published a book or been anthologised since 1970. There are more than a hundred of these and they are a very mixed group. All that they have in common is some degree of Greek descent and the fact that they have lived and published in Australia. Some are established authors in Australian literature, some are widely known as writers among the Greeks of Australia and some have received very little, if any, recognition anywhere. Some have a strong and continuing commitment to writing, and some are only peripherally involved.

The part published here is a listing of collections—bibliographies, anthologies, and literary and cultural journals—and of general studies, including those which deal with more than one author. It will give the reader or student access to some of the work of all the established writers and a large number of the others.

The titles of the items written in Greek have been transliterated. I have used a modified version of the table prepared for the Library of Congress. The modifications are the use of e for 'ita' and w for 'omega'.

BIBLIOGRAPHIES

Castan, Con 1988 'Secondary Sources for the Study of Greek Australian Literature' Spilias and Messinis (see below) 32–6. This is limited to (a) material in book form and (b) articles in literary or cultural periodicals. Book reviews are not included nor is any material from the general press. It contains items in both Greek and English.

Castan, Con 1988 'Theatrical, Cinematic, Television Material written by Greek Australians' *Australasian Drama Studies* 12/13: 26–33.

Karakostas, Alexander 1984 'Forty Years of Greek Writing in Australia, 1943–1983' *Outrider* 1.2: 138–48. It lists published volumes of poetry, prose fiction, and play scripts, and indicates the genre or genres in each volume. It is not complete but quite useful.

Bibliographical information will also be found in the introductions to each author in the anthologies *Reflections* and *Greek Voices* listed below.

ANTHOLOGIES

General

Bruns, A. and Jenkins, J. (eds) 1984 *Soft Lounges: An Anthology of New Writings from the Melbourne Fringe Arts Festival* Fringe Network: Melbourne. Includes small bilingual samples of work by George Michelakakis, Peter Lyssiotis, Dimitris Tzoumakas, George Vasilacopoulos, and Komninos Zervos.

Carroll, Margaret, and Gauntlett, Stathis, (eds) *Images of the Aegean* 2nd ed., U of New England: Armidale, n.d. This is an anthology of Modern Greek Poetry and it includes some work in Greek by Harkianakis, Kalamaras, Raftopulos, and Tsaloumas.

Couani, A. and Gunew, S. (eds) 1988 *Telling Ways: Australian Women's Experimental Writing*. Australian Feminist Studies: Adelaide. Includes some work by A. Couani and Thalia.

Goodwin, K., and Lawson, A., (eds) 1990 *The Macmillan Anthology of Australian Literature* Macmillan Co. of Australia: Melbourne. Small amounts of work by Couani, Kefala, Π.Ο., and Tsaloumas.

Hall, Rodney, (comp.) 1984 *The Collins Book of Australian Poetry* Fontana Australia: Sydney. Antigone Kefala and Dimitris Tsaloumas represented.

Rodriguez, Judith, (ed.) 1983 *Mrs Noah and the Minoan Queen* Sisters: Melbourne. Includes nine poems by Kefala.

Ethnic/Migrant/Multicultural

Gunew, Sneja, (ed.) 1987 *Displacements 2: Multicultural Storytellers* Deakin UP: Geelong. Includes work by A. Couani, Z. Giles, A. Kefala, A. Loukakis, G. Papaellinas, Π.Ο., D. Tsaloumas.

Gunew, Sneja, and Mahyuddin, Jan, (eds) 1988 *Beyond the Echo: Multicultural Womens' Writing* U of Qld Press: St Lucia. Includes work by A. Kefala, I. Vlachou, H. Massala, Thalia, Z. Giles, V., Kalamaras, and I. Krili-Kevans.

Holt, R.F. (ed.) 1983 *The Strength of Tradition: Stories of the Immigrant Presence in Australia* U of Qld Press: St Lucia. Includes work by V. Kalamaras, Z. Giles, N. Athanasou, and A. Loukakis.

Jurgensen, Manfred, (ed.) 1981 *Ethnic Australia* Phoenix Publications: Brisbane. Includes work by A. Kefala, E. Roumeliotakis, and A. Paradissis.

The Word is Round: An Anthology By the Migrant Women Writers' Group Melbourne, 1985. Significant bilingual samples of Dina Amanatidis, Joanna Nicolopoulou-Liakakou, Litsa Gogas.

Here We Are. An Anthology by the Migrant Women Writers' Group Melbourne, 1989. Roughly fifteen pages each of Amanatides, Gogas, and Demetra Koutoulis. The first two in English, the last in Greek and English.

Multilingual Authors Association of SA 1982 *The First Step* Dezsery Ethnic Publications: Adelaide. Includes four poems of T. Mazarakis in both Greek and English.

Skrzynecki, Peter, (ed.) 1985 *Joseph's Coat: An Anthology of Multicultural Writing* Hale & Iremonger: Sydney. Includes work by V. Kalamaras, A. Kefala, I. Krili-Kevans, A. Loukakis, D. Tsaloumas, and S. Zavos.

Greek–Australian

Emeis. Skorpies Elegeies gia Fovismenous Anthropous [We. Scattered Elegies for Frightened People] 1988 Themelio: Sydney. This contains the eleven prize-winning stories from a competition organised by a Sydney bookshop. The authors of the stories are Vasilis Pantzikas, Yuri Kovalenko, Yiannis Vasilakakos, Sophia Tsoutouras, Iakovos Gavriel, Kyriakos Kourasias, Nikos Piperis, Viki Doulabera, Dimitris Oikonomos, Tassos Nerantzis, D. Layiou-Panayiotopoulou.

Kanarakis, George, (ed.) 1985 *E: Logotechnike: Parousia Twn Elle:nwn Ste:n Australia* [The Literary Presence of the Greeks in Australia] Foundation for Modern Greek Studies: Athens

Kanarakis, George, (ed.) 1987 *Greek Voices in Australia. A Tradition of Prose Poetry and Drama* Australian National University Press: Sydney. There are some differences between these two, but the second esentially makes the first available to English readers. In each there is a Preface and an Introduction by the editor, followed by Part I 'Greek Language Literature' and Part II 'English Language Literature'. The material is arranged by authors in a historical sequence, and for each author there is a biographical, critical, and bibliographical introduction as well as a paragraph. In the first edition everything except the texts in Part II is in Greek; in the second all is in English. Eighty-two writers are represented, some of whom are dedicated authors who have produced a sizable body of work over a period of years, and some of whom have written (or orally composed) only very occasionally. The compiler states that the aim is 'to capture the collective face' of 'the literature of the Greeks in Australia' (1987, p.xix). In effect this has meant the representation of a large number of writers in small amounts.

Messinis, Stavros, (ed.) 1984 *Anthologia.Erga Elle:nwn Logotechnwn te:s Melbourne:s* [Anthology. Works of Six Melbourne Writers] Elikia Books: Melbourne. The writers are Iakovos Gavriel, Stavros Messinis, Ilias Mourakos, Katina Balouka, Michael Pais, and Thymios Haralampopoulos. Between six to twenty pages for each with a biographical note.

Spilias, Thanasis, and Messinis, Stavros, (eds) 1988 *Reflections. Selected Works from Greek Australian Literature* Elikia Books: Melbourne. The editors made the selection, wrote the Prologue and the notes that introduce the work of each of the thirteen authors represented. These are: A. Doukas, C. Malaxos-Alexander, V. Kalamaras, N. Ninolakis, A. Paradissis, J. Vasilakakos, A. Kefala, D. Tsaloumas, S. Harkianakis, Z. Giles, A. Loukakis, S. Zavos, G. Papaellinas. It also has an Introduction, 'Greek Australian Literature : an Essay', and a bibliography, 'Secondary Sources for the Study of Greek Australian Literature' (see above), both by Con Castan. The criteria for inclusion in this anthology were having published in book form (as some indication of a serious commitment to literature) and 'having attracted favourable criticism from authoritative critics in Australia or abroad'. All the texts are given in the first part of the book in English, regardless of the language of composition, and in Greek in the second part. In the English section each author receives from five to twelve pages, with a long story by Kalamaras boosting hers to 24.

JOURNALS DEVOTED TO GREEK-AUSTRALIAN CULTURE AND LITERATURE

Short works by many Greek-Australian writers will be found in these.

Antipodes Twice yearly, No 1 1974—25/26 1989

Chronico An Annual, Vol 1 1979—Vol 10 1988 (and following)

Epafe [Contact] Journal of the Modern Greek Students' Association University of Melbourne. Started in May 1978, continued to at least 1983.

Mozaic Published by Monash University Greek Club. I have only seen one issue, that of 1988.

To Giofyri [The Bridge] Journal of Modern Greek Students of Sydney. First appeared in 1978, seven issues being published to the end of 1980—1, 2, 3/4, 5, 6, 7/8, and 9. Issue 10 appeared in 1988.

GENERAL STUDIES AND STUDIES DEALING AT SOME LENGTH WITH MORE THAN ONE WRITER

Castan, Con 1983 'Greek Australian Literature' *AUMLA* 59: 5–25

————1986 *Conflicts of Love* Phoenix Publications: Brisbane, Part II. This section of the book has three chapters entitled 'Multiculturalism and Australian Literature', 'The Greeks in Australia', and 'Greek Literature in Austalia'. The last of these is a revised version of the AUMLA article.

————1986 'Ethnic Australian Writing. Is It Really Australian Literature?' *Outrider* 3.2: 64–79

————1987 'What is Greek Australian Literature?' *Chronico* 8/9: 4–12

————1988 'The Greeks and Australian Literature' *Afstraliotes Hellenes: Greeks in Australia* Karpadis, A. and A. Tamis, (eds) River Seine Press: Melbourne, 27–38

————Introduction, Greek-Australian Literature: an Essay, Spilias and Messinis (see above) 3–31

————1988 'Greek–Australian Plays' *Australasian Drama Review* 12/13: 17–33

————1988 'Greek Australian Literature: a Greek Way of Being Australian' *Anitpodes* (USA) 2.2: 95–97

Gunew, Sneja 1983 'Migrant Women Writers: Who's on Whose Margins?' *Meanjin* 42.1: 16–26. Also in Ferrier, C. (ed.) 1985 *Gender, Politics, and Fiction: Twentieth Century Women's Novels* University of Queensland Press: Brisbane, 163–78. Discusses Kefala, Giles and Couani among others.

Kanarakis, George 1980 'Research into the Greek Literature of Australia' *Chronico* 2:25–28 (Greek version), 28–30 (English version)

————1980 'E: Logotechnia tou Apode:mou Elle:nismou kai e: these: te:s sta Neoell:enika Grammata' [The Literature of the Overseas Greeks and Its Place in Modern Greek Letters] *Antipodes*, 12: 13–22

————Preface and Introduction, *Greek Voices in Australia* (see above), xvii–xxiii and 1–41. The original Greek versions will be found in *E Logotecnikhe: Parousia . . .* (see above)

————1987 'A Profile of the Literature of the Greeks in Australia', *Hermes* II.1: 89–94

————1989 'O Elle:nikos typos te:s Australias kai e: logotechnike: tou prosfora' [The Greek Press of Australia and its Literary Offering] *Antipodes* 25/26: 15-26

O *Krikos* [The Link] 79/80 (1957). This issue of the London-based magazine was devoted to the Greeks of Australia. While it contains no articles on Greek Australian Literature as such, the issue contains much material that is important for its study.

Krausmann, Rudi 1987 *M.A.T.I.A. Literature* Australia Council: Sydney. Contains pieces on Tzoumakas and Nomikos.

Michelakakis, George 1979 'De:me:tre:s Tsaloumas, S.S. Charkianakis, Stathis Raftopoulos. Apopseis gia to Ergo Tous' [Dimitris Tsaloumas, S.S. Harkianakis, Stathis Raftopoulos. Views on Their Work] *Chronico* 1: 43-49

————1980 'Gia to Theatro te:s Elle:nike:s Meionote:tas ste: Melbourne' [On the theatre of the Greek minority in Melbourne] *Chronico* 2: 62-64

————1981 'Gia to Elle:nofono tragoudi ste: Melbourne' [On the Greek Song in Melbourne] *Chronico* 3: 36-40

————1984 'The Cultural Structure of the Greek Minority in Australia' *Aspect* 29/30: 54-66. This goes beyond literature but has a section on it.

————'Literature and the Greek Migrants in Australia' *Writing in Multicultural Australia* Australia Council for the Literature Board: Sydney, 58-63

————1985 'Gia Ena Metanasteutiko Theatro' [For a migrant theatre] *Chronico* 4/5: 78-84

Papageorgopoulos, A. 1981 *The Greeks in Australia—a Home Away from Home* Alpha Books: Sydney. In both Greek and English. Background.

Papastergiadis, N. 1986 'Culture Self and Plurality' *Arena* 76: 49-61 (D. Tzoumakas, A. Kefala.)

————1987 'A Vision Revised. The Question of Identity, History and Language in the Writings of Kefala, Tsaloumas and Tzoumakas' *Chronico* 8-9: 13-26.

Vondra, Joseph 1979 *Hellas Australia* Widescope: Melbourne. Useful for background study. Greek–Australian literature is also discussed on pp. 105-20.

Waten, J. 1980 'Writers from Two Cultures' *Aspect* 5.1/2: 49-55 (Doukas and Kefala.)

Webby, E. 1983 'Short Fiction in the Eighties: White Anglo-Celtic Male No More?' *Meanjin* 42.1: 34-41. Discusses, among others, Loukakis and Zavos.

Wilton, J. 1985 'From 'Culotta' to Castro: The Migrant Presence in Australian Writing' *Writing in Multicultural Australia* The Australia Council: Sydney, 24-33. Includes discussion of Loukakis and Kalamaras.

Selected bibliography of Italo-Australian literature

Compiled by G. Rando

This bibliography is in two parts. Part One contains a selection of literary and paraliterary works written by Italian immigrants and visitors to Australia. Part Two contains a selection of criticism written on this topic as well as one general work on Italians in Australia. Items mentioned in the body of the chapter may be found in the appropriate part of the bibliography.

PART 1

Abiuso, J. (1984) *The Male Model and Other Stories* Adelaide: Dezsery Ethnic Publications. Collection of short stories, most set in Australia, some in Italy. Contains long short 'Diary of an Italo-Australian schoolboy' which is claimed to have served as a substantial source for the film 'Moving Out'.

Andreoni, G. (1982) *L'Italo-australiano come linguaggio letterario un racconto documento* [Quaderni del Veltro 19] Rome: Il Veltro Editrice. Contains short novel 'Cenere' which presents themes on multiculturalism and Italo–Australian identity.

Basili, S. (1982) *Would I say Hello* Sydney: Oleander Press. Poetry.

Bonutto, O. (1963) *A Migrant's story* Brisbane: H. Pole and Co. Memoirs.

Borghese, V. (1984) *La moneta e altri racconti* Melbourne: The Author. Short stories.

Bosi, P. (1971) *Australia cane* Sydney: Kurunda. Novel about experiences of an Italian migrant's first years in Australia in the 1950s.

———(1972) *Farewell Australia* Sydney: Kurunda. Critique of Australian society in the 1960s.

———(1973) *The Checkmate and other stories* Sydney: Kurunda. Collection of short stories set in various Australian ethnic communities.

———(1973) *I'll say good morning* Sydney: Kurunda. Poetry.

———(1986) *Who is afraid of the ethnic wolf?* Sydney: Kurunda. Critique of Australian society in the 1980s with special reference to multiculturalism and to various controversial issues relating to the SBS.

Cappiello, R.R. (1984) *Oh Lucky country* (Translated with an introduction by

Gaetano Rando) St Lucia: University of Queensland Press [Translation of Cappiello, Rosa R. (1981)] *Paese fortunato* Milan: Feltrinellis. Novel about the experiences of a single woman migrant worker in the 1970s.

Carboni, R. (1855) *The Eureka Stockade: The Consequence of some Pirates wanting on Quarterdeck a Rebellion* Melbourne: J.P. Atkinson & Co. Chronicle of the 1854 Eureka uprising.

——(1861) *La Santola* Turin: Derossi & Dusso. Melodrama.

——(1867) *Schiantapalmi* Naples: Gargiulio. Melodrama.

Cerquetti, W. and Phillips, G. (1987) *Australia e Umbria dorate e verdi* Perugia: Casa Editrice Sigla 3. Poetry—some poems in English, some in Italian.

Cincotta, V. (ed.) (1989) *Italo-Australian Poetry in the 80s* Department of Languages, University of Wollongong. Poetry anthology.

Cipolla, A. (1928) *Il mio viaggio in Oceania, Australia a Insulindia* Milan: Agnelli. Account of the author's travels in Australia in the 1920s.

Concas, L. (1977) *Ballata di Vento* Rome: Gabrieli. Poetry.

——(1988) *L'altro uomo Poesie 1981–1983* Gorie [BG]: Editrice Velar. Poetry.

Coreno, M. (1980) *Yellow Sun* Sydney: Saturday Centre. Poetry.

D'Aprano, C. (1986) *Old wine in new bottles* Melbourne: Winseray Pty Ltd. Short stories.

de Amezaga, C. (1885–86) *Viaggio di Circumnavigazione della Regia Corvetta 'Caracciolo' negli anni 1881–82–83–84* Rome: Forzani e Comp., Tipografici del Senato. Contains section on Australia in vol. 1 pp. 162–89.

De Scalzo, G. (1938) *La Terra dei fossili viventi* Milan: Ceschina. Account of author's travels in Australia in the 1930s.

Di Stefano, E. (1978) *Voci di lontananza* Sydney: Southern Cross Press. Poetry.

——(1988) *Se rimmarrà qualcosa,* Sydney: Southern Cross Press. Poetry.

Ercole, V. (1932) *No Escape* London: Butterworth. Novel about settlement and assimilation of an Italian doctor at the turn of the century.

Fazzolari, L. (ed.) (1985) *Visioni di donne. An anthology of Italo-Australian women* Richmond (Vic): CHOMI. Poetry.

Gagliardi, F. (1881) *Australia: lettere alla Gazzetta d'Italia* Florence: Tipografia Editrice della Gazzetta d'Italia. Account of Australia and Australian society in the 1870s.

Giliberto, G. (1939) *Raggi d'Idealismo (Poesie, poemetti e dramma)* Sydney: Tip. Tomalin. Poetry and short play.

Kahan-Guidi, A.M. and Weiss, E. (eds) (1989) *Give me strength: Forza e coraggio* Sydney: Women's Redress Press Inc. Accounts of post-1945 Italian migrant womens' experiences. Bilingual English/Italian texts.

Loh, M. (1980) *With courage in their cases* Melbourne: Filef. Oral histories of post-1945 Italian migrant worker experiences.

Luciano, G. (1959) *Italians as they are (Gli Italiani come sono)* Sydney: The Italian Press Pty Ltd. Memoirs. Bilingual English/Italian text.

Maione, O. (1979) *Bitch* Melbourne: Tusculum. Play. Bilingual English/Italian text.

Morrison, R.H. (1976) *Australia's Italian poets* Adelaide: Andor. Poetry anthology.

Nibbi, G. (1937) *Il Volto degli emigranti (scene di vita in Australia)* Florence: Parenti Short stories and memoirs.

——(1965) *Cocktails d'Australia* Milan: Martello. Short stories and memoirs.

Penninger, H.R. (1976) *Mary my hun. A novel with a purpose* Campsie (NSW): The Author. Novel.

Petrolo, R. (1986) *The Shadows of the Mystery* Warrawong (NSW): The Author. Poetry.

Pinelli, D.G. (1971) *Songs of love—Canti d'amore* Perth: Eco Printing Co. Poetry.

——(1971) *Wise thoughts of a 'mad' man—Pensieri saggi d'un pazzo* Perth: Eco Printing Co. Poetry.

Rando, G. (ed.) (1988) *Italo-Australian prose in the 80s* Department of Languages, University of Wollongong. Anthology. Bilingual Italian/English texts.

Sanciolo, N. (1983) *La Passione di Gesù Cristo (Tragedia sacra in versi su temi d'antichi motivi pololari siciliani)* Melbourne: The Author. Trilingual play.

Stormon, E.J. (1977) *The Salvado Memoirs* Perth: University of Western Australia Press. Translation of Salvado, Rudesindo (1851) *Memorie Storiche dell'Australia particolarmente della Missione Benedettina di Nuova Norcia e degli usi e costumi degli Australiani* Rome: Propaganda Fide.

Strano, A. (1986) *Luck without Joy. A Portrayal of a Migrant* (translated by Elizabeth P. Burrows) Fremantle (WA): Fremantle Arts Centre Press. Biography.

Strano, L. (1964) *Inquietudine* Sydney: Tip. Ital-Print. Poetry.

——(1970) *Mostratemi la via di gire al monte* Auckland: The University. Poetry.

——(1984) *Di qui ci son passato anch'io* Mt Wilson NSW: The Author. Poetry.

——(1986) *Fifty Years ago* Fairfield (NSW): W.R. Bright & Sons. Poetry.

Triaca, M. (1985) *Amelia: a long journey* Richmond (Vic.): Greenhouse Publications. Memoirs.

Ursino, F. (1980) *Where Two Extremes Meet* Panania (NSW), The Author.

Valli, M. (1972) *Poesie australiane: Australian poems* St Lucia: University of Queensland Press. Poetry. Bilingual Italian/English texts.

PART 2

Arrighi, M. (ed.) (1991) *Italians in Australia. The Literary Experience* Department of Languages, University of Wollongong. Contains essays and an anthology of Italo-Australian prose.

Gunew, S. 'Rosa Cappiello's "Oh Lucky Country": Multicultural Reading Strategies' *Meanjin*, 44(4), December 1985, 517–528

Jurgensen, M. 'Oh Lucky Country, Rosa R. Cappiello' *Outrider*, 2(1), June 1985, 243–6

Mitchell, T. 'Italo-Australian theatre: multiculturalism and neo-colonialism' *Australian Drama Studies*, 10 (April 1987), 31–48 and 11 (October 1987), 37–46

O'Grady, D. 'Sincerely—Gino Nibbi' *Overland*, 111 (June 1988) 2–8

Rando, G. (ed.) (1983) *Italian writers in Australia: essays and texts* Department of European Languages, University of Wollongong

——'Italo-Australian fiction' *Meanjin*, 43(3), September 1984, 341–9

——'Caste and cultural identity: the prose fiction of Pino Bosi' *Outrider*, 4:1 (June 1987), 75–84

——'Notes on the writings of Giuseppe Abiuso' *Outrider*, 4:2 (December 1987), 117–24

Serle, G. 'Introduction' in Raffaello Carboni (1975) *The Eureka Stockade* Melbourne: Melbourne University Press

Ware, H. (1981) *A Profile of the Italian community in Australia* Melbourne: AIMA/CO.AS.IT.

List of references

Abdullah, M. and Mathew, R. 1974 *The Time of the Peacock* Angus & Robertson, Sydney

Abiuso, J. 1984 *The Male Model and Other Stories* Dezsery Ethnic Publications, Adelaide

A.C.R. 1974 *Atlanta /** [Slash Asterisk] Press, Fitzroy

Adorno, T.W. and Horkheimer, M. 1971 *Dialektik der Aufklärung* Suhrkamp, Frankfurt

Anderson, B. 1983 *Imagined Communities* Verso, London

Andreoni, G. 1982 *L'Italo-australiano come linguaggio letterario: un racconto documento* Quaderni del Veltro 19, Il Veltro Editrice,Rome

Anggraeni, D. 1987 *The Root of all Evil* Indra Publishing, Victoria

———1988 *Parallel Forces* Indra Publishing, Victoria

Arthur, K.O. 1988 'Twice removed: Aboriginal and immigrant writing in Australia' in *A Sense of Exile: Essays in the Literature of the Asia-Pacific Region*, ed. Bruce Bennett, University of Western Australia Centre for Studies in Australian Literature, Perth, pp. 119–29

Aslanides, T. 1978 *The Creek Connection*, T. Aslanides, Canberra

———1979 *Passacaglia and Fugue* T. Aslanides, Canberra

———1984 *One Hundred Riddles* Angus & Robertson, Sydney

———1990 *Australian Things* Penguin Australia, Ringwood, Victoria

Assad, T. 1986 'The concept of cultural translation in British social anthropology' in *Writing Culture: The Poetics and Politics of Ethnography* eds J. Clifford et al., University of California Press, Berkeley

Bachelard, G. 1964 *The Psychoanalysis of Fire* Routledge, London

———1969 *The Poetics of Space* trans. Maria Jolas, Beacon Press, Boston

Bachman, I. 1961 *Anrufung des grossen Bären* Piper, Munich

Baggio, R.A. 1989 *The Shoe in my Cheese* R.A. Baggio, Melbourne

Baker, C. 1986 *Yacker* Pan/Picador, Sydney

———1987 *Yacker 2* Pan/Picador, Sydney

———1989 *Yacker 3* Pan/Picador, Sydney

Bakhtin, M.M. 1987 *The Dialogic Imagination: Four Essays* ed. M. Holquist, University of Texas Press, Austin

Baldick, C. 1983 *The Social Mission of English Criticism 1848–1932* Clarendon Press, Oxford

Barthes, R. 1974 *S/Z* Hill & Wang, New York

Basili, S. 1982 *Would I Say Hello* Oleander Press, Sydney

Batsleer, J. et al. 1988 *Rewriting English: Cultural Politics of Gender and Class* Methuen, London

Baudrillard, J. 1984 'The precession of simulacra' in *Art after Modernism* ed. B. Wallis, New Museum of Contemporary Art, New York, pp.253–81

———1988 *America* Verso, London

Beckett, S. 1965 *The Unnamable* in *Three Novels* Grove Press Inc., New York

Benjamin, W. 1985 *One Way Street* trans. E. Jephrott & K. Shorter, Verso, London

Bennett, B. 1979 in *The Literature of Western Australia* ed. B. Bennett, University of Western Australia Press, Nedlands

———1988 'Perceptions of Australia 1965–1988' in *New Literary History of Australia* ed. L. Hergenhan, Penguin Australia, Ringwood Victoria

Berger, J. 1984 *And Our Faces My Heart, As Brief As Photos* Writers & Readers, London

———1985 *The White Bird : Writings by John Berger*, edited with an introduction by L. Spencer Chatto and Windus, London

Bhabha, H. 1984 'Representation and the colonial text: A critical exploration of some forms of mimeticism' in *The Theory of Reading* ed. F. Gloversmith, Harvester, Sussex, pp.93–122

———1987 'Interrogating identity' in *Identity* ed. L. Appignanesi, ICA Documents no. 6, ICA London

———1988 'The commitment to theory' *New Formations* Vol. 5, Spring

———(ed.) 1990 *Nations and Narration* Routledge, London

Bloomer, K.C. and Moore, C.W. 1977 *Body, Memory and Architecture* Yale University Press, New Haven

Bonutto, O. 1963 *A Migrant's Story* H. Pole & Co, Brisbane

Bosi, P. 1971 *Australia Cane* Kurunda, Sydney

———1972 *Farewell Australia* Kurunda, Sydney

———1973 *I'll Say Good Morning* Kurunda, Sydney

———1973 *The Checkmate and Other Stories* Kurunda, Sydney

———1986 *Who is Afraid of the Ethnic Wolf?* Kurunda, Sydney

Bourdieu, P. 1987 *Outline of a Theory or Practice* Cambridge University Press, Cambridge

Brett, J. 1985 'The process of becoming' *Meanjin* vol.44, no.1

Brook, P. 1988 *The Mahabharata* trans. from the French translation by Jean-Claude Carriere, Methuen, London

Brooker, P. and Widdowson, P. 1986 'A literature for England' in *Englishness: Politics and Culture 1880–1920* eds R. Collis & P. Dodd, Croom Helm, London, pp.116–63

Cameron, D. 1985 *Feminism and Linguistics* St Martins Press, New York

Cappiello, R.R. 1984 *Oh Lucky Country* trans. Gaetano Rando from *Paese Fortunato* (1981) University of Queensland Press, Brisbane

Carboni, R. 1855 *The Eureka Stockade: The Consequences of Some Pirates Wanting on Quarterdeck a Rebellion* J.P. Atkinson & Co, Melbourne

———1861 *La Santola* Derossi & Dusso, Turin

——1987 *Schiantapalmi* Gargiulio, Naples

Carsaniga, G. 1986 'Varieties of national identity' *Arena* no.74

Carter, D. 1990 'Introduction' in *Alien Son* by J. Waten, Angus & Robertson, Sydney

Carter, P. 1987 *The Road to Botany Bay* Faber, London

Castan, C. 1983 'Greek- Australian literature', AUMLA no.59, pp.5–25

——1984 'Antigone Kefala' *Outrider* vol.1, no.2

——1985 'Form, Place and Structure in a Poem by Dimitris Tsaloumas' *Outrider* vol.2, no.2

——1986 *Conflicts of Love* Phoenix Publications, Brisbane

——1986a 'Ethnic Australian Writing. Is It Really Australian Literature?' *Outrider* vol.3, no.2

——[1987] 'What is Greek-Australian literature?' *Chroniko* 8/9

——1988 'Greece and the Greeks and Australian Literature' in *Greeks in Australia* eds A. Karpadis and T. Tamis, River Seine Press, Melbourne, pp.26–40

Castro, B. 1984 'Bridging cultural concepts' in *Writing in Multicultural Australia* Australia Council, Sydney

Cavafy, C. 1978 *Collected Poems* trans. Edmund Keeley & Philip Sherrard, Chatto & Windus, London

Caws, M.A. 1989, 'Architecture and conversation' in *The Art of Interference* Polity Press, Cambridge UK

Cerquetti, W. and Phillips, G. 1987 *Australia e Umbria dorate e verdi* Casa Editrice Sigla 3, Perugia

Cipolla, A. 1928 *Il mio Viaggio on Oceania, Australia a Insulindia* Agnelli, Milan

Clifford, J. 1986 'Introduction: Partial truths' in *Writing Culture: The Poetics and Politics of Ethnography* eds J. Clifford et al., University of California Press, Berkeley

——1989 'The others: Beyond the "salvage" paradigm' *Third Text* vol. 6 Spring

Clift, C. 1987 *Peel Me a Lotus* Fontana, Sydney (original publication 1959)

Clunies Ross, B. 1988 'Australian literature and Australian culture' in *New Literary History of Australia* Penguin Books, Ringwood Victoria

Concas, L. 1977 *Ballata di Vento* Gabrieli, Rome

——1988 *L'altro uomo Poesie 1981–1983* Editrice Velar, Gorie (BG)

Coreno, M. 1980 *Yellow Sun* Saturday Centre, Sydney

Couani, A. 1988 *Teacher Attitudes to Arabic-Speaking Students* Sea Cruise Books, Sydney

——1989 *A Genre-Based Approach to Writing Reports in Art for High School ESL Students* Sea Cruise Books, Sydney

Couani, A. and Lyssiotis, P. 1989 'Through Your Eyes' in *The Harbour Breathes* Sea Cruise Books, Sydney

Coveney, L. et al. (eds) 1984 *The Sexuality Papers: Male Sexuality and the Social Control of Women* Hutchinson, London

D'Aprano, C. 1986 *Old Wine in New Bottles* Winseray Pty Ltd, Melbourne

Daniel, H. 1988 *Liars. Australian New Novelists* Penguin Australia, Ringwood Victoria

Daniels, K., Bennett, B.H. and McQueen, H. 1987 *Windows onto Worlds: Studying Australia at the Tertiary Level* AGPS Press, Canberra

Davis, J. 1978 *Jagardoo* Methuen, Sydney

————1983 *The First-born and Other Poems* J.M. Dent, Melbourne

Daws, G. 1980 *A Dream of Islands* Jacaranda Press, Sydney

de Amezaga, C. 1885–86 *Viaggio di Circumnavigazione della Regia Corvetta 'Caracciolo' negli Anni 1881–82–83–84* Rome

De Scalzo, G. 1938 *La Terra di Fossili Viventi* Ceschina, Milan

Deszéry, A. (ed.) 1979 *English and Other Than English Anthology* Dezsery Ethnic Publications, Adelaide

Delaruelle J. and Karakostas-Seda (eds) 1985 *Writing in Multicultural Australia* Australia Council, Sydney

Davy, R. 1985 *Kenzo: A Tokyo Story* Penguin, Ringwood, Victoria

Deleuze, G. and Guattari, F. 1977 *Anti-Oedipus: Capitalism and Schizophrenia* Athlone Press, London

————1981 'Rhizome' *Ideology and consciousness* Spring, pp. 49–71

————1986 *Kafka: Toward a Minor Literature* trans. Dana Polan, University of Minnesota Press, Minneapolis

————1987 *A Thousand Plateaus* Athlone Press, London

Dimock, E. et al. (eds) 1974 *The Literature of India* University of Chicago Press, Chicago

Dirlik, A. 1987 'Culturalism as hegemonic ideology and liberating practice' *Cultural Critique* 6

Di Stefano, G. 1985 *Voci di Lontananza* Southern Cross Press, Sydney

————1988 *Se rimarrà qualcosa* Southern Cross Press, Sydney

Dodd, P. 1986 'Englishness and the national culture' in *Englishness: Politics and Culture 1880–1920* eds R. Collis & P. Dodd, Croom Helm, London

During, S. 1988 'Postmodernism or post-Colonialism today' in *Postmodern Conditions* eds A. Milner et al., Centre for General & Comparative Literature, Monash University, Melbourne

Dutton, G. 1985 *The Australian Collection: Australia's Greatest Books* Angus & Robertson, Sydney

Eagleton, T. 1987 'The End of English,' *Textual Practice* Spring, pp.1–9

Easthope, A. 1983 *Poetry as Discourse* Methuen, London

English, D. 1982 'Patrick White's Greek alter ego' (unpub.) lecture given at the University of Pisa

Ercole, V. 1932 *No Escape* Butterworth, London

Ewers, J.K. 1966 *Creative Writing in Australia* Georgian House, Melbourne

Fazzolari, L. ed. 1985 *Visioni di Donne: An Anthology of Italo-Australian Women* CHOMI, Richmond Victoria

Fischer, M. 1986 'Ethnicity and the post-modern arts of memory' in Clifford et al. (1986)

Flower, C. 1975 *The Antipodes Observed: Prints and Printmakers of Australia 1788–1850* Macmillan, Melbourne

Foster, H. 1984 'Re:Post' in *Art after Modernism* ed B. Wallis, New Museum of Contemporary Art, New York

Forster, G. 1986 *Georg Forsters Werke. Sämtliche Schriften, Tagebücher, Briefe* vol. 1 *A Voyage Round the World*, ed. R. Kahn, Akademie der Wissenschaften der DDR, Akademie-Verlag, Berlin

Foucault, M. 1986 *The Archaeology of Knowledge* Tavistock, London

Gadamer, H.G. 1975 *Truth and Method* Seabury, New York

————1976 'On the problem of self-understanding' in *Philosophical Hermeneutics* University of California, Berkeley

Gagliardi, F. 1881 *Australia: Lettere alla Gazzetta d'Italia* Tipografia Editrice della Gazzetta d'Italia, Florence

Gardner, S. 1983 *With Open Eyes* Queensland Community Press, Brisbane

Gates Jr, H.L. 1987 'Authority, (white) power and the (black) critic: Or, it's all Greek to me' *Cultural Critique* 7

Gilbert K. (ed.) 1988 *Inside Black Australia* Penguin Books, Ringwood

Giliberto, G. 1939 *Raggi d'Idealismo (Poesie, Poemetti e Dramma)* Tip. Tomalin, Sydney

Goodwin, K. 1986 *History of Australian Literature* St Martin's Press, New York

Goodwin, K. and Lawson, A. (eds) 1990 *An Anthology of Australian Literature* Macmillan, Sydney

Govinda, L.A. 1970 *The Way of the White Clouds* Shambala, Boston

Green, H.W. (ed.) 1985 *A History of Australian Literature, Pure and Applied* revised Green, D. vol.2, Angus & Robertson, Sydney

Grivas, A. 1957 'O Ellinikos typos stin Australia ke i apostoli tou' (The Greek press in Australia and its mission) *Krikos* no.79/80, pp.77–8

Guattari, F. 1984 *Molecular Revolution: Psychiatry and Politics* Penguin Books, Harmondsworth

Gunew, S. and Mahyuddin, J. (eds) 1988 *Beyond the Echo: Multicultural Women's Writing* University of Queensland Press, St Lucia

Gunew, S. 1985 'Framing marginality: Distinguishing the textual politics of the marginal voice' *Southern Review* vol.18, no.2, July, pp.142–57

————1985a 'Rosa Cappiello's "Oh Lucky Country": Multicultural reading strategies' *Meanjin* vol.44, no.4, December, pp.517–28

————1986 'Ania Walwicz and Antigone Kefala: Varieties of migrant dreaming' *Arena* no.76

————1987 'Culture, gender and the author function: Wongar's "Walg" ' *Southern Review* vol.20, no.3, pp.161–70

————1988 'Beyond the echo' in *Displaced Persons* eds K.H. Petersen & A. Rutherford, Dangaroo Press, Sydney

————1988a 'Letter' *Australian Book Review* December, pp.3–4

————1988b 'Home and away: Nostalgia in Australian (migrant) writing' in *Island in the Stream* ed. P. Foss, Pluto Press, Sydney, pp.35–46

————1989 'Authenticity and the writing cure' in *Grafts* ed S. Sheridan, Verso, London

————1990 'PostModern tensions: Reading for (multi)cultural difference' *Meanjin* vol.49, no.1, Autumn, pp.21–33

————1990a 'Denaturalizing cultural nationalisms: Multicultural readings of "Australia" ' in Bhabha (1990)

Hadgraft, C. 1960 *Australian Literature: A Critical Account to 1955* Heinemann, London

Hall, S. 1987 'Minimal selves' *Identity* ed. L. Appignanesi, ICA Documents no. 6, ICA London

Harris, A. (pseud. 'The Emigrant Mechanic') 1964 *Settlers and Convicts* Melbourne University Press, Melbourne

Hartsock, N. 1987 'Rethinking modernism: Minority vs majority theories' *Cultural Critique* 7

Heidegger, M. 1971 *Poetry, Language and Thought* trans. A. Hofstadter, Harper & Row, New York

Hergenhan, L. (ed.) 1988 *New Literary History of Australia* Penguin Australia, Ringwood Victoria

Hobsbawm, E. 1983 'Introduction: Inventing traditions' *The Invention of Tradition* Cambridge University Press, Cambridge, pp.1–14

Houbein, L. 1984 (3rd. rev. edn) *Ethnic Writings in English from Australia* ALS Working Papers, Department of English, University of Adelaide, Adelaide

Howitt, W. 1972 *Land, Labour and Gold* Sydney University Press, Sydney

Hutcheon, L. 1988 *A Poetics of Postmodernism: History, Theory, Fiction* Routledge, London

Ingamells, R. 1951 *The Great South Land* Georgian House, Melbourne

Inglis, A. 1988 'The singular voice' *Australian Book Review* November, pp.32–4

Jameson, F. 1983 'Postmodernism and the consumer society' in *Postmodern Culture* ed. H. Foster, Pluto Press, London, pp.111–25

JanMohammed, A.R. and Lloyd, D. 1987 'Introduction: Minority discourse —what is to be done?' *Cultural Critique* vol.7, Spring

Johnston, G. 1970 *Clean Straw for Nothing* World Books, Sydney

Johnston, M. 1973 *Ithaki* Island Press, Sydney

Jubilee History of Brunswick and Coburg 1907, Government Printer, Coburg

Jupp, J. (ed.) 1988 *The Australian People: An Encyclopaedia of the Nation, its People and their Origins* Angus & Robertson, Sydney

Jurgensen, M. ' "Oh Lucky Country", Rosa R. Cappiello' *Outrider* vol.2, no.1, June 1985, pp.243–6

Kahan-Guidi, A.M. and Weiss, E. (eds) 1989 *Give Me Strength: Forza e Corragio* (In English and Italian) Women's Redress Press, Sydney

Kalamaras, V. 1989 *The Same Light* Fremantle Arts Centre Press, Fremantle

Kanarakis, G. 1985 *The Literary Presence of Greeks in Australia* Foundation for Modern Greek Studies, Athens

——(ed.) 1988 *Greek Voices in Australia: A Tradition of Prose, Poetry and Drama* Australian National University Press, Canberra

Kapardis, A. and Tamis, A. (eds) 1988 *Greeks in Australia* River Seine Press, Melbourne

Kaplan, C. 1987 'Deterritorializations: The rewriting of home and exile in Western feminist discourse' *Cultural Critique* 6

Karakostas-Seda, A. (unpub.) Creative writing in languages other than English in Australia 1945–87: A bibliography, M.A. thesis, Monash University

Kastamonitis, S. 1987 *The Endless Journey* ed. M. Sophocleous, Elikia Books, Melbourne

Kefala, A. 1975 *The First Journey* Wild & Woolley, Sydney

——1984 *The Island* Hale & Iremonger, Sydney

——1988 *European Notebook* Hale & Iremonger, Sydney

——1988a 'Towards a language' in *Displaced Persons* eds K.H. Petersen & A. Rutherford, Dangaroo Press, Sydney

Kermode, F. 1988 'Canon and period' in *History and Value* Clarendon, Oxford

Kippax, H.G. 1965 'Drama' in *Australian Society, a Sociological Introduction* eds A.F. Davies & S. Encel, Cheshire, Melbourne

Kramer, L. (ed.) 1981 *Oxford History of Australian Literature* Oxford University Press, London

Krauss, W. 1979 *Zur Anthropologie des 18 Jahrhunderts: die Frühgeschichte der Menschheit im Blickpundkt der Aufklährung* eds H. Kortüm & C. Gohrisch, Hanser, Munich

Kress, G. 1985 *Linguistic Processes in Sociocultural Practices* Deakin University Press, Burwood Victoria

Lambasdaridou, E. 1986 Patrick White, magna mater, and her son lover, Thesis, University of Athens, UMI order no. DA 8626715

Lepenies, W. 1976 *Das Ende der Naturgeschichte. Wandel kultureller Selbstverständlichkeiten in den Wissenschaften de 18 und 19 Jahrhunderts,* Hanser, Munich

Lewitt, M. 1985 'Rights and problems of a writer' in *Writing in Multicultural Australia* Australia Council, Sydney

Lloyd. D. 1987 'Genet's genealogy: European minorities and the ends of the canon' *Cultural Critique* 6

Loh, M. 1980 *With Courage in their Cases* Filef, Melbourne

Loukakis, A. 1983 'A National Literature', *The Bulletin Literary Supplement* ed. G. Dutton, July 5, p.139

Luciano, G. 1959 *Italians As they Are: Gli Italiani come sono* (in English and Italian) Italian Press, Sydney

Lurie, M. 1978 *Flying Home* Outback Press, Melbourne

McKie, R. 1974 *The Mango Tree* William Collins, Sydney

Maione, O. 1979 *Bitch* (play, in English and Italian) Tusculum, Melbourne

Malouf, D. 1978 *An Imaginary Life* Picador, London

Merleau-Ponty, M. 1962 *The Phenomenology of Perception* trans. C. Smith, Routledge, London

Mitchell, A. 1981 'Fiction' in *The Oxford History of Australian Literature* ed. L. Kramer, Oxford University Press, Melbourne, pp.27–172

Mitchell, T. 1987 'Italo-Australian theatre: Multiculturalism and neocolonialism' *Australian Drama Studies* vol.10, April, pp.31–48, and vol.11, October, pp. 37–46

Mohanty, C. 1988 'Under Western eyes: Feminist scholarship and colonial discourses' *Feminist Review* no.30, Autumn

Moore, A. 1990 'Thirroul and the Literary Establishment Strike Back', *Overland* 120, Spring

Moravia, S. 1970 *La Scienza dell'uomo nel settecento* Guis Laterza, Bari

Morrison, R.H. 1976 *Australia's Italian Poets* (anthology) Andor, Adelaide

Mudrooroo (see Narogin)

Mukherjee, T. 1986 'ESL: An imported new empire?' *Journal of Moral Education* vol.15, no.1, pp.43–9

Murray, D. 1989 'Unity and difference: Poetry and criticism' in *Literary Theory and Poetry: Extending the Canon* ed. D. Murray, Batsford, London

Naipaul, S. 1985 'The myth of the third world: A thousand million invisible men' *Spectator* May 18

Naipaul, V. S. 1980 'People Are Proud of Being Stupid: Edward Behr interviews V. S. Naipaul' *Newsweek* 18 August p.38

——1991 'Our universal civilisation' *New York Review of Books* 31 January, pp. 22–5

Narogin, Mudrooroo (Colin Johnson also Mudrooroo Nyoongah) 1988 'Settled land vision: Les Murray's country poetry' *Age Monthly Review* vol.8, no.2, May

Niall, B. 1988 *Martin Boyd: A Life* Melbourne University Press, Victoria

Nibbi, G. 1937 *Il Volto degli emigranti: scene di vita in Australia* (The flight of the emigrants: scenes of life in Australia), Parenti, Florence

———1965 *Cocktails d'Australia* Martello, Milan

Noffs, T. 1983 *Childhood Memories of Henry Lawson Country and Henry Lawson's Mudgee Poems* The Wayside Foundation, Sydney

Noonuccal, Oodgeroo (Kath Walker) 1970 *My People* Jacaranda Press, Queensland

Norberg-Schulz, C. 1980 *Genius Loci: Towards a Phenomenology of Architecture* L. Rizzoli, New York

Nyoongah (see Narogin)

O'Grady, D. 1988 'Sincerely: Gino Nibbi' *Overland* no.111, pp.2–8

O'Grady, J. (Nino Culotta) 1957 *They're a Weird Mob* Ure Smith, Sydney

Owens, C. 1984 'The allegorical impulse: Toward a new theory of postmodernism' in *Art after Modernism* ed. B. Wallis, New Museum of Contemporary Art, New York

Palmer, V. 1952 'Two Australian novels' *Voice* October, p. 25

Papastergiadis, N. 1987 'A vision revised: The question of identity, history and language in the writings of Kefala, Tsaloumas and Tzoumakas' *Chroniko* 8/9, pp.13–26

———1989 'Stealing the measure' *Age Monthly Review* vol.9, no.4

Parmar, P. 1990 'Woman, native, other: Interview with Trinh T. Minh-ha' *Feminist Review* no.36, Autumn

Pascoe, R. 1987 *Buongiorno Australia: Our Italian Heritage* Greenhouse Publications, Richmond Victoria

Penninger, H.R. 1976 *Mary my hun: a novel with a purpose* H.R. Penninger, Campsie NSW

Petrolo, R. 1986 *The Shadows of the Mystery* R. Petrolo, Warrawong NSW

Pinelli, D.G. 1971 *Songs of Love: Canti d'Amore* Eco Printing Co, Perth

———1771 *Wise Thoughts of a 'Mad' Man: Pensieri saggi d'un pazzo* Eco Printing Co, Perth

Plessner, H. 1979 'Mit anderen Augen' in *Zwischen Philosophie und Gesellschaft* Suhrkamp, Frankfurt, pp.232–48

Π.O. 1978 *Panash* Collective Effort Press, Melbourne

———(ed). 1985 *Off the Record* Penguin Australia, Ringwood Victoria

———1989 *Fitzroy Poems* Collective Effort Press, Melbourne

Raisis, M. 1983 'The image of the Greek in Australian literature' in *Papers: Yugoslavia, Europe and Australia* ed. Mirko Jurak, Faculty of Arts and Sciences, Edvard Kardelj University, Ljubljana

Rando, G. (ed.) 1983 *Italian Writers in Australia: Essays and Texts* Department of European Languages, University of Wollongong, Wollongong NSW

———1984 'Italo-Australian fiction' *Meanjin* vol.43, no.3, September, pp. 341–9

———1987 'Caste and cultural identity: The prose fiction of Pino Bosi' *Outrider* vol.4, no.1, June, pp.75–84

———1987a 'Notes on the writings of Giuseppe Abiuso' *Outrider* vol.4, no.2, December, pp.117–24

————(ed.) 1988 *Italo-Australian Prose in the 80s* Department of European Languages, University of Wollongong, Wollongong NSW

Reid, B. 1989 'The unknown art: Visual poetry in Australia' in *Words on Walls: A Survey of Contemporary Visual Poetry* Heide Gallery, Bulleen Victoria, pp. 5–9

Rushdie, S. 1987 'Introduction' *Günter Grass on Writing and Politics* Penguin, Harmondsworth, pp. vii–xiii

————1988 'Minority literatures in a multi-cultural society' in *Displaced Persons* eds K.H. Petersen & A. Rutherford, Dangaroo Press, Sydney

Said, E. 1979 *Orientalism* Random House, New York; Penguin Books, London

————1984 *The World, The Text and the Critic* Faber, London

————1984a 'Reflections on Exile' *Granta* no.13, Granta Publications, London

Sanciolo, N. 1983 *La Passione di Gesu Cristo: Tragedia Sacra in Versi sui Temi d'Antichi Motivi Pololari Siciliani* (play in three languages) N. Sanciolo, Melbourne

Sangari, K. 1987 'The politics of the possible' *Cultural Critique 7*

Schütz, A. 1974 'Grundzüge einer Theorie des Fremdverstehens' in *Der sinnhafte Aufbau der sozialen Welt. Einleitung in die verstehende Sozioolgie* Fischer, Frankfurt

Seferis, G. 1969 *Collected Poems 1924–1955* trans. Edmund Keeley & Phillip Sherrard, Jonathan Cape, London

Serle, G. 1975 'Introduction' in *The Eureka Stockade* R. Carboni, Melbourne University Press, Melbourne

Silverman, K. 1983 *The Subject of Semiotics* Oxford University Press, New York

Skrzynecki, P. (ed.) 1985 *Joseph's Coat* Hale & Iremonger, Sydney

Smith, B. 1979 *Art as Information: Reflections on the Art from Captain Cook's Voyages* Sydney University Press, Sydney

Sollors, W. 1986 *Beyond Ethnicity: Consent and Descent in American Culture* Oxford University Press, New York

Spender, D. 1980 *Man Made Language* Routledge, London

Spilias, T and Messinis, S. (eds) *Reflections* Elikia Books, Melbourne

Spivak, G.C. 1987 *In Other Worlds: Essays in Cultural Politics* Methuen, London

————1990 'Questions of Multi-culturalism' in *The Post-Colonial Critic* ed. Sarah Harasym, Routledge, New York & London

Steven, M. 1988 *First Impressions: The British Discovery of Australia* British Museum, London

Stewart, D. and Davis, B. 1971 *Best Australian Short Stories* Angus & Robertson, Sydney

Stormon, E. J. 1977 *The Salvado Memoirs* (trans. of *Memorie Storiche dell'Australia particolarmente della Missione Benedettina di Nuova Norcia e degli Usi e Costumi degle Australiani* Salvado & Rudesindo, 1851) Propaganda Fide, Rome

Strano, A. 1986 *Luck Without Joy: A Portrayal of a Migrant* trans. E.P. Burrows, Fremantle Arts Centre Press, Fremantle WA

Strano, L. 1964 *Inquietudine* Tip. Ital-Print, Sydney

————1970 *Mostratemi la Via di Gire al Monte* The University, Auckland

————1984 *Di qui ci son Passato anch'lo* L. Strano, Mt Wilson NSW

————1986 *Fifty Years Ago* W.R. Bright & Sons, Fairfield NSW

Thiele, C. 1961 *The Sun on the Stubble* Rigby, Adelaide

Triaca, M. 1985 *Amelia: A Long Journey* Greenhouse Publications, Melbourne

Trinh, M.T. 1989 *Woman, Native, Other: Writing, Postcoloniality and Feminism* Indiana University Press, Bloomington

Tsaloumas, D. 1975 *To Spiti me tous Eukalyptous* (The House with the Eucalypts) AKE, Athens

——1983 *The Observatory* University of Queensland Press, St Lucia

——1985 *The Book of Epigrams* University of Queensland Press, St Lucia

——1987 'I Gnorimia mou me ton Niko Kypraio' (My acquaintance with Nikos Kypraios) *Antipodes* no.22, pp.32–4

——1988 *Falcon Drinking. The English Poems* University of Queensland Press, St Lucia

Tzoumakas, D. 1986 'Merry Sydney' *Meanjin* vol.45, no.4, pp. 453–61

——1987 *The Earth is Hollow. Merry Sydney* Leros Press, Canberra

Ursino, F. 1980 *Where Two Extremes Meet* F. Ursino, Panania NSW

Valli, M. 1972 *Poesie, Australiane: Australian Poems* (in Italian and English) University of Queensland Press, St Lucia

Veit, W. 1983 'The Topoi of the European Imagining of the Non-European World' *Arcadia-Zeitschrift für Vergleichende Literaturwissenschaft* vol.18, no.3, pp.1–20

——1985 'Überlegungen zur Hermeneutik der Germanistik in Australien' in *Das Fremde und das Eigene. Prolegomena zu einer interkulturellen Germanistik* ed. A. Wierlacher, iudicium-Verlag, Munich, pp.314–26

——1987 'The foreign and the familiar: "Deutsch als Fremdsprache" and "Interkulturelle Germanistik" ' AUMLA no.67, pp.5–24

——1987a 'Die Hermeneutik des Fremden' in *Anspruch und Widerspruch* eds E. Grassi & H. Schmale, Zürcher Gesprache (Zurich Colloquia), W. Fink, Munich, pp. 35–69

Vleeskens, C. 1981 *Orange Blizzard,* Queensland Community Press, Brisbane

——1984 *The Day the River* University of Queensland Press, St Lucia

——1987 *Het Gedrang van de Leegte* WWQSS, Amsterdam

——1988 *Sittings for a Family Portrait* Post-Neo Publications, Melbourne

Walshe, R. D. (ed.) 1975 *Speaking of Writing* Reed Education, Sydney

Walwicz, A. 1982 'Delicatessen' in *Writing* Rigmarole, Melbourne

——1985 'Buttons' in *Off the Record* compiled and introduced by Π.O., Penguin, Ringwood Victoria

——1989 'Landlord' in *Boat* Angus & Robertson, Sydney

Ware, H. 1981 *A Profile of the Italian Community in Australia* AIMA/CO.AS.IT, Melbourne

Waten, J. 1952 *Alien Son* Angus & Robertson, Sydney

——1966 Judah Waten on Commitment, interview on 'Spectrum', ABC television, 18 December

——1971 'My Two Literary Careers' *Southerly* XXXI, pp.83–92

Wierlacher, A. (ed.) 1980 *Fremdsprache Deutsch* Fink, Munich

——(ed.) 1985 *Das Fremde und das Eigene. Prolegomena zu einer interkulturellen Germanistik* iudicium-Verlag, Munich

Wilde, W. H., Hooten, J., Andrews, B. (eds) 1985 *The Oxford companion to Australian literature* Oxford University Press, Melbourne

Wolf-Phillips, L. 1987 'Why "third world"?: Origin, definition and usage' *Third World Quarterly* vol.9, no. 4, October

Yates, F. 1966 *The Art of Memory* Routledge, London

Index

This is an index of names of persons, books and journals referred to in the text. Page references in *italics* represent major contributions by the named authors.